Spinoza and the Specters of Modernity

Spinoza and the Specters of Modernity

The Hidden Enlightenment of Diversity from Spinoza to Freud

Michael Mack

continuum

NEW YORK • LONDON

The Continuum International Publishing Group Inc
80 Maiden Lane, New York, NY 10038

The Continuum International Publishing Group Ltd
The Tower Building, 11 York Road, London SE1 7NX

www.continuumbooks.com

Copyright © 2010 by Michael Mack

Library of Congress Cataloging-in-Publication Data
A catalog record for this book is available from the Library of Congress.

ISBN: 978-1-4411-7344-7 (hardcover)
ISBN: 978-1-4411-1872-1 (paperback)

Typeset by Newgen Imaging Systems Pvt Ltd, Chennai, India
Printed in the United States of America

Contents

ACKNOWLEDGMENTS

I am most grateful to Haaris Naqvi for his exceptional help as editor at Continuum. It is thanks to his invaluable advice, sincere support and strong encouragement that the book is now being published as an affordable paperback. I am also grateful to the anonymous reviewers for Continuum.

Many institutions and individuals supported the conception and the completion of this book. I am grateful to the reviews of my previous book by Wendy C. Hamblet, Barrett Pashak, Alan Levenson and Jeffrey Alan Bernstein. In different but related ways, all four reviewers helped me discover how a development of *German Idealism and the Jew* could logically be conceived within the study of Spinoza and Spinozan thought.

I am grateful to Jeffrey A Barash, Rick Rosengarten, Donald N. Levine, Andrew Benjamin, Sander L. Gilman, Jeff Malpas, Susan James, Etienne Balibar, Jonathan Israel, Marissa and Maximilian zu Bentheim-Tecklenburg, Gillian Beer, Beth Lord, Dimitris Vardoulakis, Nonica Datta, Aleida Assmann, Michael Gassenmeier, Dan Diner, Eric Santner, David Jasper, Kate Rigby, Jonathan M. Hess, Lars Fischer Manfred Walther and Oded Schechter for most helpful and inspiring conversations about critical theory, Darwin, Spinoza, Herder, Gadamer and Salomon Maimon in Chicago, Jerusalem, Berlin, Rheda-Wiedenbrück, Sydney, Melbourne, Glasgow, Cambridge, Dundee and London.

I am most grateful to Fred Beiser (Syracuse University) for his encouragement and for inspiring conversations with him about Herder. At the University of Chicago Michael N. Forster assured me of the prospect of a coming "Herder renaissance," while Robert J Richards corrected my interpretation of Charles Darwin, pointing out his open-ended and nondeterministic view of moral progress.

Much of this book is deeply indebted to longstanding discussions with Paul Mendes-Flohr (Chicago/Jerusalem) and—via email—with Willi Goetschel (Toronto). In many ways this book complements Willi Goetschel's *Spinoza's Modernity*.

I cannot thank Warren Montag (Occidental College) enough for all his generous help, advice and encouragement. Warren Montag has been a mentor in my thought about Spinoza's alternative modernity.

The conception and writing of this book was first generously supported by a Sesquicentenary Research Fellowship at the University of Sydney. I am most grateful to the support, advice and encouragement of Norelle Lickiss,

Danielle Celermajer, Suzanne Rutland, Konrad Kwiet, Nick Eckstein, Ivan Head, Tim Fitzpatrick, Moira Gatens, Vrasidas Karalis, Stephen Gaukroger, John Gumley, Paul Redding, George Markus, Vanessa Smith, Alastair Blanshard, Paolo Bartoloni, Dugald Mclellan, Stephen Garton and Deirdre Coleman.

I am most grateful to the Leverhulme Trust for awarding me a research fellowship that enabled me to complete this book in the United Kingdom. Back in the United Kingdom I am most grateful to Simon Glendining for his inspiring and very helpful thought about postmodernism and Herder. I am also grateful to Simon for inviting me to present three revisions of Europe lectures on Spinoza, Herder and Freud at the London School of Economics.

I want to dedicate this book to my mother and to the memory of my father. An earlier version of Chapter 7 appeared as "The Significance of the Insignificant: George Eliot's *Daniel Deronda* and the Literature of Weimar Classicism" in *Modern Philology. Critical and Historical Studies in Literature, Medieval through Contemporary* Volume 105 (May 2008).

Here at Nottingham I am most grateful to my Head of School, Julian Henderson, and to my Head of Department, Karen Kilby for having supported work on the index of this book. Aaron Riches has kindly agreed to do the index and I most grateful to him for his work as I am to Anthony Smith for his advanced copyediting.

It has been a pleasure working at the marvelous Herzog August Library in Wolfenbüttel. I am most grateful to its brilliant and most helpful staff.

All translations are mine if not otherwise indicated.

INTRODUCTION: SPINOZA'S ALTERNATIVE MODERNITY

Wasn't all history full of the destruction of precious things?
Henry James, The Portrait of a Lady

This work is a study in religion, literature and cultural theory: it takes its terms of reference from the seventeenth and late eighteenth century in the cultural history of the Enlightenment, but has implications for understanding global politics in the twenty-first century.

Contemporary issues are, however, not the main focus of this book. Neither is this a study in the intellectual background of Spinoza, Herder, Goethe, George Eliot, Rosenzweig and Freud. It engages with key intellectual texts not along the methodological lines of either history or cultural theory but rather reads them as forms of literature. The book is not, however, confined to the study of literature. Neither is it of exclusively historical value. This is what I have in mind when I combine intellectual history with cultural theory: I practice intellectual history that is productive of contemporary thought but the main focus is not the contemporary scene but a literary reading of "past" texts which bring to the fore their present day relevance.

This hybrid methodological approach has important implication for a new understanding of what Spinoza, and in a further intellectual shift of thought, Herder criticizes as societal self-destruction. In related but different ways Spinoza and Herder take issue with a form of self-preservation that is not sustainable and thus turns out to be self-destructive. This concern with sustainability has become an urgent contemporary issue due to certain military, economic and ecological crises which we confront in the present. Reading "past" texts in the context of present-day concerns does not necessarily mean that history transmutes into a work of fiction. On the contrary, it is the very "pastness" of Spinoza's, Herder's, Goethe's and George Eliot's work that makes it relevant for an engagement with present-day issues: it is distinct in its ethical message from the self-destructive practices that shape much of our economical and ecological current situation.

The historical texts discussed in this book have a contemporary relevance precisely because they are not products of our age but are rather distinct from it and in their distinction are thus capable of producing thought which is relevant to rethinking the problems we are facing now.[1] As a discussion of mainly "past" thought this book does not manifest a new cultural theory in its own right but it may contribute to twenty-first century thought—hence its tangential references to Derrida's work on philosophy in times of terror.

---

1 For a brilliant discussion of this see Jeffrey Andrew Barash's "Why remember the Historical Past," in Günter Fink (ed.) *Internationales Jahrbuch für Hermeneutik*, Vol. 7 (Tübingen: Mohr Siebeck, 2008) pp. 79–91 (p. 87).

The book draws new theoretical conclusions from a study of Spinoza's leg-acy in the age of Goethe and beyond, largely transmitted through the writings of Herder. It develops a cultural theory based on that legacy. By legacy I mean the ways in which a person's thought impacts on, rather than merely influ-ences, contemporary thought. In the context of this project it describes how a line of writers and thinkers reconfigured Spinoza's ideas and how these ideas thus became effective in society at large. The legacy of Spinoza is important because he was the first thinker to theorize narrative as the constitutive fabric of politics, identity, society, religion and the larger sphere of culture.

This book takes forward a novel approach toward the study of modern history and cultural theory as first developed in *German Idealism and the Jew*. That work focused on the problematic nature of Kant's autonomy-heteronomy divide. While the Kantian position of an autonomous self is intrinsically liber-ating, his stark contrast between a free society and one enslaved to 'the goods of this world' has rather violent connotations and implications. Kant's moral philosophy, however, has often come to serve as the foundation for a non-violent, and therefore rational, modern and postmodern sense of European identity. What has been overlooked in this context is Kant's exclusion of soci-etal manifestations that he associates with naturalistic contingency (African societies, Tahitians—whom he equates with cattle in his review of Herder's *Ideas*, as will be discussed in Chapter 6—Jews, Orientals etc.).[2]

For writers who critically confronted this demotion of naturalistic contin-gency and embodied life (as analyzed in *German Idealism and the Jew*), how-ever, Spinoza's anti-teleological thought became an inspiration for their literary revision of Kant's idealism. The book takes forward the analysis developed in *German Idealism and the Jew* by discussing Spinoza's writings on politics and ethics as an alternative to a Kantian conception of modernity. Spinoza pro-vides the intellectual and historical common ground where the more private

---

2 Related to this divide between rational or free and irrational or naturalistic com-munities is Kant's concern with humanity's assumed division into superior and infe-rior races. Scholars (Robert Bernasconi, among others) have recently shown how Kant was the first to legitimate racism on scientific grounds. (This topic will be discussed in Chapter 7) As John Gray has put it: "It was Immanuel Kant—after Voltaire the supreme Enlightenment figure and, unlike Voltaire, a great philoso-pher—who more than any other thinker gave intellectual legitimacy to the concept of race. Kant was in the forefront of the science of anthropology that was emerging in Europe and maintained that there are innate differences between the races. While he judged whites to have all the attributes required for progress towards perfection, he represents Africans as being predisposed to slavery, observing in his *Observa-tions on the Feelings of the Beautiful and the Sublime* (1764), 'The Negroes of Africa have by nature no feeling that rises above the trifling.'" Gray, *Black Mass. Apocalyptic Religion and the Death of Utopia* (New York: Farrar, Straus and Giroux, 2007), p. 61.

realm of literature and the public sphere of the political can meet and interact with each other. Spinozist writing and thought seems to confound binary oppositions, such as the one between private and public.

Here opposites are not fundamental. They do not oppose each other but are complementary to each other. Spinoza's legacy seems to be a ghostly one: it opens up a space where apparently incompatible entities visit each other as if one were haunting the other. The specter whom Marx conjured up in his *Communist Manifesto* (1848) had already made an appearance in the hugely influential *On the Doctrine of Spinoza (Über die Lehre des Spinoza)* with which Friedrich Heinrich Jacobi provoked the Spinoza controversy in 1785. Jacobi makes clear that he endeavors to put an end to the haunting with which Spinoza's ghost seems to keep Germany enthralled.

What is crucial here is that the haunting in question does its work by confounding clearly defined forms. Revisiting Marx's Specter of 1848, Derrida has recently argued that ghostliness disturbs and disrupts the presence of an identity that purports to be identical to itself. A specter performs this rupture so that one cannot be sure whether its disappearance is not at the same time its appearance: "a specter is always a *revenant*. One cannot control its comings and goings because it *begins by coming back*."[3] Jacobi attempts to turn the indefinable specter of Spinoza into the clearly definable doctrine of Spinoza. What makes him so uneasy about the absence of definition is that it gives rise to undecidability. It is difficult to decide against someone whose image has not been clearly depicted with definite and recognizable features. Jacobi sets out to clarify matters by pinpointing the exact structure and shape of Spinoza's teaching so that it can be opposed.

According to Jacobi only the delineation of a stable form would be capable of preventing the visitation of the ghost Spinoza. "**It would be of great use to publically represent the doctrine of Spinoza in its** true shape [Gestalt] and according to its necessary connections" writes Jacobi.[4] What follows concerns the absence of shape or the confounding of clearly defined entities—in other words, the haunting exerted by the ghost Spinoza:

> A spectre [Gespenst] has recently been haunting Germany in various shapes (I wrote to Moses Mendelssohn) and it is held by the superstitious and by the atheists in equal reverence . . . Perhaps we will witness some day that an argument will arise over the corpse of Spinoza equal to the one which arose between the archangels and Satan over the corpse of Moses . . . [bold in the German original].[5]

3　Derrida, *Specters of Mars. The State of the Debt, the Work of Mourning, & the New International*, trans. by Peggy Kamuf (New York: Routledge, 1994), p. 11.

4　Friedrich Heinrich Jacobi, *Über die Lehre des Spinoza in Briefen an den Herrn Moses Mendelssohn* (Breslau, Gottlieb Löwe, 1785), p. 168.

5　Jacobi, *Über die Lehre des Spinoza*, p. 168.

Jacobi composes and publishes the writings gathered together in *On the Doctrine of Spinoza* in order to exorcise the persistent impact of a figure that appears to be an anti-Moses of sorts. Whereas the archangels and Satan's argument over the corpse of Moses concerned a clearly defined doctrine, the impending one over the corpse of Spinoza is malicious, because no one can be sure what it is actually about. Significantly, an early eighteenth-century German translation of Johannes Colerus' Spinoza biography associates the Spinozist God with the deleterious impact of a ghost. It may well be that Jacobi enlarges this association of Spinoza's alleged atheism with the haunting of a malicious specter: "If one considers, however, his opinions one concludes that the god of Spinoza is nothing but a fictive Ghost, an imagined god, who is the opposite of God."[6] Countering such deleterious influences, Jacobi endeavors to deprive the corpse of Spinoza of its confounding and haunting power. He does so by giving a clearly defined shape to what Spinoza represents (*Gestalt*). Jacobi constructs Spinoza's *Gestalt* (shape or form) in order to banish Spinoza's *Gespenst* (Specter).

The present book shows how unsuccessful Jacobi's attempt was. Far from having put an end to Spinoza's legacy, Jacobi in fact provoked a controversy that hugely increased the appreciation of the writing, life and thought of the Dutch Jewish philosopher within the public sphere of the late eighteenth century. Indeed Spinoza became the representative for an alternative modernity that differed from the categorical and hierarchical components of Kant's modern moral and political philosophy.

Rather than whole-heartedly embracing the Kantian project of modernity, writers and thinkers in the age of Goethe put Spinoza's concept of self-preservation to creative use by highlighting the self-destruction implicit in the modern quest for unlimited power. Having Spinoza's *conatus* (self-preservation) as their point of intellectual orientation writers and thinkers in the age of Goethe discussed in different but related ways how the emerging increase in human power was accompanied by an erosion of limits toward human self-destruction. They criticized precisely this self-destructive element in a teleological and deterministic narrative of history that demoted the past and cast non-European "primitive" societies as morally debauched and epistemologically retarded.

Spinoza's vision of a non-hierarchical modernity together with its various creative inflections and revisions in the eighteenth, nineteenth and twentieth century has particular significance for contemporary political philosophy and cultural theory. The broad findings of the study center on the way in which Spinoza has endured as a major, if not to say, the major inspiration of visions of modernity that are nonexclusive—or, in other words nonideological—and non-hierarchical. The center of analysis is the contemporary relevance of Herder's thought and the creative rereading of Herder's Spinozist historiography in the work of his tutee Goethe as well as in Eliot's proto-Zionist novel

---

6　Johannes Colerus, *Das Leben des Bened. von Spinoza* (Leipzig: Johann George Loewe, 1736).

Daniel Deronda. Herder's "invention" of the concept culture is a creative development of Spinoza's notion of self-preservation (*conatus*).

The book establishes the contemporary relevance of Herder's Spinoza-inspired critique of Kantian teleology in the study of both nature and history. Rather than discuss Herder as a reader of various writers and thinkers (as is commonly done in German influence studies) this study establishes Herder as a philosopher who is capable of enjoying a remarkable contemporary relevance. His relevance consists in his divergence from the standard Enlightenment conception of history as unilateral progress and his reinterpretation of history as diverse. In this account history does not find its fulfillment in a single goal (as is argued in teleological thought).

In the seventeenth and eighteenth centuries Spinoza was infamous for having pulled down the hierarchical divide between the realms of the transcendent (God and the mind) and the immanent (Nature and the body). Goethe and his former mentor Herder set out to adapt this Spinozisit undertaking to the changed life world of the end of the eighteenth and the beginning of the nineteenth century. They took issue with some tendencies in Enlightenment thought which condemned the historical past to insignificance. A new reading of Herder's writing and thought contributes to an understanding of temporality as a non-hierarchical, gradual development of diversity out of and within a common substance of interconnectedness and interdependence.

This discussion is important because it offers a way out of the self-destructive social set up that drives much of contemporary global policies.[7] The new cultural theory that informs my approach toward the study of modernity is a timely response to what has recently been characterized, in the philosophical analysis of both Islamic fundamentalism and "the war on terror," as autoimmunity or the self-destruction of our contemporary global society. Jacques Derrida in an interview with Giovanna Borradori characterized autoimmune processes as "the strange behaviour where a living being, in quasi-*suicidal* fashion, 'itself' works to destroy its own protection"[8] and they thus invariably refer back to their opposite: to the Spinozist theory of self-preservation. These self-destructive processes result from triumphal declarations of moral, epistemological, military and religious superiority of one societal formation over the one which functions as its "enemy." Here clearly the spheres of religion and politics meet in a rather disturbing manner.

I

Whether one agrees or disagrees with Nancy Levene's assessment of Spinoza's oneness with the biblical conception of God, she may have a point in

---

7   See Gray, *Black Mass*, 73.

8   Giovanna Borradori, *Philosophy in a Time of Terror. Dialogues with Jürgen Habermas and Jacques Derrida* (Chicago: The University of Chicago Press, 2003), p. 94.

emphasizing the validity of a Spinozist contribution to the study of religion.[9] The present book, however, does not only discuss Spinoza (as well as thought inspired by Spinoza) in the context of religious studies because it has a much wider reach. In addition to religious studies, it engages with the disciplines of literature, philosophy, history as well as with the political and social sciences.

It is worth emphasizing that Spinoza refuses secular radicalism because he values those aspects that in different forms of religion give rise to ethical actions. This brings us to one of the main wagers of this book; Spinoza introduces a non-hierarchical vision into the conception of modernity. Spinoza does not privilege one religion over another or one ethical system over another, because one of his main endeavors is to do away with privilege and other forms of hierarchical rankings—be it between reason and revelation or between different ethnic and/or religious groups. As Levene has put it,

> unlike many of Spinoza's medieval precursors, for whom reason and revelation were hierarchically related, and unlike many of his contemporaries, for whom reason and revelation agreed in all important respects except for the supernatural claims of the latter (to which reason gives uniformed but deferential assent), Spinoza attempted to put the perennial question on a footing which leaves both sovereign.[10]

Contrary to his geometrical method, the content of Spinoza's thought is filled with uncertainty. He argues for the coexistence of different ways of life.

The historical context in which Spinoza developed his thought is clearly pertinent for a better understanding of his skepticism toward certainty in political life. He was born into a confused cultural set up. He was a Jew of Marrano origin. The situation of the Marranos was far from being "certain" in that it "favored doubt of Christianity quite as much as doubt of Judaism."[11] It was "disposed to alienation from all revealed religion."[12] Within the wider sphere of Amsterdam politics Spinoza encountered the uncertain power struggle between orthodox Calvinist and *Remonstrants*.[13] Even though he clearly sided with the egalitarianism of the *Remonstrants*, Spinoza did not attempt to overcome a state of epistemological, religious and political uncertainty.

It seems an egalitarian approach allows for a certain amount of ambiguity. Indeed, Spinoza makes the limitations of human knowledge the basis of his thought: he focuses on the discrepancy between empirical reality and our conception of it. He argues for the indistinguishable unity of body and mind so

---

9 See Levene, *Spinoza's Revelation. Religion, Democracy, and Reason* (Cambridge: Cambridge University Press, 2004), p. 240.

10 Levene, *Spinoza's Revelation*, p. 234.

11 Strauss, *Spinoza's Critique of Religion*, translated by E. M. Sinclair (Chicago: The University of Chicago Press, 1997), 53.

12 Ibid.

13 For a brilliant discussion of the wider political context see Etienne Balibar's *Spinoza and Politics*, translated by Peter Snowdown (London: Verso, 1998), 16–31.

that bodily distractions emerge not as the opponent of thinking but as its proper core. In this way uncertainty encapsulates philosophical inquiry. Spinoza blurs the distinction between conceptual boundaries: the corporeal is not the imperfect, because there is no such thing as imperfection. We are all equally imperfect or, rather, perfect.[14] Spinoza radically breaks down the hierarchical divide between those who succeed and those who seem to fail. Warren Montag refers to this conscious espousal of ambiguity when he interprets Spinoza's *Ethics* as follows:

> The idea of a God or nature which does not in any way pre-exist its own realization (E I, Prop. 33, scholium 2) forces us to reject the notion of imperfection: "By reality and perfection I mean the same thing." The notion of final causes, like that of free will, however, is no less real for being false.[15]

Part of Spinoza's critique of final causes, and teleology in general, is his critique of an anthropomorphic conception of God. Here he confirms the gap between humanity and divinity; not, however, to uphold a hierarchical conception of God but in order to upend attempts by specific religious groups to claim quasi-divine authority in their struggle for economic and military power against other social formations.

II

Spinoza's rational inquiry is concerned with the avoidance of violence. He analyzes the ways in which anthropomorphic conceptions of God further violent forms of social interaction. This book discusses the long life of the Spinozist critique of anthropomorphism. The critique of anthropomorphism emerges as a political theology that has abandoned the institution of sovereignty. It is this theological and political engagement that gives rise to a Spinozist conception of modernity. It is an alternative to the dualist notion of modern rationalism as propounded by Descartes and Kant.

Spinoza was of course to some extent a Cartesian.[16] Similarly Spinoza and Kant's respective projects share many features. Both are rationalists and universalists. They arrive, however, at their respective conceptions of both reason and universalism rather differently. Pauline Phemister has justifiably argued that "Spinoza often opposes Descartes while Leibniz, in opposition to both, nevertheless forges a path midway between the two, melding truths from each

---

14 For a brilliant discussion of this point see Montag's *Louis Althusser* (New York: Palgrave, 2003), 53.

15 Montag, *Bodies, Masses, Power. Spinoza and his Contemporaries* (London: Verso, 1999), 40.

16 For detailed discussion of Descartes' influence on Spinoza see Tammy Nyden-Bullock's *Spinoza's Radical Cartesian Mind* (London: Continuum, 2007).

into a new theory." [17] Crucially—and in striking contrast to Descartes—there is lack of binary oppositions in Spinoza's formulation of a radical Enlightenment. He does not play off the mind against the body, nor does he oppose the particular with the universal. While Spinoza has a strong commitment to rationalism in common with Descartes, Hobbes and Kant, his version of reason is more inclusive of what is considered lowly, bodily or even irrational than any other philosopher in the rationalist tradition.

There is another important difference between the modernity shaped by Kant's moral philosophy and Spinoza's modern ethology. It is a difference, which Constantin Brunner has analyzed in his 1909 introduction to K. O. Meinsma's *Spinoza and his Circle*. Brunner argues that Kant's rationalism has ironically fallen prey to what Spinoza criticizes as superstition and anthropomorphism. How can we account for a superstitious Kant? Brunner pinpoints Kant's superstition in his belief in progress (*Entwicklungsglaube*). He traces the way how "the transformation of superstition out of religion emerges in the doctrine of progress as part of Immanuel Kant's philosophy." [18] The central part of this book (Chapters 3 to 7) analyzes Herder's important critique of Kant's doctrine of progress.

We may justifiably describe Herder as the inventor of the concept "culture". This study offers the first analysis of how Herder's notion of culture is a creative development of Spinoza's *conatus*. Spinoza's *conatus* describes the ways in which the particular participates in the universal: by preserving oneself one contributes to the preservation of the entire universe of which we all are an infinitesimal part. This book articulates a line of thought which has often been silenced in standard accounts of modernity: that of an inclusive rather than exclusive universalism—one that does not condemn the particular and one that does not oppose it to the universal but rather makes the two dependent on each other.

This book focuses on Spinoza's rupture with the metaphysics of God or nature and Herder's shift away from Cartesian and Kantian categories of the cogito. The rupture and shifts introduced by Herder and Spinoza revolve around a doubling of thought where we first radically separate entities that have become conflated with each other—this is precisely what Spinoza does when he says that we superimpose our conception of nature or God onto nature and God; thus distorting truth while proclaiming to have found "the truth." In the second doubling movement of thought this separation performs unity. We are part of God or nature precisely because we are aware of being separate from it. This awareness of separation makes us realize that we are part of that from which we are separated. We are a part of nature but just

---

17   See Phemister's, *The Rationalists. Descartes, Spinoza and Leibniz* (Cambridge: Polity, 2006), p. 18.

18   Brunner "Spinoza Gegen Kant und die Sache der geistigen Wahrheit," in K. O. Meinsma, *Spinoza und sein Kreis. Historisch-Kritische Studien über Holländische Freigeister*, trans. into German by Lina Schneider (Berlin: Karl Schnabel, 1909), pp. 1–83 (p. 5).

that: only a part and not the whole and hence we are not able to comprehend the whole of which we are a part.

Franz Rosenzweig calls this principle of holistic separation Spinoza's paganism. The chapter following the discussion of Herder's Spinozist account of reason introduces the reader to Goethe's related critique of an exclusive type of rationality which understands itself as being separated from and opposed to the "primitive," "uncivilized," "merely natural and thus irrational." Rosenzweig defines paganism in terms of Spinoza's abandonment of categories. Notional thought is prone to fall prey to anthropomorphism. Anthropomorphic conceptions of God enact the distortion of categories in its most glaring form as they conflate human deficient logic with the logic of being. The logic of being, however, is nature as it exists undisturbed by the partiality of limited human thought. According to Rosenzweig paganism is Spinozism: both distinguish between thought and being while nevertheless not opposing one against the other.

Rosenzweig establishes an intriguing link between the new thinking of phenomenology and Spinoza's retreat from traditional metaphysical thought that remains mired to the fixity and timelessness as encapsulated by the term essence. According to Rosenzweig Spinoza inaugurated a revolution within metaphysics. This may sound strange, because Spinoza is often seen as a disciple of Descartes. Yet Spinoza's discussion of the anthropomorphic conception of God in traditional theological and philosophical discourse introduces not only a shift within but also, more radically, a break from traditional metaphysics. What makes his thought so radical is the fact that it instantiates the crucial phenomenological differentiation between our limited human categories and the being of nature or God. Within traditional metaphysics the categories are meant to grasp the true existence of world. According to Spinoza, and Herder afterwards, we are, however, never fully able to fathom the laws of the cosmos. If we presume to do so we have already fallen prey to anthropomorphism and anthropocentricism.

Our inability to grasp nature's complete set of laws does not mean that we are incapable of reaching an adequate view of our limited world. This is precisely what George Eliot sets out to do in her Spinozist characterization of literary realism as the performance of an inclusive universalism.[19] Chapter 8 discusses the ways in which Eliot presents a critique of ideology in *Daniel Deronda* when she argues for the Spinozist right of a universal particularism. In related but different ways Eliot, Herder, Rosenzweig and Goethe conceive of reason in narrative terms. The writers and thinkers discussed in this study further develop Spinoza's shift away from the nonnarrative and static toward

---

19 For a study of Spinoza's influence on George Eliot see Dorothy Atkins' *George Eliot and Spinoza* (Salzburg: Salzburg Studies in English Literature, 1978). Arkins, however depicts Spinoza in light that contradicts recent assessments of his nonhostile approach to the emotions (Moira Gatens, Genevieve Lloyd and Damasio's recent studies, for example).

the complementary and diverse. Mental awareness that goes so far as to be mindful of the mind prepares an alternative conception of modernity and rationality. The concluding chapter to this book connects with the opening chapter by discussing the ways in which Spinoza and Freud are rationalists with a difference. It is so far an unarticulated conception of another modernity and rationality that the following study attempts to uncover. As has been intimated above, the uncovering in question is not only historical. The conclusions of the study do not lose their intellectual significance and impact within the context of the late nineteenth century. The work of historical exegesis does not confine itself to the rather closed sphere of philological influence study. By unearthing and delineating the blueprint of a truly universalist Enlightenment this book also unfolds a novel social and cultural theory.

CHAPTER 1

DESCARTES, SPINOZA OR THE GOAL THAT DESTROYS ITSELF

No philosopher of the seventeenth century has acquired more literary buzz in the twenty-first century than Benedict de Spinoza, who lived from 1632 to 1677.
Don Garett, Times Literary Supplement *19 October 2007*

1. Introduction: *Spinoza and the Critique of Hierarchy*

Why did Spinoza prove to be such a vital source of inspiration for both the romantic approach toward diversity and for the contemporary philosophical discussion about politics and ethics? This chapter will delineate the ways in which Spinoza's philosophy offers a novel conception of what it means to be enlightened at precisely those points where it diverges from Descartes' conception of rationality.[1] Chapter 2 will then discuss how Spinoza's notion of self-preservation (the *conatus*) encloses in itself a blueprint of a cooperative vision of society. The possible ramifications of this vision are the subject of the discussion in the chapters that follow chapter 2. They will mainly focus on how Herder creatively reconfigured Spinozist philosophy in his critique of goal-oriented conceptualizations (i.e. teleologies) of history as well as in his various controversies with what he thought to be monolithic formations within the eighteenth-century enlightenment. This chapter offers an introduction to the ways in which Spinoza' *Ethics* lays the foundation for various visions of a type

---

1   Spinoza's reading of Descartes' is a complex topic of research. Genevieve Lloyd has ingeniously analyzed how Spinoza calls into question the connections established by Descartes' in particular, and the philosophic tradition in general, "between individuality and the concept of substance." Lloyd, *Part of Nature: Self-Knowledge in Spinoza's Ethics* (Ithaca, NY: Cornell University Press, 1994), p. 10. Lloyd argues that Spinoza diverges from Descartes by paradoxically pushing Cartesian thought to an extreme point where it is no longer Cartesian. In this way Spinoza undermines Descartes's distinction between will and intellect by widening the cracks which have already developed as part of the traditional philosophical concept of autonomy: "But there are for Descartes restraints on this power of autonomous choice; and Spinoza exploits them to collapse the Cartesian distinction between will and intellect into his own doctrine that the power of the mind resides in understanding only—an understanding that is itself subject to the necessities that govern the rest of nature. In the lack of accompanying will, however, understanding does not remain a bare cognitive state. It becomes conative, though not in a way that could be summed up in Descartes's idea of the will as wishing or shunning, seeking or avoiding. The essence of Spinoza's conative understanding becomes not choice but acquiescence. And this is at the center of his difference with Descartes." Lloyd, *Part of Nature*, p. 62.

of enlightenment that rather than rejecting, embraces cultural diversity and the plurality of the material viz. embodied world.

Does the ethology which Spinoza advanced in his *Ethics* have singular significance for the formulation of a viable contemporary social theory?[2] Spinoza's presence can be found in the thought of divergent twentieth- and twenty-first century thinkers. Spinoza's thought seems to exert a peculiar sense of contemporaneousness.[3]

This is not to claim that Spinoza anticipated the social problems that haunt our seemingly inclusive global society. Instead of dislocating Spinoza's thought from his particular historical setting, this chapter analyzes how his *Ethics* delineate the project of a kind of modernity that offers an alternative to the current Kantian approach toward defining the modern. Within the latter part of the eighteenth century—under the immense influence of Kant's transcendental philosophy—history came to represent modernity: the future of humanity seemed to promise its immanent perfectibility. In my recent book *German Idealism and the Jew. The Inner Anti-Semitism of Philosophy and German Jewish Responses*[4] I have shown how these attempts at constructing a "perfect" otherworldly world within this one were premised on the exclusion of worldly imperfections. Judaism and the Jews represented these bodily remainders of contingency as well as political and ethical deficiency: it was thought that with the progress of history, worldly imperfections would vanish from the world just as Jews and Judaism would cease to exist in the perfect modern state of the future.

---

2 The term "ethology" describes the broad reach of Spinoza's *Ethics* which is not concerned with a narrow conception of the ethical but includes the political, medical, and the larger sphere of culture. Genevieve Lloyds has intriguingly argued that Deleuze's term "ethology" emerges from a political reading of the *Ethics* as a work which is closely related to the *Theological-Political Treatise*: "Whether or not we accept Deleuze's direct political explanation of the interruption, the insertion of the *Theological-Political Treatise* into the chronology of the writing of the *Ethics* should alert us to the importance for Spinoza of the relations between the metaphysical, the ethical, and the political." Lloyd, *Spinoza and the Ethics* (New York: Routledge, 1996), p. 26.

3 See Louis Althusser's, "The Only Materialist Tradition, Part I: Spinoza," trans. by Ted Stolze, in Warren Montag and Ted Stolze (eds), *The New Spinoza* (Minneapolis: University of Minnesota Press, 19997), 3–19; Etienne Balibar's *Spinoza and Politics*, trans. by Peter Snowdown (New York: Verso, 1998); Gilles Deuleuze's *Expressionism in Philosophy: Spinoza*, trans. by Martin Joughin (New York: Zone Books, 1992) and his *Spinoza: Practical Philosophy*, trans. by Robert Hurley (San Francisco: City Light Books, 1988); Antonio Negri's *The Savage Anomaly: The Power of Spinoza's Metaphysics and Politics*, trans. by Michael Hardt (Minneapolis: University of Minnesota Press, 1991) and his recent, *Subversive Spinoza (un)Contemporary Variations*, ed. by Timothy S. Murphy, trans. by T. S. Murphy, M. Hardt, T. Stolze and C. T. Wolfe (Manchester: Manchester University Press); Martha C. Nussbaum's *Upheaval's of Thought: The Intelligence of Emotions* (Cambridge: Cambridge University Press, 2001).

4 (Chicago: The University of Chicago Press, 2003).

For writers who critically confronted this demotion of naturalistic contingency and embodied life, Spinoza's union of mind and body became an inspiration for their literary revision of Kant's idealism.

This chapter implicitly discusses Spinoza's writings on politics and ethics as an alternative to the Cartesian legacy within a predominantly Kantian conception of modernity. Spinoza upends the hierarchical dualism between mind and body that prepares the ground for the construction of Kant's moral philosophy. As Stuart Hampshire has put it: "The union of mind and body is so close because the mind monitors changes in the body, and the brain is both the instrument and the object of the monitoring."[5] There is a non-hierarchical relationship between mind, brain and body so that neither "is more fundamental than the other."[6] This chapter focuses on the ways in which Spinoza overturns fundamental oppositions and makes them complementary until we reach a reach state of the coexistence of the diverse.[7] It analyzes how Spinoza's *Ethics* delineates the blueprint for a non-hierarchical and nonexclusive understanding of human sociability. Accordingly, it takes issue with a recent trend in scholarly literature that attributes a hierarchical framework to Spinoza's understanding of ethics.[8] Recently, Steven B. Smith has thus argued that the *Ethics* radicalizes Descartes' divide between the biological viz. natural realm of the body and the intellectual sphere of the mind.

There is some scholarly disagreement as to how radical the divide was that Descartes established between mind and body. Susan James has taken some critics to task who overemphasize the divisiveness of this divide: "By treating *The Meditations on First Philosophy* as Descartes's philosophical treatment, scholars have created a one-sided interpretation of Cartesianism in which the division between body and soul is overemphasized and sometimes misunderstood."[9] Stephen Gaukroger, in contrast, has argued that, even though his

---

5 Hampshire, *Spinoza and Spinozism* (Oxford: Clarendon Press, 2005), p. xlii.

6 Ibid., p. lii.

7 In this respect my argument further develops and radicalizes Genevieve Lloyd's discussion of Spinoza's philosophy as outdoing the false opposition between the individualistic and the communitarian. Lloyd has ingeniously analyzed the way in which Spinoza's notion of the self includes that of the other and thus offers a striking contrast to the philosophical tradition: "The self evoked in Epicurus's discussion of death is an all-or-nothing affair—solidly there during life, totally absent at death. For Spinoza, in contrast, the mind's self-awareness during life involves, as we have already seen, a blurring of the boundaries between its own body and that of the others that impinge on it. To the extent that a mind comes to an adequate understanding of itself as an individual—that is, of the essence of the body of which it is the idea—it must understand other things together with itself." Lloyd, *Spinoza and the Ethics*, p. 120.

8 Compare Don Garrett's "Teleology in Spinoza and Early Modern Rationalism" in Rocco J. Gennaro and Charles Huenemann (eds), *New Essays on the Rationalists* (Oxford: Oxford University Press, 2003), pp. 310–335.

9 James, *Passion and Action: The Emotions in Seventeenth-Century Philosophy* (Oxford: Clarendon Press, 1997), p. 106.

thought underwent significant changes throughout his life, Descartes did "at no stage" abandon the belief "that human perceptual cognition, still less human behavior, could be explained fully without reference to an immaterial intelligence."[10] Gaukroger astutely historicizes Descartes' emphasis on the immaterial and, associated with it, his highly ambivalent attitude to embodied life. He traces Descartes' mind-body divide to the Christian religious renewal of the sixteenth and seventeenth centuries that attempted to recuperate qualities which it associated with the origins of Christianity: "hatred of the body and the world, the pervasiveness of sin, and a sharp sense of the fleetingness of time."[11] John Cottingham has certainly abstained from overemphasizing Descartes's divide between body and mind,[12] but he none the less acknowledges Spinoza's striking departure from a Cartesian mind-body dualism:

> When Spinoza himself speaks of the mind and body as being "united", or of their "union", he emphatically rejects the Cartesian idea of union as an intermingling or joining together; what is meant, rather, is that mind and body are *unum et idem*, one and the same.[13]

Recently Steven Nadler has confirmed this crucial difference between Descartes' and Spinoza's philosophy in relation to their respective writings about mind and body: "For Spinoza, there is a fundamental identity between mind and body—and thus a fundamental unity to the human being—that goes much deeper than any difference there may be between them."[14] According to Smith, however, Spinoza seems to emphasize the difference rather than the unity between the corporal and the cerebral.[15]

---

10 Gaukroger, *Descartes: An Intellectual Biography* (Oxford: Oxford University Press, 1995), p. 7.

11 Ibid., p. 25.

12 See Cottingham's *The Rationalists* (Oxford: Oxford University Press, 1990), p. 131.

13 Ibid., p. 132.

14 Nadler, *Spinoza's Ethics. An Introduction* (Cambridge: Cambridge University Press, 2006), p. 135.

15 Smith claims that Spinoza's critique of teleology devalues nature in order to celebrate human goals as the pinnacle of moral achievement. Here nature represents the immorality of the corporeal which Smith opposes to the morality of humanity's cerebral life: "The belief in divine teleology, we have seen, is a prejudice that is itself explained by the tendency to attribute to nature or God the same kinds of purposes that we have as human beings. We are, Spinoza appears to say, teleological beings and we cannot help fancifully ascribing similar ends to other objects in nature and history." Smith, *Spinoza's Book of Life: Freedom and Redemption in the Ethics*, (New Haven, CT: Yale University Press, 2003), p. 53. Smith ignores that what he is describing is precisely the object of Spinoza's critique: Spinoza certainly does not approve of ascribing human purposes to either God or nature. On the contrary he unmasks such ascriptions as deluded, anthropomorphic fantasies. Spinoza is far from endorsing a "we cannot help" approach which Smith seems to be advocating here.

Instead of critically questioning this binary opposition between nature, on the one hand, and intellect, on the other, Spinoza here appears to reaffirm the supremacy of the latter over the former. This hierarchy of values results from imputing a deterministic teleological agenda to the underlying conception and structure of the *Ethics*. On this view, Spinoza's denial of teleology on the part of both nature and God only paves the way for his enthronement of humanity as the agent of moral progress in the universe.[16]

Rather than endorsing human goals as part of the telos of the universe, Spinoza tries to separate our particular endeavors from any grand scheme of God or Nature. Even though we are part of nature, Spinoza takes great care to emphasize that we *are not* nature (but only a tiny part of it). Our cognitive faculties are far too inadequate to comprehend the world in its necessity and complexity. Clearly, Spinoza does not share Descartes's elevated view of the mind's adequacy. In this context it is pertinent to draw attention to Genevieve Lloyd's ingenious analysis of how Spinoza conceptualizes inadequacy in terms of being an inalienable ingredient of the human condition: "The Cartesian mind is completely knowable to itself regardless of the existence of the body— the most accessible of all objects of knowledge. Spinoza's self-knowledge, in contrast, is mediated through bodily self-awareness and must share its inadequacy."[17] The inadequacy of our minds—being ideas of our bodies—should make us mindful of our minds. The mindfulness of the mind also involves a critical engagement with absolutist conceptions of teleology.

Spinoza does of course not deny that we need to have goals. However, he emphasizes that we must stay cognizant of the particularity of these goals. We must not conflate our particular everyday tasks with what we take to be the goal of the universe at large. A conflation of the two takes place in anthropomorphic conceptions of God or nature. Anthropomorphism elevates human goals. Spinoza, in contrast, demotes these goals to the sphere of the passions or, in other words, the appetites. Demotion is the wrong word here, because Spinoza does not refute the validity of the passions. What he takes issue with is the aggrandizement of human inclinations into the quasi-objectivity of the truth of nature or God. The term demotion thus only relates to its antonym, elevation: demotion serves to balance out the effects of elevation without establishing a hierarchical structure. Spinoza attempts to put the human into its proper place—but not within a hierarchical order—and hence he counteracts an elevation with demotion. He does, however, not necessarily rank the one (the universe in its entirety or God/Nature) over the other (humanity as being only a part of the universe without representing the universe).

So Spinoza does not deny that we need goals but crucially he describes our lofty aspirations as appetitive. He does so as part of his larger attempt at disentangling the confusion of our intellectual, but always already particular, goals with the universal state of God or nature. As Spinoza states in the preface to the fourth part of the *Ethics* "Nature does nothing on account of

---

16   See Nadler's, *Spinoza's Ethics*, p. 199.
17   Lloyd, *Part of Nature*, pp. 20–21.

an end."[18] He goes on to detect behind the teleology of a universal "final cause nothing but human appetite."[19] It is important to note that Spinoza does not berate us for having appetites. He criticizes, however, the projection of our particular goals or appetites onto the whole of the universe. This confusion of the particular with the universal is dangerous because it makes absolute what is only a part of the whole but not the whole itself. The promulgation of any given teleology of the universe serves to both justify and enthrone as absolute value the hierarchical validation of what is only a part (i.e. humanity or rather one prioritized fraction of it) but not the whole of nature. Moreover, the confusion of our particular goals or appetites with nature or God is deceptive and leads to a loss of reality.

A deterministic conception of the world as predictable is the offspring of this loss of reality. Contrary to common perception, Spinoza is not a determinist, as the term is commonly understood. As Hampshire has astutely pointed out:

> A determinist, as this label is commonly understood, has the single idea that any human behavior is to be explained by well-confirmed natural laws which, taken together with a statement of initial conditions, exhibit the behavior, whatever it may be, as always in principle predictable. This is not the kind of understanding, and of self-understanding, that is proposed by Spinoza and Freud.[20]

Here Hampshire establishes an intriguing account of both Spinoza and Freud as nondeterministic and non-teleological thinkers. Both Freud and Spinoza unmask the mind's construction of a universal goal as the anthropocentric and anthropomorphic projection of particular appetites onto the world in its entirety (see Chapter 9). Both thinkers focus their ethical work on how a "man's discrimination between good objects and bad objects will be explained to him as imaginative projection upon reality of unconsciously remembered incidents in his personal history."[21] Both trace quasi-absolute and quasi-universal accounts of reality back to their source within the sphere of personal, particular appetites. Significantly both focus their analysis onto the sphere of religion, because it is here that humanity is perhaps most prone to confuse its limitations with God or nature.

Clearly, Spinoza's critique of a certain kind of theology is directed against the elevation of human teleology into a quasi-divine sphere (i.e. what Spinoza calls anthropomorphism). This anthropomorphic conception of God/nature renders absolute human conceptions of teleology that are intrinsically egoistic. As Hampshire has astutely pointed out, reflection, in contrast, "entails the suppression of egotism in our relation with the external world."[22] According to

---

18 Spinoza, *Ethics*, edited and translated by Edwin Curley with an introduction by Stuart Hampshire (London: Penguin, 1996), p. 114.
19 Ibid.
20 Hampshire, *Spinoza and Spinozism*, p. 195.
21 Ibid.
22 Ibid., p. xxiii.

some strands within recent Spinoza scholarship (i.e. Smith and to some extent Nadler) the *Ethics* ultimately extols rather than questions humanity's egoistic and teleological superiority over the heteronomy of God/nature. No wonder then that Spinoza emerges as a Kantian *avant la lettre* (as we will see, this Kantian view of Spinoza's *conatus* is based on a reading of Spinoza as Hobbesian thinker).[23]

This view argues that the *Ethics* reaffirms the centrality and superiority of human agency which the Copernican revolution had threatened to overturn. The earth might no longer be the center of the universe. Human epistemology and morality, however, vouches for the supremacy of man's rational constitution over anything that might be subsumed under the category of the merely natural (the body) or irrational (God). Smith thus argues that Spinoza only undermined teleology in order to debunk the role of God or nature in the life of the world: "The denial of any sort of natural teleology or divine providence has an ethical corollary. The *Ethics* deflates the idea that our moral judgments of approval and disapproval have any counterpart in nature."[24] From the perspective of this interpretation, Spinoza indeed anticipates Kant's further development of Descartes' mind-body divide. Spinoza does not question this divide. "Rather", writes Smith, "Spinoza maintains that there are at least two different and irreducible conceptual vocabularies, a language of bodies in motion and a language of minds with reasons and purposes."[25] Smith conflates Spinoza's approach with a Cartesian hierarchy that subjects the assumed irrationality of the body to the purported purposefulness of the mind in order to "challenge" contemporary thought and scientific inquiry.[26]

Instead of marshalling Spinoza as bulwark for the defense of an antiquated conception of what should constitute rationality, this chapter follows the approach of the neurologist Antonio Damasio. While having previously discussed the scientific inadequacy of the Cartesian mind-body divide in his study *Descartes' Error: Emotion, Reason, and the Human Brain*,[27] Damasio in his new book argues that Spinoza's *Ethics* develops a social theory that dovetails with recent scientific findings about the homeostatic relationship between the mind and the body. According to Damasio, Spinoza's anti-teleological thought helps advance a non-hierarchical understanding of humanity's place within nature. In what sense does Spinoza criticize teleology? His philosophy is anti-teleological in so far as it refuses to recognize a purposeful design in nature. As a corollary of his critique of teleology Spinoza abandons a prioritization of the mind over and above the body. This non-hierarchical stance moves his

---

23 In this way Spinoza's *Ethics* seems to anticipate the austerity of Kant's categorical imperative: "Like Kant's categorical (moral) imperative, the dictates of reason transcend personal differences and make universal demands on human behaviour." Nadler, *Spinoza's Ethics*, p. 227.

24 Smith, *Spinoza's Book of Life*, p. 52.

25 Ibid., p. 80.

26 Ibid., p. XII.

27 (New York: Grosset/Putnam, 1994).

thought into close vicinity of that of Darwin and Freud.[28] Following Damasio's approach, this book focuses on Spinoza's attempt to abandon a mind body dualism. It is this element in Spinoza's thought that accounts for his centrality in philosophical as well as literary discussions about an ethics that embraces rather than discards the diversity of embodied life.

Spinoza did not only align the life of the mind with that of the body. He also established an invariable link between the equilibrium of the individual and that of the society to which he or she belongs. As Genevieve Lloyd has astutely put it: "The mind is the idea of a body which is what it is, and does what it does, by virtue of being part of wider wholes reaching up to the totality of the material world."[29] The connection between the biological and the epistemological on the individual scale thus prepares the ground for the larger sphere of intersubjective relations that connect the preservation of the self to the survival of the other. As a neurologist Damasio emphasizes the scientific validity of Spinoza's social philosophy. "The biological reality of self-preservation", writes Damasio, "leads to virtue because in our inalienable need to maintain ourselves we must, of necessity, help preserve *other* selves."[30] The two related expressions "perfection" and "virtue" within the *Ethics* serve to amplify the signifying field of that concept that describes the future viability of life's ongoing existence, namely, the central word *conatus*.

Spinoza's understanding of the *conatus* does not prioritize either the mind or the body: "The *conatus*, the drive to self-maintenance and coherence, is a universal feature both of any person's mind and of his body."[31] Hampshire here lists coherence and self-maintenance as crucial elements of the *conatus*: they describe not a teleological form of development but a perpetual state of perfection throughout the ebb and flow of life's generation and regeneration. What Spinoza understands by perfection is precisely the *conatus* as the future viability (rather than plan or goal) of life's endurance and duration. Hence this book interprets Spinoza's notion of perfection not in terms of teleology, but in terms of sustainability on both an individual and a social scale.

An analysis of Spinoza's biological approach toward social theory paves the way for a novel account of human agency which does not prioritize the concerns of the mind over those of the body. Rather, both entities emerge as being intrinsically interconnected. This interdependence of mind and body does not mean that they are identical or perform indistinguishable tasks.

Spinoza famously characterizes the mind as the idea of the body. This view establishes an isomorphism between the two entities while at the same time not questioning their distinct identities. As the idea of the body, the mind is responsible for actions performed within the external and material world of embodiment. The mind does, however, also depend on the well being of the body.

---

28 Damasio, *Looking for Spinoza: Joy, Sorrow and the Feeling Brain* (London: Harcourt, 2003), p. 13.

29 Lloyd, *Spinoza and the Ethics*, p. 96.

30 Damasio, *Looking for Spinoza*, p. 171.

31 Hampshire, *Spinoza and Spinozism*, p. xxix.

According to Spinoza there is therefore not a hierarchical relation in which one commands the other. Rather the mind has to take care of the body and the body has to take care of the mind in order to ensure the preservation of the self (*conatus*). This equilibrium between the cerebral and the material by no means calls into question Spinoza's status as a rationalist. On the contrary this interpretation confirms Spinoza's rationalist credentials while also illuminating the originality of his approach.

Spinoza is a rationalist with a difference. He is a rationalist because the mind is central to his understanding of humanity. Nevertheless he conceives of the mental as being not opposed to but intrinsically linked with the physical. What the mind does is important because it has a considerable impact on the material world. This does, however, not mean that it is an unquestionable authority. The mind's work has to be questioned, because if its operations go wrong many things are likely to result in destruction in the embodied world of politics and society at large.

Anticipating Freud's analytical approach towards the ambiguities of the psyche, Spinoza argues that we have to be mindful of our minds. This is the originality of his approach: it is not hierarchical in so far as it does not prioritize one side over and above another; but at the same time it places a strongly rationalistic emphasis on the mind's central position as a place where one has to be on one's guard in order to ensure the preservation of embodied life. It is this close relationship that Spinoza establishes between the cerebral and the biological that moves his philosophy to the center of contemporary scientific discussion in the field of neurology and psychology. As Stuart Hampshire has pointed out, Spinoza "gives the strong impression of thinking like a biologist."[32] This intermingling of the biological with the mental implies that Spinoza does away with the boundaries that divide the natural sciences from the humanities. Spinoza's hybrid (boundary-crossing) approach has significant repercussions for a novel conception of the relationship between philosophy and social criticism. The aims of this undertaking are accomplished through an analysis of how different communities may come to realize that their respective truth claims are not absolute, but have a certain narrative element to their foundation. Toward this end, this book analyses Spinoza's as well as some Spinozist attempts at building a society in which the self and the other are not in competition but are instead dependent on each other. Does this narrative notion of identity deserve to be called relativist? Rather than being a relativist Spinoza is a realist. He is anti-relativist, because he criticizes an epistemology that trims down reality to its conception of the world.

A suspicious reader would object that Spinoza's philosophy had a revolutionary impact only within the self-enclosed field of Biblical hermeneutics. The innovative force of Spinoza's thought was, however, not confined to the realm of Bible criticism—it had a much larger reach. As Jonathan I. Israel has recently pointed out, Spinoza's revolution "overtly challenged the three principle pillars of medieval and early modern society—monarchy, aristocracy, and

---

32 Ibid., p. xlvii.

the Church—going some way to overturning all three."[33] For an accurate discussion of his critique of theology as politics, it is therefore necessary to discuss Spinoza's ontological critique of all kinds of epistemological mediations (be they theological, economic, sociopolitical or scientific). At this point he breaks with Cartesianism. It is therefore worth presenting a brief account of Spinoza's departure from the epistemological foundations which Descartes inherited from Plato.

2. Spinoza's Critique of an Absolutist Epistemology

The middle of the seventeenth century witnessed the emergence of a new age. This new era set out to introduce philosophy as the master-discourse that would, from then on, increasingly shape the outlook of Western European society on an all-encompassing level. It would have an impact not only on academic matters, but would saliently contribute to new developments in divergent fields such as the applied sciences and economics. From the mid-seventeenth century onwards, philosophy attempted to dethrone theology as master narrative. This attempted dethronement of theology provided the ideological basis for critical inquiry into all kinds of areas within society.

Whereas Descartes affirmed the validity of the established order in both political and theological matters (as he preeminently did at the opening of his *Meditation on First Philosophy* of 1641),[34] Spinoza's *Tractatus Theologico-Politicus* (1670) advocated the application of a scientific method to the study of biblical texts. In the *Ethics* (which was published posthumously in 1677), Spinoza would extend Descartes' rationalist approach from the field of Bible criticism to that of theology, anthropology, politics and social analysis.

While emphasizing the distinction between philosophy, on one hand, and theology as well as politics on the other, the metaphorical description with which Descartes characterizes the novelty of his philosophical method nevertheless implies the totalizing potential of his undertaking. In what ways does Descartes' use of metaphor undercut his seemingly humble self-limitation of philosophy as a self-enclosed entity which pays its respect to the spiritual and worldly powers that be? In his *Discourse on Method* (1663), Descartes compares his philosophical approach to the pulling down of an old house:

> And just as in pulling down an old house we usually preserve the debris to serve in building up another, so in destroying all those opinions which I considered to be ill-founded, I made various observations and acquired many experiences, which have since been of use to me in establishing those which are more certain.[35]

---

33 Israel, *The Jewish Enlightenment*, p. 714.
34 Gaukroger emphasizes "Descartes' strong adherence to Catholicism and his general avoidance of theological questions [. . .]." Gaukroger, *Descartes*, p. 4.

The destruction of the old building serves as the foundation for the construction of the new, which promises a more all-encompassing sense of certainty.

A house, however, symbolizes a unified whole made up of particular entities. Descartes is thus at pains to emphasize that the abolition at work in his philosophy does not threaten the theological foundations of the body politic. So Descartes is tearing down the house while leaving its foundations intact. Scholars have in fact analyzed the ways in which Descartes' writing supports rather than undermines the cultural and social relevance of the Catholic Church. He supports the status of the Church through his adhesion to Suarez's novel theological argument, according to which there is radical divide between the world of nature and the sphere of divine grace. This theology has been dubbed a theology of "pure nature" in order to distinguish it from the Augustine's and Thomas Aquinas's conception of nature as being capable of receiving the divine gift of grace.

Descartes' philosophical dualism between body and mind may be the offspring of the theological divide between the realms of pure nature and grace. According to Jean-Luc Marion, Descartes in fact radicalized Suarez's theology of pure nature. How did he do so?—by erasing a certain semantic meaning from the term *capacitas*: Augustine and Aquinas used this expression not to denote nature's and humanity's autonomous capabilities (i.e. nature's/humanity's independent power) but its openness towards the reception of the gift of divine grace. Marion argues that Descartes pushed "the semantic variation until *capacitas* was de facto understood as a strict synonym of *potentia*."[36] *Potentia*, however, describes a purely natural sphere: the realm of nature's autonomy which Suarez and, following him, Descartes strictly separate from the workings of divine grace. Could it be that Descartes' rationalist approach is in fact a theological one, one that radically departs from Augustine's and Aquinas's theology of grace but none the less develops and radicalizes Suarez's "modern" theology of "pure nature"?

Descartes endeavored to sever the union between theology and philosophy—as illustrated by his immanent use of the traditionally theological term *capacitas*. Has his undertaking been successful? Marion polemically asks "could Descartes be an unacknowledged theologian of pure nature?"[37] This seems to be the case. Marion points out that "starting with Descartes, the relation between man and God is apprehended by modern metaphysics in terms of power (*pouvoir*) and capacity (*puissance*)"[38] and he argues that this Cartesian

---

35 Descartes, *Discourse on Method and Meditations on First Philosophy*, ed. by David Weissman with essays by William T. Bluhm, Lou Massa, Thomas Pavel, John F. Post and Stephen Toulmin (New Haven, CT: Yale University Press, 1996), p. 19.

36 Marion, *Cartesian Questions: Method and Metaphysics* (Chicago: University of Chicago Press, 1999), p. 91.

37 Ibid.

38 Ibid., p. 95.

development "is in large part thanks to the theology of pure nature."[39] What are the implications of this discussion for a better understanding of Descartes' revolution? It may well be that Descartes attempts to demolish one theological dwelling space (the one built by Augustine and Aquinas when they formulated a theology which allows for nature's openness towards the gift of divine grace). He preserves its debris, however, in order to have the necessary materials for the construction of a new one.

Indeed, Descartes avers that the house he is in the process of tearing down has nothing to do with the societal architectonics of both an absolutist monarchy and the Catholic Church's claim to infallible truth. At the opening of his *Meditation on First Philosophy* he thus takes great care to depict the philosophical as a self-enclosed field of inquiry whose critical potential stops short at questioning the political and theological powers that be. He then proceeds to emphasize that his mind-body divide serves as an epistemological bastion in support of Leo X's orthodoxy. "As regards the soul," Descartes argues,

> although many have considered that it is not easy to know its nature, and some have even dared to say that human reasons have convinced us that it would perish with the body, and that faith alone could believe the contrary, nevertheless, inasmuch as the Lateran Council held under Leo X (in the eighth session) condemns these tenets, and as Leo expressly ordains Christian philosophers to refute their arguments and to employ all their powers in making known the truth, I have ventured in this treatise to undertake the same task.[40]

The supremacy of the mind over the body proves the immortality of the soul and thus reaffirms the social order that divides those that work menially from those who are engaged in non-menial work.

By 1660, however, Spinoza—due to his Marrano background[41] and no doubt spurred by his expulsion from the Jewish community in 1656—abandoned Descartes' purported differentiation between philosophical discovery, on one hand, and religious as well as social life, on the other. In order to improve the welfare of humanity, Spinoza argued, the philosopher cannot avoid addressing human issues in their entirety. He thus did away not only with the traditional philosophical-theological dualism between body and mind, but also with philosophy's self-restriction to a limited field of social influence. As J. Samuel Preus has shown, Spinoza "attacks" philosophy for its "elitism."[42] In the *Theological-Political Treatise* Spinoza questions the social and political repercussions of both a superstitious kind of theology and philosophy:

39　Ibid.

40　Descartes, *Discourse on Method and Meditations on First Philosophy*, p. 50.

41　Spinoza's Portuguese ancestors were forced to convert to Catholicism in the early part of the sixteenth century. Marrano was originally a swear word—denoting "pig"—which became common usage as a label for these New Christians. As Yirmiyahu Yovel has described with considerable detail, religious uncertainty characterizes the Marrano experience: Yovel, *Spinoza and Other Heretics: The Marrano of Reason* (Princeton, NJ: Princeton University Press, 1989), p. 24.

Spinoza's attack on the philosophers has a novel twist: they were traditionally the sworn enemies of "superstition," but here he accuses them of perpetuating it by conniving with the theologians. Superstition, more or less harmless by itself, can have dire political consequences, as already noted. Hence, Spinoza's critique of the philosophers is an integral part of his argument in the cause of liberty and a democratic hermeneutic.[43]

Spinoza attempted to make philosophy relevant for the life of the people and as we shall see, Herder radicalizes Spinoza's undertaking by attempting to dissolve philosophy into the social and natural sciences. It was therefore no longer the occupation of a privileged group. Instead philosophy became a democratic endeavor. Nadler argues that Spinoza's support of democracy is one of the reasons why he originally set out to ensure that a Dutch translation of the *Ethics* was available.[44]

By questioning a hierarchical divide between mind and body, Spinoza in fact undermined the societal force of various ideologies that have their foundation in specific epistemological assumptions (be they theological, philosophical, scientific or economic). In this manner he opened the way for an understanding of humanity that does not force abstract standards upon the specific contexts of human minds and bodies. He therefore did not merely differentiate theology from philosophy. If he had done so he would simply have followed in Descartes' footsteps. Crucially, Spinoza marked off philosophical strivings and scientific claims to epistemological certainty from the inevitable uncertainties of embodied social life. These inevitable uncertainties are the result of the incompleteness of our knowledge. Had Spinoza only driven a wedge between theology and philosophy he would have been close to replacing the monolithic assumptions of the former with those of the latter. Instead, Spinoza questioned the validity of all kinds of human epistemologies, thus encouraging us to be mindful of our minds.

The Spinozist critique of various kinds of intellectual endeavors (not just those of "theology") thus resulted in a blurring of the boundaries which demarcate the realm of sensuous enjoyment from that of cerebral work: "All these things [relating to both bodily enjoyment and cerebral work]," Spinoza argues,

indeed, show clearly that both the decision of the mind and the appetites and the determination of the body by nature exist together—or rather are one and the same thing, which we call a decision when it is considered under, and explained through, the attribute of thought, and which we call determination when it is

---

42 Preus, *Spinoza and the Irrelevance of Biblical Authority* (Cambridge: Cambridge University Press, 2001), p. 178.

43 Ibid.

44 Jonathan Israel as well as Steven Nadler rightly emphasize Spinoza's democratic outlook. See Nadler's *Spinoza. A Life* (Cambridge: Cambridge University Press, 1999), pp. 226–227.

considered under the attribute of extension and deduced from the laws of motion and rest.[45]

As corollary, and as has been intimated above, Spinoza reveals "the decisions of the mind" as "nothing but the appetites themselves."[46] In this way he reveals how purposeful viz. teleological thought emerges as what is seemingly opposed to it, namely, the sphere of the appetitive: "By the end for the sake of which we do something I understand appetite"[47] ("*Per finem, cujus causa aliquid facimus, appetitum intellego*").[48] Unpacking this short sentence helps us understand the relationship between Spinoza's critique of teleology and his deconstruction of the Cartesian mind-body divide. The *telos* of the final (*finem*) aim itself constitutes the motif force of the appetitive (*appetitum*). In order to be able to do something (*facimus*) we rely on the bodily function of the visceral (*appetitum*). The geometrical method thus serves as an instrument for the self-reflection of the mind (*intellego*) from its dependence on bodily desire. Self-consciousness can therefore not do without desire, precisely because it is desire's self-awareness. Spinoza's philosophical inquiry into the dependence of the mind on the body has crucial consequences for a reanimation of his social and cultural theory. This issue will be discussed in the following section.

3. The Theological Foundations of Teleological Thought

Critics have so far not sufficiently discussed how Spinoza's critique of theology works as social criticism.[49] Why does Spinoza broach the issue of anthropomorphism? What exactly is the target of his critical inquiry? He takes issue with the teleological thought inherent in anthropomorphic conceptions of God. According to Spinoza, neither philosophy nor theology exists in a self-enclosed sphere of influence. Rather any type of epistemology that plays a dominant role in a particular society at a particular time inevitably shapes specific social relations. Significantly, Spinoza discusses theological anthropomorphism in the context of prejudices that permeate different societal fabrics. He analyzes how social prejudices

> depend on this one: that men commonly suppose that all natural things act, as men do, on account of an end; indeed, they maintain as certain that God himself directs all things to some certain end, for they say that God has made all things for man, and man that he might worship God.[50]

---

45 Spinoza, *Ethics*, p. 73; Spinoza, *Opera* Vol II, ed. by Carl Gebhardt (Heidelberg: Carl Winter, 1925), p. 144.
46 Ibid.
47 Ibid., p. 117.
48 Spinoza, *Opera*, Vol. II, p. 210.
49 My argument builds on that developed by Antonio Negri, Etienne Balibar and Warren Montag.
50 Spinoza, *Ethics*, pp. 25–26. Spinoza, *Opera*, Vol. II, p. 78.

Here Spinoza criticizes not so much the worship of God but human self-adulation. The parallelism between the phrases *hominess . . . ut ipsos* and *Deum . . . ut ipsum* serves to emphasize precisely this point: humans attribute human forms of behavior to God's nature, since they perceive themselves as divine. Spinoza thus reveals "religious" worship of God as deification of the self.

This adulation of the self by the self hinges upon the espousal of teleology as the *sine qua non* for the definition of what distinguishes the human from the nonhuman and thus the divine from what lacks divinity. Everything that belongs to the order of nature, as perceived in terms of God's creation, supposedly strives toward a *telos*, toward an end [*omnes res naturales . . . propter finem agere . . . ipsum Deum omnia ad certum aliquem finem dirigere, pro certo statuant*]. Various social prejudices gain momentum, thanks to the philosophical positing of teleology as the certain criteria by means of which we have to distinguish between logical viz. theological forms of life and those which are illogical and are thus excluded from the order of God's creation. In this way social prejudices result from the equation of the rational (and thus Godly) with teleology. Only those forms of life alone are worthy of sustenance which evince a goal-oriented structure. The teleological thus functions as the lynchpin around which the anthropomorphic conception of God and nature revolves.

Spinoza's *Ethics* focuses on how it comes that dichotomous ways of thinking are an outcome of perceiving the divine from the perspective of teleology. By enthroning the finality of the goal as the main criteria of rational action, society intellectually justifies all kinds of exploitative power-relations. Under Spinoza's scrutiny, teleology emerges as a cover-up for the pursuit of self-interest that disregards the well-being of the other. The end of purpose-driven action coincides with the single-minded pursuit of one's advantage in the present without paying attention to the disadvantageous consequences that might accrue in the future. The anthropomorphic conception of a goal-directed God thus provides theological justification for man's domination over nature:

> It follows, *second*, that men act always on account of an end, namely on account of their advantage, which they want. [. . .] Hence they [humans] consider all natural things as means to their own advantage. [. . .] For they considered things as means, they could not believe that the things had made themselves; but from the means they were accustomed to prepare for themselves, they had to infer that there was a ruler, or a number of rulers, of Nature, endowed with human freedom who had taken care of things for them, and made all things for their use.[51]

The end (*finem*) of human action describes that which the self conceives of as being useful (*utile*) for itself. Spinoza does of course not devalue self-advantage. What he thus criticizes in teleological thought is not self-interest *per se*. Rather he excoriates those modes of perception that represent the self as the center of life. According to Spinoza it is certainly not wrong that

---

51 Spinoza, *Ethics*, p. 26. Spinoza, *Opera* Vol. II, pp. 78–79.

humanity lives on the fruits of nature. He criticizes certain teleological modes of thought, then, for divinizing a utilitarian relationship toward the external natural world. While it is worth emphasizing that Spinoza does not take issue with utilitarianism as such, it is equally important to show how he warns against both the loss of perspective and the logical fallacies that go along with a self-inflation of humanity. The target of Spinoza's critique of anthropomorphism is not theology as such but Descartes' conception of "pure nature" that subjects the merely mechanical natural world to the power and will of God's representative on earth: humanity.

Countering the anthropomorphism within the theology of pure nature, Spinoza makes clear how humanity's will and power (as manifested in teleology) self-destroys itself at the point where it loses track of human limitations. It thus sacrifices the sustainability of life to the quasi-divine power of redemption that posits in the future the attainment of its goals. Spinoza's rationalism is not hostile to theology as such.[52] Why is this so? Because Spinoza understands by reason a faculty that limits the unlimited reign of the passions and thus curbs the exhilarating presumptions of humanity's omniscience and omnipotence. Infinity describes the void that separates our limited human perception from the unlimited view of nature or God. The appearance of the concept describes the disappearance of the being that it names.

Spinoza's infinite mode denotes this abyss that separates our limited power of comprehension (concepts and categories) and the being of nature or God. What Spinoza thus criticizes as theology is that element that endows humanity with the domination over nature. Spinoza does not berate humanity's rule over nature. What he takes issue with is the forgetfulness of the limit that makes such rule possible. Humanity's domination comes at the cost of being mindful of our particularity within the infinity of Nature or God. Teleological thought denies that the natural world has an independent existence. Instead nature (*omnia naturalia*) serves exclusively as means (*media*) for the self-preservation of humanity. Spinoza therefore unmasks Suarez's and Descartes' theology of pure nature as anthropomorphism and as an exclusive teleology.

At this point, self-preservation appears in a rather ambiguous light. Crucially, an exclusive teleology instantiates an irrational kind of *conatus*: here the self preserves itself to the detriment of those circumstances and forces that enable the survival of the other, but this exclusive strategy has the potential to hit back, mirroring the flight trajectory of a boomerang. Spinoza's understanding of self-preservation discloses a critique of violence. The self that does violence to the other will be hit by violence whose force is equal to that perpetrated by the self in the first place. Jean-Paul Sartre's questioning of colonial violence is pertinent here. Sartre refers to the image of the boomerang in order to

---

52 Rather than denying the social relevance of religion and theology, Spinoza subjects theological inquiry to historical analysis. As J. Samuel Preus has put it, "Spinoza construed all scriptures and religions as natural products of history rather than as things supernatural." Preus, *Spinoza and the Irrelevance of Biblical Authority*, p. 158.

illustrate the social and cultural repercussions of a presumptuous kind of self-preservation that is in actual fact nothing but self-destruction: "It is the moment of the boomerang; it is the third phase of violence; it comes back on us, it strikes us, and we do not realize any more than we did the other times that it's we who have launched it."[53] Unlike Sartre, however, Spinoza does not maintain that "violence, like Achilles' lance, can heal the wounds that it has inflicted."[54] Spinoza argues that wounds can only be healed through the realization that self-preservation is tantamount to assisting rather than injuring the other.

One might counter this argument about the political relevance of the *Ethics* saying that Spinoza does not explicitly talk about self-destruction. Does Spinoza's notion of the *conatus* adumbrate a critique of societal self-destruction? T. W. Adorno has implicitly raised this question while discussing Elias Canetti's response to the Nazi-genocide.[55] In an important conversation with Canetti, Adorno has drawn attention to Spinoza's thought on self-preservation:

> Horkheimer and I have in fact analysed the problem of survival in the *Dialectic of Enlightenment*. In so doing we came upon the realisation that this principle of survival, which you [i.e. Canetti] in your terminology call the moment of survival, namely the situation of survival in the succinct sense—as it was for the first time, one could say in a classical manner, formulated by Spinoza—that this motive of survival, transforms itself into a destructive force, into the destructive and always at the same time into the self-destructive force if it turns wild, as it were, if it thus abandons the relationships to those others which stand opposed to it.[56]

Adorno here astutely points out that Spinoza is careful to emphasize that the will to survival is a social phenomenon. It has to be inclusive of others. If it turns exclusive it paves the way for self-destruction. Then the immunity of the individual disintegrates into autoimmunity. (Adorno underscores this point when he says, "that this motive of survival, transforms itself into a destructive force, into the destructive and always at the same time into the self-destructive force if it turns wild, as it were, if it thus abandons the relationships to those others which stand opposed to it.") Adorno's interpretation of Spinoza's *conatus* has an illuminating bearing on an accurate understanding of the autoimmunity or self-destruction inherent in some aspects of our contemporary global society. Thus Derrida has recently discussed how autoimmune processes such as "the strange behaviour where a living being, in quasi-*suicidal* fashion, 'itself'

---

53 Sartre, "Preface" in Frantz Fanon, *The Wretched of the Earth*, trans. by Constance Farrington (New York: Grove Press, 1979), p. 20.

54 Ibid., p. 30.

55 For a detailed discussion of this topic see, M. Mack, *Anthropology as Memory. Elias Canetti's and Franz Baermann Steiner's Responses to the Shoah* (Tübingen: Niemeyer, 2001).

56 Canetti, "Gespräch mit Theodor W. Adorno," in Canetti, *Aufsätze, Reden, Gespräche*, (Munich: Hanser, 2005), pp. 140–163, p. 141.

works to destroy its own protection"[57] invariably refer back to their opposite: to Spinozist attempts at self-preservation. These self-destructive processes result from triumphal declarations of moral, epistemological, military and spiritual superiority of one societal formation over the one that poses, or is seen to pose, as its enemy. This awareness of one's own triumph accompanies the perceived increase of one's power. Spinoza shows how proclamations of one's own superiority often go hand in hand with a loss of reality.

How does the occurrence of a loss of reality dovetail with Spinoza's philo-sophical writing about the *conatus*? As the discussion of Adorno and Derrida has shown, the theme of self-preservation combines medical and political concerns. Thought about a loss of reality clearly derives from psychoanalysis. The emotive, or in other words the psychological, and the political meet in Spinoza's discussion of the *conatus*. His work on self-preservation is highly interdisciplinary: here philosophical inquiry vibrates in a force field where political, medical, theological, psychological and literary currents crisscross each other.

Politics, medicine, theology and psychology focus on the self and its rela-tion with others. The self cannot survive without others and vice versa. This is precisely Spinoza's approach. He ties self-preservation to an engagement with the well-being of others. If self-preservation remains folded in upon itself the preservation of the self turns self-destructive (i.e. what Adorno has called self-preservation turned wild). This exclusive and all absorbing concern of the self with itself precisely describes the psychoanalytical phenomenon of a loss of reality. As the psychoanalyst and Hannah Arendt scholar Elisabeth Young-Bruehl has pointed out, "a psychotic person is one who cannot recognize real-ity, cannot become oriented in space and time, and is not mentally connected to other people; the mind of a psychotic is enwrapped in itself as if it were the whole world."[58] Spinoza attempts to remedy a loss of reality not through a psychological technique but via a philosophical investigation into its political, social and emotive causation.

What causes the societal drift towards unreality? A given society that seeks to establish its supremacy over and above other societies' claims to signifi-cance attempts to make reality conform to its epistemological standards. An inability to engage with epistemologies that differ from that of one's own con-ception thus does not evince realism. On the contrary, it indicates relativism, precisely, because it does not come to terms with the differing and always changing complexities of diverse social realities. The denial that the external world exists as an inviolable entity—as formulated by Descartes in his radical-ization of Suarez' theology of pure nature—justifies political actions based on

---

57 Jacques Derrida in Borradori (ed.), *Philosophy in a Time of Terror. Dialogues with Jürgen Habermas and Jacques Derrida* (Chicago: University of Chicago Press, 2003), 94.

58 Young-Bruehl, *Why Arendt Matters* (New Haven, CT: Yale University Press, 2006), pp. 170–171.

the principle of domination (*aliquos rectores*).[59] This hegemony deprives nature of animation (i.e. Descartes' mechanical understanding of the non-human world) turning it into a zombie-like means that does not have a life of its own [*Nam postquam res, ut media, consideraverunt, credere non potuerunt, easdem se ipsas fecisse*].[60]

The anthropomorphic or teleological conception of God does not only give rise to the ruthless and self-destructive exploitation of nature, but it also lays the foundation for violence and ethnocentric discrimination within society itself. Teleological thought pitches the *telos* of one community against that of another. The difference in religious worship thus furthers war between different social units; each of which deifies its specific way of life that goes along with its specific (anthropomorphic) conception of God. Under this teleological-theological constellation, particularity comes into conflict with universality. Self-preservation mutates to self-destruction at the point at which goal-directed behavior turns exclusive. Within this process, the self ignores the fact that the pursuit of perfection does not coincide with the single-minded attainment of a goal that it sets for itself as self-enclosed entity. Perfection has rather to do with what enables the sustainability of life, that is to say, with the avoidance of social exclusion and the abandonment of defensive reactions that aim to affirm one's superiority over another. How Spinoza conceptualizes perfection not in terms of a particular goal but in terms of the sustainability of the entire universe will be discussed in the following chapter.

---

59 Spinoza, *Opera* Vol. II, p. 79 (see previous quote ftn. 45). For a critique of auto-nomy as domination see Mack's, *German Idealism and the Jew*, pp. 42–62.
60 Spinoza, *Opera* Vol. II, p. 79 (see previous quote ftn. 48 and 49).

CHAPTER 2

SPINOZA'S *CONATUS* OR THE CRITIQUE OF POLITICAL SELF-DESTRUCTION

Everything that is, considered in itself, and without regard to anything else, includes perfection, which always extends in each thing as far as does the essence of the thing itself.

Spinoza, letter of 5 January 1665 to William van Blyenbergh

1. Spinoza's Critique of Theology as Teleology

The previous chapter focused on how Spinoza developed his novel theory of the self and its relation to the other within the larger philosophical context of the seventeenth century. This chapter pays particular attention to the precise formulation of Spinoza's social thought in his *magnum opus*: his *Ethics*. The following discussion revolves around the twin issues of self-preservation and self-destruction. It does so mainly by addressing the relationship that enfolds the particular within the horizon of the universal.

A particularity that seeks to realize its goals while defending itself against the aspirations of other political and cultural formations endangers its own survival precisely by focusing exclusively on its own *telos*. As Etienne Balibar has pointed out, Spinoza employs the term *ingenium* in order to denote the singularity not only of individuals but also of ethnic groups.[1] This deification of a specific teleology that structures the life of a particular social group eventuates in the war of all against all. Spinoza thus argues, *contra* Hobbes, that violence does not originate within the state of nature. Rather, it is the outcome of confusing those intellectual constructs that serve to represent a singular entity with the expression of reality as such. The real, however, is not only singular but also diverse.[2]

Teleological constructions about "all final causes are nothing but human fictions"[3] (*omnes causas finales nihil, nisi humana esse figmenta*).[4] Spinoza does not want to abolish these fictions. If he did he would be hostile to diversity, because it is exactly in the figuration of these *figmenta* that the imagination shapes the singular cultural formations of different ethnic groups. Instead, Spinoza critiques an inability to detect the fictional elements that underpin human modes of reasoning. As Genevieve Lloyd has put, "imagination can be

---

1 See Balibar's *Spinoza and Politics* (London: Verso, 1998), p. 37.
2 For detailed comparison between Descartes' theory of representation and Spinoza's philosophy of expression see Deleuze, *Expressionism in Philosophy: Spinoza*, trans. by Martin Joughin (New York: Zone Books, 1992).
3 Spinoza, *Ethics*, p. 27.
4 Spinoza, *Opera* Vol. II, p. 80.

a source of delusion; but we delude ourselves also if we deny its role in knowledge."[5] Anticipating Freud's rational investigation of irrationality, Spinoza takes seriously what the philosophical tradition dismisses as inadequacy. According to Spinoza inadequacy is a worthy subject of serious study, because it shapes much of our life. Inadequacy is the limit of knowledge that separates us from God: "God may have an adequate understanding of the essence of my body in its total context; but inadequacy is integral to the complex of ideas that constitutes the individual *me*."[6] Self-awareness delineates the difference between my limitations and the omniscience of God.

Spinoza makes teleological forms of thought responsible for a lack of self-awareness. Self-reflexivity makes the self aware of the fictional foundations of what it takes to be the truth (be that nature or God). A social unit which makes absolute its specific teleological conception of the world deifies itself and thus loses self-consciousness of its limited capacity. Self-reflexivity, in contrast, illuminates the desire based texture of its epistemes. Spinoza explicitly unmasks the touting of political and cultural superiority as perverted form of religious worship: "So it happened that each of them [individuals as well as ethnic groups] has thought up from his own temperament different ways of worshipping god, so that God might love him above all the rest, and direct the whole of Nature according to the needs of their blind desire and insatiable greed"[7] [*unde de factum, ut unusquisque diversos Deum colendi modos ex suo ingenio excogitaverit, ut Deus eos supra reliquos diligeret, & totam naturam in usum coecae illorum cupiditatis, & insatiabilis avatitiae dirigeret*].[8] Here Spinoza analyzes how teleology qua theology, which justifies man's domination over nature, has an immediate impact on the way in which different communities interact with each other. Instead of recognizing the fictional character of their specific social imaginings, each group claims superiority over other groups (*ut Deus eos supra reliquos diligeret*). This touting of supremacy refers to theology in order to bolster the assumed accuracy of its statements via the absolute authority that only the name of the deity seems to be able to provide.

Significantly, Spinoza focuses on the mind (*excogitaverit*) as the source of this confusion of particular inclination (*ex suo ingenio*) with the absolute value of the truth supposedly issuing from God (*Deus*). Rather than providing an accurate account of reality as it could be, here the mind qua will transforms potentially peaceful interactions between humanity and nature, as well as potential types of cooperation between different ethnic groups, into violent encounters in which particular entities destroy themselves while fighting for their predominance.

Critics have so far ignored the way in which Spinoza's critique of theology as teleology (and thus anthropomorphism) ironically relates to Descartes' and

---

5   Lloyd, *Spinoza and the Ethics*, p. 137.
6   Ibid.
7   Ibid., p. 27.
8   Spinoza, *Opera* Vol. II, p. 79.

Hobbes' voluntarism. A notable exception is Jerome B. Schneewind who has drawn attention to the fact that Spinoza's philosophy restored the split, perpetrated by voluntarist natural lawyers, between politics (prefigured by Duns Scotus' view of God's unlimited and arbitrary power) and ethics. Spinoza replaced Descartes' will with a notion of wisdom that strives for both the joyful and the virtuous: "Each increase in perfection is an increase in both our joy and virtue."[9] In contrast to Descartes, Spinoza maintained that virtue was not superimposed on nature by reason, God or political power. Rather the virtuous coincides with the joyful fulfillment of each individual's different natural potential. This appreciation of an infinite variety of different forms of life makes for the *differentia specifica* of Spinoza's understanding of self-preservation (*conatus*) from that of Hobbes.

Hobbes's political philosophy is based on a dualism between the state of nature, on the one hand, and the politics of reason, on the other. Kant transforms Hobbes's dualism between *status naturalis* and a *status civilis* into one between the state of nature and the state of freedom. By freedom, however, Kant understands a radical independence from any reliance on the "goods of this world."[10] Kantian rationality, with its unbridgeable gulf between the realms of freedom and nature, sets out to demonstrate the worthlessness of bare life (as "pure nature"). Kant thus adheres to Suarez' and Descartes' theology of pure nature. Reason dominates and overcomes nature by humiliating desires for objects in the external world. Kant deemed these desires "pathological." Kant's famous law of autonomy helped enact such subjugation of the forces of the body to the body politics. Here Hobbes clearly meets Kant.

Both Kant and Hobbes attempt to distill a moral kernel out of the Christian heritage. This moral essence should thus form the basis of their respective political philosophies. Both emphasize conscience over and against action. Spinoza's ethology, in contrast, focuses on actions and their outcome rather than on the inward sphere of conviction.

In his work on politics and religion Spinoza is heavily indebted to Averroes in that he does not completely reject the religious dimension within political life.[11] Why does Spinoza abstain from secular radicalism? He values those aspects in different forms of religion that give rise to actions which are supportive of what he understands by ethics. Hobbes and Kant, however, do not allow for a religious element that would contradict their conviction about the absolute supremacy of the secular state. In this way Spinoza's "break with the

---

9 Schneewind, *The Invention of Autonomy: A History of Modern Moral Philosophy* (Cambridge: Cambridge University Press, 1998), p. 221.

10 For a detailed discussion of this point see Mack, *German Idealism and the Jew*, pp. 23–41.

11 See Strauss's *Spinoza's Critique of Religion*, p. 101.

immediately preceding tradition was much less radical than that of Hobbes."[12] It is to some extent due to Spinoza's non-hostile attitude toward religion that his understanding of the *conatus* differs from that of Hobbes.

In contrast to Hobbes Spinoza argues that the self-preservation of a given human community depends on the preservation of the whole of humanity and nature. Spinoza's is thus a holistic approach. There is an important link between Spinoza's abandonment of a human centered universe and his holism. As Hampshire has astutely put it, "Spinoza, alone of the great figures of that age [i.e. seventeenth century], seems somehow to have anticipated modern conceptions of the scale of the universe, and of man's relatively infinitesimal place within the vast system."[13] Hampshire goes on to establish a connection between humanity's insignificant position within nature or God and a holistic view of the universe: "To Spinoza it seemed that men can attain happiness and dignity only by identifying themselves, through their knowledge and understanding, with the whole order of nature, and by submerging their individual interests in this understanding."[14] Spinoza's universalism also shapes his view of one tiny spot within the universe: humanity. Unlike Hobbes' he does not divide humanity into different groups, differentiating between a state of nature and a state of civilization or between religious communities and those who have attained the state of Hobbes' rational absolutist monarchy.

True to his universalism, Spinoza appreciates a plural world consisting of different social and religious ways of life. As Schneewind put it: "Knowledge of God is the highest good, and one person's possession of that knowledge obviously does not lessen another's share. We need not compete for the true good. We would not be led into conflict if we all understood this."[15] Spinoza critiques teleology on account of its exclusivity. The mind turns passionate and thus prone to violence if it focuses on the exclusive rather than on the inclusive. By combining virtue with joy, Spinoza bridges the gulf between the universal and the singular as well as the apparent gap that lies between the ethical and the political. Descartes perpetuates this separation between politics and ethics. This is squarely in line with his conception of philosophy as a self-enclosed entity (as discussed in the previous chapter).

Whereas Schneewind analyzes the differences between Descartes and Spinoza, Michael Allen Gillespie tends to see both philosophers as representative of the voluntarist heritage with which modernity had to come to terms at its inception in the seventeenth century. As Gillespie (following Hans Blumenberg) has shown, Descartes idealizes the power of the human will in order to create a bastion that could prove capable of fending off God's deleterious interference

---

12 Ibid.
13 Hampshire, *Spinoza and Spinozism*, p. 123.
14 Ibid.
15 Schneewind, *The Invention of Autonomy*, p. 222.

with the workings of the mind.[16] The feared *potentia absoluta* that had been a divine prerogative in the voluntaristic theology of Ockham and Duns Scotus became a human attribute in Descartes' confirmation of the will's/mind's superiority over the body.[17]

Whether it is the human mind as will or the absolute power of God within teleological constructions, nature always figures as that remainder of imperfection that has to be overcome. Only the subjugation of nature under the willful agency of either the divine (Ockham and Scott's voluntarism) or the human (Descartes' rationalism) guarantees the implementation of a purposeful scheme of things. Spinoza analyzes the fictional element within either theological or philosophical types (or both) of teleology that profile themselves as objective proofs of nature's deficiency. His critique of theology thus amounts to a critical inquiry into the fallacy of the mind that takes itself to be absolute and affirms its supremacy over that from which it sees itself separated: be it the body or the external material world.

Spinoza subjects the emotions to the style of geometric analysis in order to circumscribe their potential violence. Hence his implicit concern with self-destruction. This subjection to the geometric analysis does not, however, serve to discard the emotions as such. He clearly knows that this would be impossible.[18] Instead, the point of his dissection of feelings consists in showing how they are closely tied to the workings of the mind. He thus addresses (*nam ad illos revertere volo*) those who "prefer to curse or laugh at the affects and actions of men, rather than to understand them"[19] (*qui hominum affectus & actiones detestari, vel ridere malunt, quam intellegere*).[20] Anthropological research has shown that laughter functions as symbolic transposition of a feeling of superiority in precisely those contexts, in which the one who laughs abandons a relationship of empathetic understanding that can be found in

---

16 Blumenberg argues that the nominalism of late scholasticism distances itself from a biblical understanding of God. It subscribes to Aristotle's understanding of an "unmoved mover," whereas the Bible depicts God as always being engaged with humanity. According to Blumenberg, Descartes turns this view of a transcendent absolute into the sphere of immanence. The "cogito ergo sum" thus instantiates the emergence of the human as the immanent "unmoved mover." Against this background Blumenberg accounts for the two-faced character of the Enlightenment. It is at once teleological (thus clinging to a great design theory that inhabits a certain theological sphere) and atheistic. Blumenberg, *Säkularisierung und Selbstbehauptung* (Frankfurt a. M.: Suhrkamp, 1974), pp. 209–211.

17 See Gillespie's *Nihilism before Nietzsche* (Chicago: University of Chicago Press, 1995), p. 33.

18 Compare Warren Montag's *Bodies, Masses, Power: Spinoza and His Contemporaries* (New York: Verson, 1999) and Moira Gatens' and Genevieve Lloyd's *Collective Imaginings: Spinoza, Past and Present* (New York: Routledge, 1999).

19 Spinoza, *Ethics*, p. 69.

20 Spinoza, *Opera* Vol. II, p. 138.

enlightened and thus enlightening forms of humor.[21] When it precludes comprehension laughing at affections amounts to an assumption of supremacy, which, as we have seen, Spinoza critiques as an anthropomorphic conception of God. This touting of superiority accompanies defensive reactions as regards perceived threats either in nature or in the intra-human social sphere. The effects of these actions are equal to those of aggressive offences: they appear to be defensive to the one who perpetrates them but they are clearly offensive to the one who has to endure them.

2. Voluntarism as the Autoimmunity of Teleology

Descartes' voluntaristic rationalism reinforces the defensive strategies which an anthropomorphic conception of God justifies theologically. Spinoza emphasizes the originality of his appraisal of the affects. Descartes did not pay much attention to the emotive aspects of humanity:

> But no one, to my knowledge, has determined the nature and powers of the affects [. . .] the celebrated Descartes, although he too believed that the mind has absolute power over its own actions, nevertheless sought to explain human affects through their first causes, and at the same time to show the way in which the mind can have absolute dominion over its affects. But in my opinion, he showed nothing but the cleverness of his understanding, as I will show in the proper place.[22]

Spinoza reveals Descartes' declaration of the absolute dominion (*absolutum imperium*) of the mind over the affects as nothing else but a sign of subjective preference rather than objective analysis. In a subtle move, he contrasts the acknowledgement of his perspective (*mea sententia*) with Descartes' confirmation of the mind's absolute domination over arbitrary and merely subjective emotions. The polite style of the excerpt quoted above does not diminish the force of its ironic tone. This becomes abundantly clear if one reads the original Latin text. The showiness (*ostendit*) of Descartes' intellectualism mirrors the imperial (*imperium*) gesture with which the mind affirms its supremacy (*absolutum*) over the affects that it associates with the body. Spinoza praises Descartes' intellect (*acumen*) while in the same breath belittling it as a sign of a temperamental attitude (*sui ingenii*) rather than an instrument to be employed in the quest for objective knowledge.

---

21 For a detailed discussion of this point see, M. Mack, *Anthropology as Memory: Elias Canetti's and Franz Baermann Steiner's Responses to the Shoah* (Tübingen: Niemeyer, 2001), pp. 25–29.

22 Spinoza, *Ethics*, p. 69. Spinoza, *Opera* Vol. II, pp. 137–138.

To be sure, Spinoza does not excoriate individual inclinations and idiosyncratic preferences. What he takes issue with is the endeavor to dress up particular opinions as if they were universally valid truths which make everything that contradicts them or opposes them appear intellectually inferior. As he shows later on (*ut suo loco demonstrabo*), namely at the opening of Book V, Descartes' enthronement of the will as the mind's absolute control over the body, radicalizes a Stoic belief in the intellectual control over the life of the emotions.[23] In a quasi-objectivist mode, Descartes locates the dictatorial powers of the mind or, in other words, the will in a specific anatomical point, namely in the pineal gland, "*by whose aid the mind is aware of all the motions aroused in the body and of external objects, and which the mind can move in various ways simply by willing.*"[24] By pinpointing the source of the will's power in the specific cerebral location of the pineal gland, Descartes objectifies his subjective theory of voluntarism. Here the brain (of which the pineal gland forms a part) serves as a concrete location by which we can quasi-experimentally fathom the anatomical mechanism that enacts the omnipotent working of the mind (*cujus ope Mens motus omnes*). In Spinoza's account, Descartes' objectivist method mirrors that which it describes: the will's absolute domination over the inclinations of the body.[25] Spinoza characterizes the salient point of his own originality as precisely the abandonment of any teleological opposition between that which is to be dominated and the dominant, the inferior and the superior, the perfect and the imperfect, the goal and the goalless.

By employing a non-prejudicial approach in his analysis of the emotions, Spinoza sets out to question a hierarchical divide between superiority and inferiority, which structures philosophical, scientific and theological forms of teleology. He thus detects in the teleological the structural kernel that shapes superstitious kinds of actions and thoughts. According to Deleuze's interpretation of the *Ethics* "superstition is everything that keeps us cut off from our

---

23   At the opening of Book V of the *Ethics* Spinoza emphasizes this philosophical trajectory that connects Descartes with the Stoics as follows: "*Here, then, as I have said, I shall treat only of the power of the mind, or of reason, and shall show, above all, how great its dominion over the affects is and what kind of dominion it has for restraining and moderating them. For we have already demonstrated above that it does not have an absolute dominion over them. Nevertheless, the Stoics thought that they depend entirely on our will, and that we can command them absolutely. But experience cries out against this, and has forced them, in spite of their principles, to confess that much practice and application are required to restrain and moderate them [. . .] Descartes was rather inclined to this opinion.*" Spinoza, *Ethics*, pp. 160–161.

24   Spinoza, *Ethics*, p. 161. Spinoza, *Opera*, Vol II, p. 278.

25   As Damasio has shown the identification of the brain with the mind in direct opposition to the merely bodily has until recently been the accepted creed as regards the perception of human intelligence, See Damasio's *Looking for Spinoza*, p. 190.

power of action and continually diminishes it."[26] What, however, is the superstitious in Spinoza's view? As the discussion above has shown, Spinoza defines teleology as the deification and thus universalization or objectification of subjective thoughts and opinions. This making absolute of one's own will and desire characterizes the anthropomorphic conception of God, which Spinoza criticizes as both theology and superstition. In this way, he unmasks the superstitious foundations of Descartes' voluntaristic rationalism, which in turn is a secular (i.e. philosophical) translation and transmutation of Ockham's and Duns Scotus' theological discourse about a voluntaristic God.

Like the teleological, the superstitious thrives on the hierarchical divide between superiority and inferiority. That which opposes the willing subject becomes demoted to the inferior. Countering such supposition of a divide in the sublunar world between what is faulty and what is perfect, Spinoza abandons a terminology that aligns embodied life along a hierarchical horizon. Rather than arguing that particular objects have particular shortcomings, Spinoza affirms the flawless character of each living being. Spinoza makes this point clear in his letter of 5 January 1665 to William van Blyenbergh when he writes that "everything that is, considered in itself, and without regard to anything else, includes perfection, which always extends in each thing as far as does the essence of the thing itself."[27] What may strike us as imperfect amounts in reality to nothing else but an organism's vulnerability to specific internal as well external effects. In this way, there is nothing in nature that is evil or poisonous as such.

The deleterious effects of any particular substance do not make up its constitutional core. Rather, an individual proves destructive not through his or her existence, which we might construe abstractly as the essence of his or her character, but rather by the particular violent turn his or her actions take in any given situation. Likewise, a mushroom is not poisonous as such, otherwise it would poison itself. Spinoza tries to persuade us that we distinguish between abstract concepts and our understanding of ever-changing particular entities that form a substantial part of our everyday lives. We might be harmed by eating a poisonous mushroom, but Spinoza warns us of taking this effect it has on us as the static character of the plant itself.[28] The mushroom in question proves deleterious to our digestive system. In does not, by contrast, damage our sense of eyesight while observing it.

---

26 Deleuze, *Expressionism in Philosophy: Spinoza*, p. 270.

27 Spinoza, *The Correspondence of Spinoza*, translated and edited with introduction and annotations by A. Wolf (London: George Allen & Unwin, 1928), p. 147.

28 This is why Deleuze with his Nietzschean opposition between good and bad might partially reinstate the hierarchical structure which Spinoza critiqued in his analysis of the dichotomy between good and evil. In Deleuze's account of Spinoza evil seems to reemerge with the abstract and universal concept of badness. See Deleuze's, *Spinoza. Practical Philosophy*, trans. by Robert Hurley (San Francisco: City Lights Books, 1988), p. 72.

As it is, nature has already come into being within a state of perfection. "But my reason is this," Spinoza affirms,

> nothing happens in Nature that can be attributed to any defect in it, for nature is always the same, and its virtue and power of acting are everywhere one and the same, that is, the laws and rules of Nature, according to which all things happen, and change from one form to another, are always and everywhere the same.[29]

Thus differentiating his thought from that of Descartes, Spinoza draws the reader's attention to sociological, political as well as medical and psychological factors which vitiate both the well-being of individuals and the welfare of entire societies. Significantly, Spinoza does not frame his analysis in an objectivist style. On the contrary he opens his remarks by paying attention to the subjective position of his argument (*Sed mea haec est ratio*). There is an apparent paradoxical tension between the subjective formulation of his reasoning and the content of the reasoning itself. For what Spinoza advances in this dense paragraph is not an argument for the separateness of individual subject positions but an affirmation of their intrinsic interconnectedness, of their underlying unity (*& ex unis formis in alias mutantur, sunt ubique & semper eadem*).

A hierarchical form of teleological thought denies this interrelationship between different subject positions. For it attributes a praiseworthy goal to a single and thus specific entity, whose *telos* it contrasts with the faultiness of purpose within another social foundation. Teleology as superstition thus sheds light on the destructive passions of the mind. The mind operates via affects at precisely that point at which it turns exclusive. This exclusivity is only seemingly rational. In fact, it not only undermines the welfare of the other which it sees as either a threat or a competitor. In the end it destroys the self together with the other, because both are intrinsically interconnected. This is why calculation and friendship cannot be separated from each other in Spinoza's account of intersubjectivity. Clearly Spinoza advocates instrumentalism but his social thought is so intriguing precisely because he affiliates the instrumental with the altruistic and the altruistic with the instrumental: We help ourselves by assisting others and by assisting others we do not vitiate our well-being but instead promote it.

From the perspective of self-interest, the defensive reaction of war-like behavior is not an option. Rather, friendship truly instantiates the dictates of self-preservation (*conatus*). In striking contradiction to Hobbes's anthropology according to which man is a wolf to man (*homo homini lupus*), Spinoza argues that we are in need of each other as if we depended on the help of a deity. Once the anthropomorphic conception has been abandoned, which gives rise to the exclusivity of teleological thought, we realize that not one of

---

29 Spinoza, *Ethics*, p. 69. Spinoza, *Opera* Vol. II, p. 138.

us is able to survive independently. We are all in need of each other. The anthropomorphic conception of God attempts to cover up this needfulness by endowing a specific social and ethnic group with a redemptive teleology (and thus with quasi-divine support), which it posits as a lack in other human communities.

In this way Spinoza's dictum that "man is a God to man"[30] (*hominem homini Deum esse*)[31] only attains its full significance if one bears in mind Hobbes' proclamation that man is a wolf to man.[32] Spinoza does not deny that humanity sometimes tends to act in a self-destructive manner as if it were its own carnivore (i.e. a wolf). However, he emphasizes the "as if" factor. Destructive and therefore self-destructive behavior does not come naturally. Unlike Hobbes, Spinoza does not posit a state of nature that is characterized by unrestrained violence. He does not share Hobbes' conception of the state of nature as the war of all against all,[33] because his understanding of nature is different from that of Hobbes: Hobbes describes the state of nature as violence, whereas according to Spinoza nature is a force that connects rather than divides. Spinoza emphasizes his holistic and nonviolent conception of nature in his letter of October 1665 to Henry Oldenburg:

> I do not think it right for me to laugh at nature, much less to weep over it, when I consider that men like the rest, are only part of nature, and that I do not know how each part of nature is connected with the whole of it, and how with the other parts.[34]

Rather than being the product of the state of nature, violence is the off-spring of a specific cultural formation that shapes a social world in which war and social exclusion are accepted as anthropological givens.

How does it come then that human society revolves around violence and exclusivity? In his answer to this crucial question Spinoza focuses on the auto-immunity of teleology. The *telos* of a specific group turns, over time, into the cause of its own destruction. Spinoza's work on the relation between the passions of the mind and the medical phenomenon of autoimmunity has a special significance in the context of contemporary cultural and social theory. In that context Gilles Deleuze has drawn attention to Spinoza's discussion of auto-immunity in Part IV of the *Ethics*.

---

30 Spinoza, *Ethics*, p. 133.
31 Spinoza, *Opera* Vol. II, p. 234.
32 As Nadler has pointed, Spinoza studied "Hobbes political writings, especially the Dutch (1667) or Latin (1668) translation of *Leviathan*" in the early 1670s. Nadler, *Spinoza's Ethics*, p. 244.
33 Nadler has argued that "like Hobbes's state of nature, Spinoza's pre-political condition is one of unrestrained pursuit of self-interest." Nadler, *Spinoza's Ethics*, p. 245.
34 Spinoza, *The Correspondence of Spinoza*, p. 205.

Deleuze's analysis of Spinoza and autoimmunity focuses on death:

> Death is all the more necessary because it always comes from without. To begin with, there is an average duration of existence: given a relation, there is an average duration in which it can be realized. But, further, accidents and external affections can interrupt its realization at any moment. It is death's necessity that makes us believe that it is internal to ourselves. But in fact the destruction and decomposition do not concern either our relations in themselves or our essence. They only concern our extensive parts which belong to us for the time being, and then are determined to enter into other relations than our own. This is why the *Ethics*, in Part IV, attaches a good deal of importance to the apparent phenomenon of self-destruction; in reality what is involved is always a group of parts that are determined to enter into other relations and consequently behave like foreign bodies inside us. This is what occurs with the "autoimmune diseases." A group of cells whose relation is disturbed by an external agent, typically a virus, will be destroyed by our characteristic (immune) system.[35]

Deleuze focuses on the way in which autoimmunity blurs the boundaries between self and other, and between good (food) and bad (poison): "poison or food?—with all the complications, since a poison can be food for part of the thing considered."[36] According to Deleuze, Spinoza's discussion of autoimmunity in Part IV of the *Ethics* thus illustrates the blurring of the subject-object distinction that characterizes Deleuze's non supplementary "plane of immanence" where there is "no longer a form, but only relations of velocity between infinitesimal particles of unformed material"; and where there "is no longer a subject, but only individuating affective states of an anonymous force."[37] Spinoza's discussion of autoimmunity thus questions the existence of autonomous individuals: instead of instantiating a unified entity there are hidden forces within the self that destroy the self. Clearly, this view undermines the commonsense understanding of a distinctly delineated boundary that separates the self from others.

Spinoza reveals self-destruction as a wish for the destruction of others. The medical boundaries between self and other are fluid and so are the emotional/affective boundaries. Spinoza illustrates this in Part IV (Paragraph 34) of the *Ethics* when he discusses the case of envy and hate between Peter and Paul. This discussion demonstrates how the affects (i.e. envy and hate) bring about a division between self and other (i.e. between Peter and Paul) in the first place. Without the quasi-autoimmune influence of the affects Peter's self-preservation could be identical with that of Paul and vice versa. According to Spinoza, we are only opposed to each other when we are torn by affects/passions. Spinoza foregrounds his discussion of self-preservation via an analysis of autoimmunity and self-destruction in order to bring to the fore the potential coincidence

---

35 Deleuze, *Spinoza: Practical Philosophy*, trans. by Robert Hurley (San Francisco: City Lights Books, 1988), p. 42.
36 Ibid., p. 126.
37 Ibid., p. 128.

of the two elements. In doing so Spinoza wants to sensitize his readers as to the deleterious and truly irrational consequences of such coincidence. At this point self-preservation mutates into its opposite: into autoimmunity. Derrida has recently analyzed the political and ethical consequence of self-preservation become self-destruction.

As has been intimated above, Derrida has defined "an autoimmunitary process" as "that strange behavior where a living being, in quasi-*suicidal* fashion, 'itself' works to destroy its own protection, to immunize itself *against* its 'own' immunity."[38] Significantly, Derrida puts the terms "itself" and "own" into quotation marks, thus pointing to the unstable character of this self that tries to preserve itself while working against itself. In his reading, autoimmunity is not only a medical, but also a social, political and economic process that is one-dimensional and in its one-dimensionality furthers precisely that *against* which it sets out to work.

The linearity of teleological reason thus becomes explosive. In this way "autoimmunitary movements [. . .] produce, invent, and feed the monstrosity they claim to overcome."[39] Offering an alternative to social practices that turn suicidal (i.e. autoimmune) Spinoza shows how teleological conceptions of perfection contrast with the perfected state of sustainability. Politicians as well as religious leaders who attempt to set their society on the path toward the establishment of some transcendent and thus non-embodied ideational construct often do so with the concomitant aim of proving the imperfections of neighboring states, depicting these in terms of the devalued body and the merely material. By proclaiming the purported superiority of their own society they work, however, for its destruction. Here the mind runs amok and has ceased to be mindful of its own operations. This malfunction of the mind has detrimental consequences in the embodied world of politics and religion.

A recent example of such moralistic and religious justification of violence is of course September 11. As Bruce Lincoln has shown, the suicide attackers described their "chosen adversary not in terms of national, racial or political alterity, but as people to whom one is opposed on strictly religious grounds."[40] These religious grounds are themselves grounded in a mentalistic or moralistic discourse that opposes Al-Qaeda's ideals with the perceived "savage materialism" of the United States and the West: "Conversely, the United States becomes the contemporary incarnation of *jahiliyyah*: the barbarism and spiritual ignorance that preceded Islam and offered savage—but misguided and unsuccessful—resistance to the Prophet [i.e. Mohammed], his armed followers, and his message."[41] The contrast between spiritualism and spiritual ignorance is a mental or theoretical one. Here it is used to justify the ruthless employment of violence against groups of people that are depicted to be morally and

---

38 Borradori, *Philosophy in a Time of Terror*, p. 94.
39 Ibid., p. 99.
40 Lincoln, *Holy Terrors: Thinking about Religion after September 11* (Chicago: University of Chicago Press, 2003), p. 13.
41 Ibid.

religiously inferior. The insistence on the supremacy of one's own telos does not only potentially justify the employment of violent means for the attainment of this aim.[42] It also provokes the resentment, if not hate, of those upon whom one seeks to triumph.

This becomes abundantly clear in Spinoza's discussion of the passions and, as contrast to them, the third kind of knowledge. Crucially in his account of the human affects that form the heart of the discussion of Book IV, Spinoza analyzes the universal abstractions which the mind generates. He discusses these abstract universals in terms of a given society's passion to triumph over another. Here hierarchy emerges as the tyranny of universal ideas. The mind as driven by passions for distinction and exclusivity constructs an ideal of universality by means of which it passes judgment on nature's deficiency. Here, the end justifies the employment of violent means. Everything that deviates from the model of the universal constitutes imperfection. The term "sin" describes this deviation. According to Spinoza, the moralistic language of sinfulness gives rise to the hierarchical dichotomy that values what is perceived as perfect and devalues what appears as imperfect:

> But after men began to form universal ideas, and devise models of houses, buildings, towers, and the like, and to prefer some models of things to others, it came about that each one called perfect what he saw agreed with the universal idea he had formed of this kind of thing, and imperfect what he saw agreed less with the model he had conceived, even though its maker thought he had entirely finished it. Nor does there seem to be any other reason why men also commonly call perfect and imperfect natural things, which have not been made by human hands. For they are accustomed to form universal ideas of natural things as much as they do of artificial ones. They regard these universal ideas as models of things, and believe that Nature (which they think does nothing except for the sake of some end) looks to them, and sets them before itself as models. So when they see something happen in Nature which does not agree with the model they have conceived of this kind of thing, they believe that Nature itself has failed or sinned, and left the thing imperfect.[43]

As in his critique of theology, in his analysis of teleological reason Spinoza focuses on the fictional fallacy to which an epistemology that takes its ideational constructs as absolute invariably falls prey. The extract quoted above opens with human cognition and ends with the uncertainty of belief systems. Societies as well as individuals construct particular models (*exemplari excogitari*) that give shape to their peculiar preferences and idiosyncratic inclination. Here again Spinoza does not take issue with subjectivity as such. Instead he excoriates a cognitive fallacy, which elevates an individual construct into an absolute assessment of reality as it should be. The conceptual (*concepto*) turns out to be a matter of belief (*crederunt*). Spinoza detects a theological opposition

---

42   See Lincoln's *Holy Terrors*, p. 17.
43   Spinoza, *Ethics*, p. 114, Spinoza, *Opera* Vol. II, p. 206.

between sin and immaculateness behind the cognitive value judgment that contrasts perfection with imperfection.

The important extract quoted above shows how Spinoza analyzes the ways in which theology and teleology meet. Teleological reason in a crucial respect coincides with the anthropomorphic construction of God, which Spinoza critiqued at the opening of the *Ethics*. Both teleology and Spinoza's understanding of theology inflate the sense of power with which any given society sees itself endowed. According to teleological reason, a future goal sets those who subscribe to it apart from the rest of the human community in terms of moral and intellectual superiority. This sense of cognitive superiority could then serve as justification for the usage of unrivalled military force that could in turn pave the way toward the attainment of a redemptive future.

In a related manner, anthropomorphic conceptions of God commingle the spiritual with the political. In this way the God of a specific community functions as a device that separates this group from other groups in terms of superiority and inferiority. According to Spinoza, theological conceptions thus serve to trump up rather than to critically reflect upon a sense of human omnipotence. The self here merges with the deity it worships. Spinoza sees in this kind of self-preservation turned wild the ultimate cause of different forms of violent conflict. Bloodshed results from the self's touting of superiority. The self who revels in his own supremacy, derives joy from the inferiority of the other:

> For whenever anyone imagines his own actions, he is affected with joy (by P 53), and with greater joy, the more his actions express perfection, and the more distinctly he imagines them, that is (by II40S1) the more he can distinguish them from others, and consider them as singular things. So everyone will have the greatest gladness from considering himself, when he considers something in himself which he denies to others.[44]

True perfection, by contrast, does not separate between the self and the other. This is exactly what Spinoza means by the intellectual love of God or the third kind of knowledge which guarantees the eternity of the soul:

> This love toward God is the highest good which we can want from the dictate of reason (by IVP28), and is common to all men (by IVP36); we desire that all should enjoy it (by IV37). And so (by Def. Aff. XXIII), it cannot be stained by an affect of envy, nor (by P18 and the Def. of jealousy, see IIIP35S) by an affect of jealousy. On the contrary (by IIIP31), the more men we imagine to enjoy it, the more it must be encouraged, q.e.d.[45]

Here Spinoza explains why the truly rational love of God represents the highest good. The *deum amor ex dictamine rationis* (the love of God out of the

---

44 Spinoza, *Ethics*, p. 99, Spinoza, *Opera*, Vol. II, p. 183.
45 Spinoza, *Ethics*, p. 170, Spinoza, *Opera* Vol. II, p. 292.

instruction obtained from rational inquiry) enables social and political interactions that are free from violence precisely because they are not accompanied
by feelings of envy and jealousy which, as the previous discussion has shown,
arise from touting teleological claims of superiority. The *summum bonum* thus
coincides with what is common, rather than exclusive, to the diversity of all
peoples (*omnibus hominibus commune est*). Here we come to understand ourselves as modes of substance, as tiny parts of an all-encompassing but, from a
limited human point of view, incomprehensible universe.

3. Conclusion: Communality as the Eternity of the Soul

As corollary of the discussion advanced in this chapter, it becomes clear that it
is exactly this communality which Spinoza understands by the eternity of the
mind.

Critics have often asked why Spinoza subscribed to the concept of the soul's
eternity while at the same time affirming the parallelism between mind and
body. How can the soul be immortal if it is intrinsically tied to the decay of the
body? In order "to deal with this mess," Aaron V. Garret has recently argued
that, according to Spinoza, "only a *part* of the mind is eternal."[46] This statement might reconcile the apparent contradiction of Spinoza's writing on the
parallelism of body and mind, on one hand, and the eternity of the soul, on the
other.

Yet at the same time it gives rise to another paradox. How does the separation of the mind into an inferior and thus perishable part and into a superior
and thus immortal essence square with Spinoza's focus on communality and
interconnectedness (an element which Garret otherwise emphasizes in his
study)?[47] Spinoza defines reason as that aspect of the mind that proves capable
of understanding the necessary causes of various experiences the body undergoes in communal life. It can thus only operate as part of a bodily entity. What
happens if the body to which the mind belongs has perished? As we have seen
above, the mind, as the rational love of God, does its work in a communal
manner. There is not a single body that can rationally claim reason as its exclusive possession. Rather, it forms part of the whole of humanity in every aspect
of its diversity.

The mind, as reason (rather than as affect) asks us to look out for our self-
interest. But the "us" in question here does not denote a singular and exclusive
group. On the contrary, it describes humanity in its entirety. The mind's eternal
nature thus introduces a novel conception of what it means to be a unity.

---

46   Aaron V. Garret, *Meaning in Spinoza's Method* (Cambridge: Cambridge Univer-
     sity Press, 2003), p. 195.

47   Thus Garret defines interconnectedness as the hallmark of Spinoza's philosophical
     approach: "That this is the case, i.e. that apparently unrelated concepts are inter-
     connected in often surprising ways is itself one of the hallmarks of Spinoza's
     method." Garrett, *Meaning in Spinoza's Method*, p. 18.

As unified form, the eternity of the mind at the same time constitutes a plurality. Once a particular body perishes, the mind keeps on living in relation to the diversity of other bodies that are still alive. As unity it thus inhabits plurality. How, however, is the plural capable of promising the eternal? In order to better understand Spinoza's notion of eternity it is worth recalling the link Walter Benjamin establishes between death and survival when he writes "to dwell means to leave traces."[48] The tenant who passes away leaves traces in either an obvious or in a less visible manner; his or her name may not be clearly indentified with what she or he leaves behind. Spinoza, does, however, not attach any importance to marks of a clearly distinct identity. What concerns him is how the traces of passed mentalities shape the makeup and setup of our minds in the here and now. These traces constitute the eternity of the mind, linking the past with the present either in a clearly recognized or in a more or less incognito mode.

The mind is an unceasing and therefore eternal hermeneutic network: it deciphers traces of the past within the present. The mind is engaged in a continual process of understanding various modes of substance—of which past traces form a part. It can, however, never reach an all-comprehensive view of substance due to its limited cognition. According to Spinoza, and according to Herder afterwards (see the following chapters), God or nature seems to be scattered throughout the universe and only the collective work of all parts of the universe would yield a view of substance that could come close to a certain standard of adequacy. The mind attempts to understand substance but always falls short of its goal, because it cannot achieve complete communality. There is a constant gap between the partial effort of hermeneutical work and the impartiality of substance. As Genevieve Lloyd has astutely put it:

> To be a mode is, by definition, to be dependent on substance; and to understand ourselves as eternal is to understand ourselves as modes of an eternal substance. To understand ourselves truly is to understand ourselves in relation to substance, which is eternal. We are not—and can never be—substance. But we cannot fully understand ourselves without reference to substance, whose modes we are. In the full understanding of ourselves as modes of substance, thought, emotion and imagination come into a powerful synthesis which makes both dying and immortality cease to matter.[49]

Dying and immortality cease to matter, because we come to understand how our partial existence is bound up with that of an all-comprehensive substance, which we, however, are not able to comprehend. We are nonetheless able to discern traces that link isolated instances to a larger whole.

To understand these linkages our mind collaborates with the emotions and the imagination. Spinoza's mind could be compared to Benjamin's flaneur,

---

48 Walter Benjamin, *The Arcades Project*, trans. by Howard Eiland and Kevin McLaughlin (Cambridge, MA: Belknap Press, 1999), p. 9.
49 Lloyd, *Spinoza and the Ethics*, p. 131.

who walks the streets of Paris while trying to comprehend how absence haunts the life of presence. This intellectual detective work relies as much on imaginative and emotive forms of intellection as it depends on mathematical calculations. Its hermeneutical endeavor is to understand how seemingly separate entities communicate with each other. In order to detect these seemingly secret transmissions it needs to have attained a certain level of imaginative and affective intelligence.

The eternity of the mind works via transmission and what is transmitted survives in changed form within different and diverse contexts. Rather than being linear and one-dimensional, the mind as rational love of God is ever-changing. This continuity of change makes for its eternity. In contrast to Hobbes and Descartes who see, in true Aristotelian fashion, change as a characteristic of a deficient world, Spinoza revalues what the philosophical tradition up to the Copernican revolution devalued: he appreciates the diverse and the ever-changing as forces not of death but of life.

Why is this change of perception as regards 'change' related to Copernicus and the accompanying transition from a geocentric to a heliocentric worldview? In order to address this question it is helpful to discuss Spinoza's theory of nature in the context not of Hobbes's or Descartes's thought but in close proximity to Galileo's natural philosophy and natural theology. As his letters to Henry Oldenburg attest, Spinoza was deeply interested in Galileo's work.[50] Galileo described the Copernican universe as one that is dependent not on Aristotle's unmoved mover but on the ever-changing force of the sun. As Mario Biagioli has pointed out, Galileo "treated change as positive notion linked to movement, life, and generation."[51] Similar to Spinoza, in his discussion of the sun, Galileo focused on how different aspects of nature depend on each other. Decay is thus not necessarily lethal: it could be part of nature's regenerative and ever-changing process. The sun as center of the universe sets in motion a novel interpretation of transformation. In a letter of March 23, 1615 to Piero Dini, Galileo argues "that there is in nature a very spirited, tenuous, and fast

---

50 In a letter of May 1665 to Oldenburg, Spinoza refers to the telescopes from which Galileo gained credit in terms of both money and reputation. In this letter Spinoza discusses Galileo's "certain Telescopes, constructed in Italy, with which they could observe eclipses in Jupiter caused by the interposition of his satellites, and also a certain shadow on Saturn, as if made by the ring." He then goes on to criticize Descartes' abstract theories with the empirical evidence offered by the work performed by Galileo's Italian telescopes: "On the occasion of these things I cannot wonder sufficiently at the rashness of Descartes, who says that the reason why the Planets next to Saturn (for he thought that its projections were Planets, perhaps because he never saw them touch Saturn) do not move may be because Saturn does not rotate around its own axis. For this does not agree with his principles, and he could very easily have explained the cause of the projections from his principles, if he had not laboured under a prejudice, etc." *The Correspondence of Spinoza*, pp. 198–199.

51 Biagioli, *Galileo's Instruments of Credit: Telescopes, Images, Secrecy* (Chicago: University of Chicago Press, 2006), p. 215.

substance that spreads throughout the universe, penetrates everything without difficulty, and warms up, gives life to, and renders fertile all living creatures."[52] The sun both instantiates and represents this transformative force of nature, which Spinoza would later denote *deus sive natura*: to Galileo "the senses themselves show us the Sun to be by far the principle receptacle of this spirit" of unceasing change.[53]

Change and decay no longer distinguishes the sublunar world from the life of the stars. The planet of the sun is not only the "the vital center" of Galileo's cosmos but it also displays the mundane characteristics of earthly existence: "the consumption of food and the production of excrements" which Galileo detected with his telescope as the reason behind the sunspots. We "live in continuous change" (*quod nos in continua vivimus variatione*)[54] Spinoza affirms.[55] Spinoza's notion of the mind as a plural, sustainable and ever-changing unity could thus serve as a blueprint for an inclusive universalism that would be truly beneficial for the nonviolent solving of problems that global societies are facing at the dawn of the twenty-first century. The following chapters focus on Herder's Spinozist readings of history. Even though he belongs to the eighteenth century, Herder's ever changing crisscrossing from the particular to the universal and back from the universal to the particular is pertinent to contemporaneous renegotiations of what it means to be a universalist.

---

52 Quoted from Biagioli's *Galileo's Instruments of Credit*, p. 215.
53 Quoted from Biagioli's *Galileo's Instruments of Credit*, p. 215.
54 Spinoza, *Opera, Vol II*, p. 305.
55 Spinoza, *Ethics*, p. 178.

Chapter 3

Herder's Spinozist Understanding of Reflection

The philosopher who deserves most credit for reviving the philosophy of the mind in eighteenth century Germany is Johann Gottfried Herder. By questioning the hegemony of mechanism, his vitalist theory of mind promised a middle path between the extremes of a reductivist materialism and supernaturalist dualism.
Frederick Beiser, The Fate of Reason

1. Herder's Ethics of Difference

The following chapters attempt to establish the contemporary relevance of Herder's Spinoza-inspired conception of diversity and sustainability. How did Herder extend and radicalize the Spinozist critique of an epistemology turned absolute? The following analyzes how Herder questions the Enlightenment ideal of a divide between irrational nature and rational humanity via an innovative account of humanity's capacity for reflection. Herder turns the problems associated with various forms of divergence (mainly those between the empirical and the conceptual) into opportunities: at his hands divergent forms of life and thought become part and parcel of his plea to respect human and natural diversity. How do these seemingly separate fields of inquiry—one epistemological (the conceptual-empirical divide) and one sociopolitical (i.e. social diversity)—relate to each other? Herder's concern with the divergence between actual things and their conception in the mind prepares for his insight into the necessity of a type of reflection that is not fixated on one side of any given inquiry but ranges from the past to the present, from the poetic to the prosaic and from touch to perception without tilting the balance into either one or the other direction.

From his youthful writings onwards Herder criticized cognitive accounts of culture and society. His early differentiation between the existential and the cerebral was the first step toward a critique of a separation between people who are perceived as "primitive" or savage in the sense of the irrational and as "civilized" in the sense of the rational. From his first encounter with Spinoza's works during his student days onwards, Herder criticized types of thinking that confused the logical with the existential or the real and thereby superimposed the former onto the latter. In his early aphoristic *Essay on Being*, he discussed the gulf that separates logic from reality. By the early 1760s he thus already developed his distinctive cultural theory. This theory sheds light on what I call the "logical fallacy of culture."[1] In his *Essay on Being*, Herder

---

1   As F. M. Barnard has recently pointed out, in contrast to Kant, Herder does not distinguish between civilization and culture. See Barnard's "Introduction", in Barnard, *Herder on Nationality, Humanity, and History* (Montreal: McGill-Queen's University Press, 2003), pp. 3–17, p. 10.

defines existence as a non-divisible, monistic entity, as something not grasp-able in its entirety but which nevertheless lays the foundation for conceptual-ity as such.

By formulating a concept we attempt to grasp being. This conceptualization forms the main part of various cultural activities. Herein resides the root of our logical fallacy. Herder wrote his *Essay on Being* while studying with Kant at the University of Königsberg in the 1760s. Here he encountered the early Kant who was roused out of his metaphysical slumber by Hume's skepticism. As John K. Zammito has deftly put it, this

> is hardly an instance of an "all-destroying" skepticism (along the lines that alarmed Mendelssohn and offended Hamann in the *Critique of Pure Reason* and led Hamann to call Kant the "Prussian Hume"), but rather a moderate skepti-cism that seemed to bode well *both* for the pragmatic pursuit of empirical science *and* for restraint in speculative metaphysics.[2]

Herder deepens and develops the early Kant's skeptical stance toward dog-matic thought.

How does he do so? He accepts what strikes Hume and later Kant as an unacceptable but yet unavoidable impediment for the practice of philosophy: the primacy of sensual perception over the formulation of concepts and cate-gories or as Hume has put it, the stubborn fact "that our impressions are the causes of our ideas, not our ideas of our impressions."[3] Hume's skepticism threatens the validity of metaphysics which is premised precisely on the prior-ity of ideas over the mere collection of empirical data. The mature Kant can-not accept that sense impression precedes the conception of ideas. He attempts to bypass this impasse via his formulation of the priority of *a priori* reason, or, in other words, autonomy over and above the original heteronomy of our nonphilosophical encounter with the world as accurately captured by Hume's skepticism.

Herder does not follow Kant's attempt to salvage metaphysics through a transcendental system that lays down limits to any possible interference of sense impression with the autonomous work performed by "pure reason." He does not do so, because he is not interested in philosophy understood as an academic and therefore independent discipline. Instead he attempts to dissolve philosophy into the natural and the social sciences. He thus closes his early essay "How Philosophy can become more Universal" with the conception of a Copernican revolution which would evaporate philosophy as a distinct disci-pline and would dissolve it into anthropology:

> All philosophy which is supposed to belong to the people must make the people its central focus, and if philosophy's viewpoint gets changed in the manner

---

2   Zammito, *Kant, Herder & the Birth of Anthropology* (Chicago: University of Press, 2002), p. 188.

3   Hume, *Treatise of Human Nature*, analytically indexed by L. A. Selby-Bigge (Oxford: Clarendon Press, 1978), p. 5.

in which out of the Ptolemaic system the Copernican developed, what new fruitful developments must not occur here, if our whole philosophy becomes anthropology.[4]

Once philosophy has discarded its metaphysical baggage and has become submerged into the empirical realm of history and nature, the gap separating concept and thing remains intact. And it can remain intact with impunity, precisely because the cognitive side (the concept) no longer has to perform the task of shaping the empirical realm—the world of things—as it has to in the critical Kant's reconstituted metaphysics of the a priori.

In contrast to the critical Kant, Herder does not attempt to shape the given world of things via human cognition. It is this shaping of the merely empirical realm of things which Kant's critical philosophy promises to enable via the conceptual work of the autonomous a priori. Herder begs to differ here. He is content to remain in the empiricist realm of things be they historical—an outcome of human society—or be they natural—part and parcel of the development of the cosmos at large.

In his 1778 essay *On the Cognition and Sensation of the Human Soul* Herder formulates his empiricist stance along the line of a Spinozist critique of anthropomorphism. He argues that it is wrong to attempt to grasp God via "pure thinking": "All so called *pure thinking* into the deity is deception and game, the worst mysticism, which only fails to recognize itself as such. All our thinking arose from and through sensation, also still bears, despite all distillation, rich traces of it."[5] We are not able to reach a transcendent purity via pure thinking, because we are simply incapable of doing away with our reliance on the body. Herder has clearly taken on board Spinoza's conception of the mind as the idea of the body. As idea of the body the mind cannot leave behind the embodied world of the senses.

Herder shifts the emphasis from Spinoza's concern with nature to that of history. This shift does not imply an opposition between the natural and the historical, because Herder comes to read the anthropological as part of natural history. As in his critique of religious dogmatism, Herder takes issue with dogmatic conceptions of history. Dogmas remove us from the senses, because they do not tolerate the diverse and divergent world of embodied life. In his *Older Critical Forestlet* of 1767/68 Herder argues that doctrinal history reduces the complexity of historical events to a single and simple structure: "A history can be a doctrinal structure to the extent that it represented to us a *single* occurrence, in its entirety, like a structure."[6] He goes on to differentiate this doctrinal approach from history proper. The doctrinal is not historical but philosophical, because it does its work via inference only, while neglecting observation: "This bond is not seen, but inferred, and the art of inferring

---

4   Herder, *Philosophical Writings*, edited and translated by Michael N. Forster (Cambridge: Cambridge University Press, 2002), p. 29.

5   Herder, *Philosophical Writings*, p. 242.

6   Ibid., p. 266.

concerning it is no longer history but philosophy."[7] This differentiation between history and philosophy was a common topic in the eighteenth century.

As Zammito and Arno Seifers have shown, in early modern thought the term "*cognitio historia* represented the most embracing concept of an *empirical* form of inquiry, in other words, a method based on observation and experience in all the various fields touching upon human experience."[8] Herder criticizes in both traditional metaphysics (i.e. Wolff and Leibniz) and in Kant's revolution of the metaphysical a priori what he sees as the neglect of the *cognitio historica*: "Herder believed that 'philosophy' as an academic endeavor had leaped far too swiftly past *cognitio historica* into *cognitio philosophica*."[9] This leap from the empirical to the metaphysical describes the trajectory of the voyage over the abyss which opens between the conceptual and the factual.

By trying to grasp the essence of being, the concept lays open a gulf between the logical and the existential. Herder does not take issue with the distance that separates the epistemological (of which logic forms a central part) from the existential. The fallacy does not lie in the separation. On the contrary *what is fallacious is the refusal to acknowledge the distance that lies between thought and that which it tries to grasp: i.e. being.* What I call "logical fallacy of culture" results from a denial of human epistemological limitations (as discussed in the previous chapters). This denial of limitations as regards morals and norms is the dogmatic aspect of Kant's moral philosophy. One could say that Herder is a critical philosopher not in a Kantian but in a Spinozist sense. Yirmiyahu Yovel has astutely described the difference between a critical Spinozist approach and dogmatic Kantian one as follows:

> On the question of normativeness then, it is Kant who represents the dogmatic view of immanence whereas Spinoza offers a critical one. Reason in Kant cannot be construed, as in Spinoza, as part of the actual world but constitutes a second, separate world over and above it, with man participating as 'citizen' in both. This is a secular vestige of Christian dualism, endowing man with a divine faculty emanating from heaven.[10]

We are only a part of nature's incomprehensible vastness and therefore our epistemological capacity is ineluctably limited if we set out to grasp the universe in its entirety. Herder adapts Spinoza's discussion of nature to the sphere of historical inquiry: our limited present perspective precludes any attempt to say how things actually were in the past or will be in the future. This does not mean that there is no cohesion—however long-winded or tiny these cohesive points might be—in either nature or in history. The crucial point here is that we are not able to comprehend how what may strike us as arbitrary and non-determined events are in actual fact phenomena that are determined by the workings of (to us) invisible determinants that regulate causation.

---

7 Ibid.
8 Zammito, *Kant, Herder & the birth of anthropology*, p. 223.
9 Ibid., p. 313.
10 Yovel, *Spinoza and other Heretics*, p. 177.

What is separate may not necessarily be dualistically opposed with each other. Herder in particular criticizes Descartes for confusing limited human thought with existence as such. Descartes equates thinking with being while at the same time promulgating a dualism between the material and the cerebral. Herder sees this dualistic opposition in the empirical idealism of Descartes (and he criticizes a similar kind of dualism in Kant's transcendental idealism). He affirms the distinctiveness of the ideal and the existential while not confronting them with each other as if they were binary opposites: "with us being already separates itself into the ideal and the existential; both are distinctive notions, and none can be explained through the other. I therefore think that Descartes wrongly inferred 'I think, therefore I am.'"[11] Herder here implicitly criticizes identitarian ways of thought. More importantly, Herder maintains that being is a split and fractured entity. Being does not coincide with itself. It is divergent. Descartes's *cogito ergo sum*, in contrast, ignores this divergence in both thinking and being. The rationalism of Descartes results in a loss of reality. By establishing an identity between being and thinking, he sacrifices realism for an ideational construct. Herder thus questions rationalism in order to defend a realist rather than a relativist position. Consequently, he uncovers relativism behind rationalist presuppositions that posit a unity between the real and the logical.

Like Spinoza, Herder does not deny that there is a correspondence between thought and reality. An adequate correlation between logic and reality can, however, only be found in the Godhead. As Herder put it in *This too a Philosophy of History*,

> incidentally, I know as well as you do that every *general image*, every *general concept*, is only an *abstraction*—it is only the Creator who *thinks* the whole *unity of one, of all*, nations in all their *manifoldness* without having the *unity* thereby fade for him.[12]

There is indeed a complete correspondence between thought (*unity*) and being (*manifoldness*).

Herder is a rationalist in the Spinozist rather than Cartesian tradition, because he differentiates between the particular human position and the truly universal one of God or nature where there is indeed an adequate correlation between logic and reality. Our human capacity is too limited to accomplish this feat. Radicalizing Spinoza's critique of anthropomorphism Herder argues that Descartes's *cogito* assumes the position of an omniscient God in whose mind being and thought does not diverge. Divergence, however, is one of the main characteristics of our human condition.

This divergence between being and concept forms the structural foundation of Herder's philosophy of diversity. Being at home on the side of being's

---

11 Herder, *Frühe Schriften 1764–1772* (ed.) by Ulrich Gaier (Frankfurt a. M.: Deutscher Klassiker Verlag, 1985), p. 21.
12 Herder, *Philosophical Writings*, p. 293.

empirical factuality does not provide us with the whole truth but neither does ensconcing within the sphere of the concept. What is required of thought is instead a restless movement between these divergent and diverse poles. This restlessness stipulates a mobile self that allows for and encourages indeterminacy rather than relying on strictly determined entities which are separated from each other (mirroring the human-nature or body-mind dualism). In an important essay John K. Noyes has uncovered an ecological and postcolonial sensibility in Herder's and Goethe's Spinozist approach that has the capacity to respond to questions and concerns articulated by contemporary thinkers such as Gayatri Spivak:

> If we are to imagine a planet fit for human habitation, we need to think of it in different terms, terms which support what Spivak calls a "more ecological practice of living, where the opposition between the human and the natural is made indeterminate". This describes precisely the epistemological ground which was being tested by a number of German writers 200 years ago.[13]

Noyes argues that Herder is an ecological and postcolonial thinker *avant la léttre* precisely because he focuses on difference not as a way to promulgate dualisms but on the contrary as the opportunity for the emergence of a mobile self that journeys back and forth between what is different.

Herder's seemingly traditionalist notion of *Humanität* describes the formation of the self (or *Bildung*) in terms of mobility and indeterminacy:

> *Humanität* allows the common goals of humankind to unfold their specific local expressions, and it could be described as the spatial manifestation of human restlessness, of the urge for mobility that, in the mind of this age [i.e. Herder's, Hegel's and Goethe's age], makes human beings human.[14]

Herder's humanistic concept is "a modern solution to a modern problem," because it describes "the potential for cross-cultural communication, allowing different peoples in different parts of the world to activate their common humanity and engage in dialogue bridging their differences."[15] What is important to emphasize here is that this bridging of difference does not flatten out what is different. In true Spinozist fashion each entity has the right and duty to preserve itself in its distinctiveness but crucially this act of self-preservation is only possible through cooperation. What diverges requires precisely what it diverges from in order to flourish in its difference. The self is only sustainable in its distinctiveness if it cooperates with what is different from itself.

In other words, Herder's seminal insight is that we cannot discover the truth anywhere and yet this impossibility is an opportunity because it encourages

---

13 Noyes, "Commerce, Colonialism, and the globalisation of action in late Enlightenment Germany," *Postcolonial Stuides* 9 (Spring 1998), pp. 81–98 (p. 82).

14 Ibid., p. 92.

15 Ibid.

us to seek for facets of truth everywhere. The stubborn incongruity between fact and concept does not need to be overcome. On the contrary it is the defining moment for a true appreciation of the complexity of the universe in its infinite diversity. In a sense Herder is saying that we were created to be diverse and to have a divergent and not a unitary view of the universe. Unity is with God and divergence makes us truly human. In an early version of *This Too* Herder defines goodness as a scattering rather than a unitary entity:

> The Good is strewn about on the earth; because no single form or century could contain it, it got distributed among a thousand forms and roams forth slowly through all the centuries. If we are unwilling to follow it on this thousand-formed Prometheus-course, then we do ourselves and the truth the greatest harm.[16]

This quote could be read as variation of Spinoza's critique of the categories "good" and "evil" in the *Ethics*. Spinoza argues that our conception of the good needs to be seen in its specific contexts. Spinoza's thought is one of different and differing perspectives. What may be food or a medicine for someone may be poison for someone else. Spinoza encourages us to be conscious of our particular perspective from which we formulate what is good and bad. This does not mean that Spinoza is a moral relativist. An awareness of different needs and different orientations does not necessarily instantiate moral relativism. As we can now see, Herder radicalizes this Spinozist appreciation of difference and diversity.

Significantly, Herder calls humanity "the diverging family" (*divergierenden Geschlecht*): "Nature provided a huge space for this divergent family: the rich and wide earth throughout which humanity should be scattered on the most diverse parts and differentiated into the most diverse ways."[17] Mirroring the divergence between fact and concept, the truth of humanity resides in the unity and yet incongruity of the diverse.

The unity of divergence means that we cannot get close to the truth if we settle only on one side of the equation, precisely because the divergent is also united with what it is not. Any given entity can only be true to itself if it is not itself. We have seen how Spinoza sees the preservation of the self as dependent on the sustainability of life at large. Herder extends Spinoza's notion of the *conatus* from the sphere of nature to the social realm of history and aesthetics. Any given historical period or any given aesthetic genre relies on its apparent opposite. Consequently, the word requires the divergent trajectory that separates itself from the thing it describes in order to be a word and vice versa things are only things by not being words. This divergence between word and thing does not force us into a decision between either of them. Rather it encourages us to move from one to the other while staying cognizant of their

---

16 Herder, *Philosophical Writings*, p. 296 footnote 40.
17 Herder, *Ideen zur Philosophie der Geschichte der Menschheit. Werke Vol. III/1. Text*, ed. by Wolfgang Pross (Darmstadt: Wissenschaftliche Buchgesellschaft, 2002), p. 286.

difference. According to Herder, our minds are mobile and it is the awareness of difference that allows for mental mobility.

2. Herder's Hermeneutics

So Herder does not lament the gulf that separates word and thing. Neither does he pitch the historical past against the present. To be sure, he enthuses about the bygone age of speech, touch and poetry. Thus in his essay "On the Ode" in Rousseau like manner Herder evokes the "age of nature, when one did not think, but felt, when one did not speak but acted, when one was poor in words but rich in action through facial expression, accent and deeds."[18] In his *Fragments on Recent German Literature* he characterizes language qua performance as poetry and contrasts it with prose, which he defines by the generation of abstractions. The age of nature, to which poetry belongs, has given way to the bourgeois age: "the more bourgeois and abstract words are introduced, the more a language receives rules, the more perfect it in fact becomes, but the more it equally loses true poetry."[19] Significantly Herder here acknowledges that the loss of "true poetry" makes for gain in the perfection of language if understood as a set of linguistic rules. It is important to point out that he does not dismiss either one or the other. What he is saying is that neither represents language in its entirety. Language's rules are its linguistic perfection. Its rules, however, do not constitute the whole of our verbal capacities of which poetry forms a substantial part. The point of this contrast between grammar (rules) and poetic irregularity is to show how both are in need of each other. They are both, in their own particulars ways, in a state of incompletion. Herder, to be sure, sympathizes with what he calls the "true poetry" of humanity the birth of which he posits at what he sees as its archaic origins. Yet he also underscores that such primeval language has been lost once and for all. In his *Fragments* he makes it clear that we cannot return to the original: "Now to be sure we are groping in dark fields when we creep off in pursuit of the voice sounding to us from afar: 'How did this arise?'"[20] We cannot return to the origin, because the origin itself is covered in darkness.

In his *Fragments* Herder accentuates the irreparable difference between antiquity and modernity. "But could those poets have written their works in our language? In our time? With our ethics?" he asks and responds with a clear: "Never! As little as we Germans will ever receive a *Homer* who is in all respects for us that which Homer was for the Greeks."[21] This divergence between ancient and modern literature does not give rise to nostalgia but instead calls for the development of a new consciousness that understands its

---

18 Herder, *Frühe Schriften 1764–1772*, p. 66.
19 Ibid., p. 183.
20 Herder, *Philosophical Writings*, p. 53.
21 Ibid., p. 42.

difference from the past while at the same time learning from and appreciating what is different (i.e. ancient Greece and antiquity in general).

Art has become a second nature. The age of poetry has passed. Within modernity, prose is as vivid a force as poetry once had been in Herder's imagined age of nature. The time in which poetry ceased to be both "the only language of writing and the language of life" went hand in hand with the birth of "prose, which now *became* the natural language of writing, because it alone was the natural language of life."[22] Far from embodying the stereotype of "the romantic" (even though he is often seen as stereotypically romantic), Herder does not believe in the resuscitation of a bygone age.[23] Nor does he esteem a clinging to tradition for tradition's sake.[24] Historical Reason, in Herder's view, does not advocate the sublation of the present in the past. Instead it recognizes an open-minded study of the past as the precondition for an accurate understanding of contemporary concerns. As Zammito has astutely put it, the "crucial innovation in Herder's hermeneutics is recognizing the openness of the subject, not simply of the object, of interpretation."[25] Only a contemporaneous subject that does not assume a state of completion can appreciate the way the past differs from the present.

The study of history therefore requires the hermeneutics of an interpreter who is open to a sense of incompletion. It is precisely this divergence between past and present which Herder accentuates but not in order to encourage nostalgia: rather the gulf between the two entities calls for an open-minded journey back and forth between them on the side of the interpretative subject. Separation understood not in terms of opposition but as non-coincidence precludes the principle of hegemonic sovereignty: each part of the separation sends out signals to its opposite that it is not complete. This consciousness of being incomplete furthers attempts at bridging the gap separating opposed entities. The bridge building in question here is an ongoing process; a continual back and forth which, importantly, leaves the state of separation intact.

Indeed it is only the fact of disconnection which enables connection. Neither the connected nor the disconnected are static phenomena. They are in fact so mobile that they continually switch places. This mobility is called for precisely by the consciousness of incompletion. Without it oppositions would turn violent. Herder, however, attempts to limit the power exerted by sovereignty and violence by characterizing humanity as lack. It is this state of lack that concomitantly requires mobility. In his *Treatise on the Origin of Language* Herder describes humanity as the most miserable of animal species:

---

22 Herder, *Frühe Schriften 1764–1772*, p. 620.

23 Robert E. Norton has argued that for Herder there is no way back to a bygone age of poetry. In contrast to Hamann, Herder does not believe in the romantic return to the past: Norton, *Herder's Aesthetic and the European Enlightenment* (Ithaca, NY: Cornell University Press, 1991), pp. 68–69.

24 For a discussion of the point see Vicki Spencer, "Towards an Ontology of Holistic Individualism: Herder's Theory of Identity, Culture and Community," in *History of European Ideas* 22 (March 1996): 245–260.

25 Zammito, *Kant, Herder & the Birth of Anthropology*, p. 339.

Considered as a naked, instinctless animal, the human being is the most miserable of beings. Here there is no obscure, innate drive which pulls him into his element and into his circle of efficacy, to his means of subsistence and to his work. No sense of smell or power to scent which pulls him towards plants so that he may state his hunger! No blind, mechanical master craftsman who would build his nest for him! Weak and succumbing, abandoned to the contention of the elements, to hunger, to all dangers, to the claws of all stronger animals, to a thousandfold death, he stands there! lonely and alone!, without the immediate instruction of his creatress [nature] and without the sure guidance of her hand, thus lost on all sides.[26]

This lack of instinct or of an innate drive which would guarantee certainty is compensated by the faculty of reflection or *Besonnenheit*: "His center of gravity, the main direction of his soul's efficiencies, fell as much on this *understanding*, on *human awareness* [*Besonnenheit*], as with the bee it falls immediately on sucking and building."[27] Herder describes reflection as an activity comparable to the bee's—the bee being a traditional symbol of work—sucking and building. The mobility in question here is first of all a hermeneutic one. It is the activity of listening: "The human being" is a "listening, noting creature."[28] Listening enacts hermeneutic mobility; it traverses the distance between speaker and listener. Metaphorically it moves from the distant past to the presence of the present. Herder contrasts past and present not to make one rule the other but rather in order to establish neighborly relations between them where one learns from the strengths and weaknesses of the other. The past renders the present incomplete; it does not question its existence.[29] So Herder enthuses about times gone by not in order to replace the present with the past. Rather

---

26 Herder, *Philosophical Writings*, pp. 127–28.

27 Ibid., p. 128.

28 Ibid., p. 98.

29 One could describe Herder's hermeneutics as partaking of a "political theology of the neighbour" as Kenneth Reinhard has put it describing Eric L. Santner's, Slavoj Žižek's and Alain Badiou's attempt to go beyond the opposition between particularism and universalism: "The political theology of the neighbour is the *decompletion* of the political theology of sovereignty, the *supplement* that both supplies something that was lacking and inserts something heteronomous into political economy. As Eric Santner has argued, if the politics of sovereignty is defined by the exception, the neighbour constitutes the exception to the exception, the interruption of sovereignty. The politics of the Not-All can be thought as the decision to say no to the superegoic insistence on All, on jouissance as an *obligation*; as Slavoj Žižek has recently formulated it, this is to reserve the right *not to enjoy*, to desist from the insistence of the sovereign exception. If there is a mode by which Sovereign and Neighbor come together, it can only be by means not of sex, but of love—that is, as the production of something new, what Alain Badiou calls a new open set, a new open part of the world." Reinhard, "Toward a Political Theology of the Neighbor," in Žižek, Santner, Reinhard, *The Neighbor. Three Inquiries in Political Theology* (Chicago: University of Chicago Press, 2005), pp. 11–75 (p. 60).

he attempts to defend the validity of the past against snuck value judgments that demean it as outdated and intrinsically valueless.

Why, however, does Herder stress the importance of the past as an aspect of life that cannot be recuperated? If the past is past why not go on with life in the immediacy of the present? Herder argues that precisely because the evolution of the human has parted ways with that of the animal from which it sprang, the study of history compensates for the loss of instinct and intuition. Undermining conceptions of humanity's centrality in the universe and its superiority over the animal Herder speaks of "the delusion of occupying a pivotal point" (*im Wahne als Mittelpunkt*).[30] In Spinozist fashion Herder questions both anthropocentrism and anthropomorphism by ironically supplementing the notion of centrality (*Mittelpunkt*) with the definition of humanity as a hybrid or mediocre entity (*Mittelding*). This term *Mittelding* is highly ambivalent, because it denotes not only the middle—rather than the centre—but also instrumentality (*Mittel* as a means) and the qualitative assessment of being mediocre (*mittelmässig*).

Significantly Herder emphasizes humanity's middle rather than central position in his critique of Enlightenment conceptions of history's progressive goals. In his *This Too* Herder refutes any demonization and equally any spiritualization of humanity. We are neither devils nor angels but both at the same time. "The depiction of the human as either an angel or a devil is fictitious," writes Herder, "the human occupies a hybrid/mediocre position between the two" and he goes on to emphasize the contingent nature of humanity's supposed telos by saying we are mere means (*Mittel*), mere instruments of something we cannot fathom: "*the human—always merely a tool.*"[31] A tool for what one might ask. Herder attends to this question in his late philosophy of history (in *Adrastea*) when he introduces his concept of nemesis. *Nemesis* is the negative aspect, which Herder introduces into his historical revision of Spinozist ontology. The notion describes the limitations of creaturely life. In his Spinozist dialogues *Gott* Herder discusses Nemesis or Adrastea as force of nature. Here he speaks of "ADRASTEA or THE LAWS OF NATURE insofar as these are based on wisdom, power and grace as much as on inner necessity" (*auf innerer Notwendigkeit beruhen*).[32] The term "laws of nature" refers back to Spinoza's discussion of God or nature in the *Ethics*. We cannot comprehend these laws but our incomprehension does not dispute their existence. Later on Herder broadens the sphere of these laws so that they encompass the history of human communities.

Herder focuses on the term *nemesis* in his late work *Adrastea* (1801–1803). Here he argues that "from the first Greek historian Herodotus onwards, history

---

30 Herder, *Werke: Band 1 Herder und der Sturm und Drang 1764–1774*, ed. Wolfgang Pross (Munich: Hanser, 1984), p. 659.
31 Pross (ed.) *Herder und der Sturm und Drang*, p. 659–60.
32 Herder, *Gott. Einige Gespräche* (Gotha: Karl Wilhelm Ettinger, 1787), p. VII.

is governed by the measure and scepter of the goddess Nemesis-Adrastea."[33] This may sound as if Herder associates nemesis (as is commonly done) with the finality of judgment day. Herder is, however, not so much interested in world history as means by which we can judge the past (to accomplish that the knowledge and expertise of the historian is far too limited), but rather as the work of recollection that is capable of saving the past and the dead from oblivion. The two attributes of Adrastea-Nemesis—"justice and truth (*Recht und Wahrheit*)—step in front of the immense and terrible (*ungeheuer*) image" of the past "and revive the figures."[34] Herder goes on to correct himself: "Not figures; they (i.e. Adrastea-Nemesis) bring the dead out of their graves back to life and they judge in their heart with a serious gaze between unreason and reason, between justice and injustice."[35] This judgment between justice and injustice, between reason and unreason needs to be distinguished from moralistic righteousness.

Herder is not interested in the construction of an abstract standard of morality. He clearly has taken on board Spinoza's critique of abstract moral categories such as good and evil or perfect and imperfect. In the fourth part of the *Ethics* Spinoza discusses this topic as follows:

> the true knowledge we have of good and evil is only abstract, *or* universal, and the judgment we make concerning the order of things and the connection of causes, so that we are able to determine what in the present is good or evil for us, is imaginary, rather than real.[36]

Our moral categories establish an imaginary order of things, which we take to be "real". Herder excoriates precisely this projection from the categorical or imaginary to the complexities of reality.

In his Spinozist dialogues entitled *Gott* he paraphrases Spinoza when he writes that

> *good* and *evil* are only relational terms (*nur Beziehungsweise gesagt werden*), so that one and the same thing could be called good and deleterious in a different context and the same goes for *perfect* and *imperfect*; because nothing can be called perfect or imperfect according to its nature.[37]

Categories such as good and evil are imaginary. Spinoza warns against the imposition of an idea with an object with which it does not agree (as he does

---

33 Herder, *Sämtliche Werke*, Vol. 23, ed. by Bernhard Suphan (Berlin: Wiedmannsche Buchhandlung, 1885), pp. 50–51.
34 Ibid., p. 50.
35 Ibid.
36 Spinoza, *Ethics*, p. 149.
37 Herder, *Gott*, p. 31.

in his critique of the anthropomorphic conception of God). Therein consist the realism of his rationalism. This attempt to employ ideas in agreement with objects—rather than in terms of an imposition onto objects—also characterizes Herder's critique of categories (such as perfect and imperfect). Crucially both Spinoza and Herder distinguish between reason and an abstract or categorical moralist discourse. Herder's Spinozist suspicion of categories is neither antirationalist nor is it immoral and anti-ethical.

It is important to realize that nemesis is itself an intrinsic part of humanity's natural—and not only historical-religious condition. Nemesis is a negative or destructive principle within history, which sets right the imbalance, caused by the overweening consequences of military conquests. Nemesis causes lack where humanity has lost a sense of its condition or, in other words, of its given shortcomings. The ambivalence of Herder's quasi-biological notion *Mittelding*, denoting a range of limited meanings (the hybrid, the mediocre and the instrumental) describes his understanding of the human condition.

In his commentary to the German original of *This Too* Wolfgang Pross has brilliantly shown how Herder's conception of humanity as a compensating, hybrid/mediocre/and tool-like species is in fact a variation of Spinoza's determinism.[38] How is this so? While unfolding his understanding of the human in terms of the middle rather than the centre, Herder argues that in the universe there is no such thing as privilege or neglect. "Who of my brothers had a privilege before he was born?"[39]—he asks and then he goes on to say that he as well as everyone else is determined by his or her position within the whole of nature. Determinism here is a positioning of sorts.

Herder is a determinist in a Spinozist sense, because he shares with Spinoza the realization that the ethical choices we are accustomed to make should be informed by our knowledge of the position we occupy in the universe. Herder's notion of *Besonnenheit* describes reflection as thought about humanity's place in the cosmos. As Stuart Hampshire has convincingly shown, "to Spinoza it seemed that men can attain happiness and dignity only by identifying themselves, through their knowledge and understanding, with the whole order of nature, and by submerging their individual interests in this understanding."[40] Knowledge is thus preconditioned on the cognizance of the external world. It is preceded by submergence into the laws of the universe. Herder describes reflection as such mindful submerging into the external world of sense data (as we shall see later, Herder's term *Besonnenheit* significantly centers on the senses). By being submerged into the outside world, reflection is, however, determined by what Kant would critique as heteronomy (which literally means the law of what lies outside).

---

38   For Pross's brilliant commentary on the Spinozist baggage of Herder's understanding of human reflection as a *Mittelding* see Pross (ed.), *Herder und der Sturm und Drang*, p. 861.

39   "Wer meiner Brüder hatte *Vorrechte ehe er war?*" Ibid. p. 661.

40   Hampshire, *Spinoza and Spinozism*, p. 123.

Unlike Kant's moral philosophy, Spinoza and Herder's ethology is deterministic, in the sense of being determined not by the centrality of human standards but by humanity's position within the universe at large. Determinism here does not dispute that we have a choice. The major book in which Spinoza develops his peculiar determinism is after all called *Ethics* and it does indeed provide guidelines as to how we should behave. As Hampshire has deftly put it:

> Admittedly passages can be found in the *Ethics* which, when quoted (as they often are) out of their context, give the impression that Spinoza was denying that there is anything to be found in our experience corresponding to the notions of "will" or "choice". Such denial would be plainly absurd; but it is certainly not a necessary consequence of his deterministic argument; and he did not (I think) intend it.[41]

Hampshire goes on to show that will and choice have no place in Spinoza's non-anthropocentric account of the universe. This does not mean, however, that Spinoza denies the importance of ethical decisions in everyday life. On the contrary he articulates his idiosyncratic type of determinism in order to exemplify that we are part of an interdependent whole where we cannot do as we please with impunity.

Herder further develops and radicalizes Spinoza's *ethical and holistic determinism* in both his philosophy of mind (where he describes the concept of reflection) and in his philosophy of nature/history (focusing on the concepts of compensation and nemesis). If we become so full of ourselves that we do violence to our surroundings, the force of our aggressive actions determines the response we will receive for our aggression. We are determined in the sense of being irrevocably dependent on others, because we occupy not the center but the middle. Concomitantly human capacity is not located in one person but is infinitely spread throughout the whole of humanity (as, at least according to Herder, it is throughout the entire universe): "I am not neglected, nor am I privileged; sensibility, activity and capacity is *scattered* throughout humanity."[42] Following Spinoza, Herder here argues that what we perceive as either favors (in Spinoza's words "good") or disfavors (in Spinoza's terms "evil") is our personal distortion of reality. Our strengths and our weaknesses are not determined by a providence that privileges some and neglects others. Rather they are part of cultural and natural diversity.

What we are lacking we are able to find in others and vice versa; some may find those qualities in us whose absence they may register in themselves. In his *Ideas* Herder elaborates on this idea of a middle ground as characterized by incompletion and dependence (i.e. the opposite of sovereignty). Here he clearly enmeshes humanity as a *Mittelding* into natural history when he writes

---

41   Hampshire, *Spinoza and Spinozism*, p. 118.
42   Pross (ed) *Herder und der Sturm und Drang*, p. 661.

of "nature's compensation" (*die Compensation der Natur*).[43] Nature compensates loss and diminishes gain by distributing its infinite arsenal of qualities throughout a diversity of species. "Where it (i.e. nature) refused to give something, it was generous and where she had to confuse, she confused wisely— that is to say in harmony with the exterior organization of the creature and of its way of life."[44] Refusal of granting a special capacity prepares for the generous bestowal of another talent in another sphere.

Herder illustrates nature's "wise confusion" with a description of human physiology. Humanity lacks the nimbleness that is characteristic of other animals, which walk on four feet rather than two. Instead of the adroitness and quickness, which often accompany animals, what distinguishes humanity is the "upright position" (*aufrechten Stellung*).[45] As has been intimated above, Herder argues that it is this physiological position that paves the way for the formation of mental capacities. Unlike Kant and Hegel, Herder denies the primordial status of reason. This refusal to describe reason as a gift bestowed by nature runs parallel to Herder's rejection of Hamann's position that (as will be discussed below) assumes language to be God's present to humanity: "The fact is therefore a wrong one," proclaims Herder in his *Essay on the Origin of Language*, "and the conclusions drawn from it are even falser: it [i.e. language] does not derive from a divine but from an animalistic origin."[46] This is the young Herder of the early 1770ies but the mature Herder of the *Ideas* (1790s) has not abandoned his youthful endeavor to enmesh the cultural sphere within lower spheres of the animalistic (language) or the physiological (reason).

What nature originally bestows upon humanity is not its cerebral position but the physiological position of standing upright. Out of this physiology develops reason. Herder makes it clear that the "advantage of the human brain's formation" *depends* on the peculiar physiology of standing upright.[47] By differentiating itself from other animals through its confusing and, in some respects, debilitating, physiology, humanity is capable of doing cerebral work. The work performed by the mind may have advantageous and disadvantageous results in a way similar to which the body may be nurturing or destructive. As highly complex animal, humanity relies on its reflective powers to coordinate its activities so that they do not turn calamitous.

Reflection focuses on how to balance out lack and superabundance. It does so by reflecting upon human and natural diversity. Human diversity runs parallel to natural diversity and what is diverse in both cases is nothing else but infinitesimal divisions and subdivisions from the whole of the universe. What may strike us as privilege or neglect is in actual fact only a given part of a whole where lack and superabundance is balanced out via the determining

---

43   Herder, *Werke Vol III/1. Ideen*, p. 90.
44   Ibid., p. 117.
45   Ibid.
46   Herder *Frühe Schriften 1764–1772*, p. 704.
47   Herder, *Werke Vol III/1. Ideen*, p. 117.

laws of interdependence and compensation. So what the human loses in animalistic instinct it is capable of regaining as reflection.

Immediacy, which characterizes the instinctual life of the animal, makes room for reflection (*Besonnenheit*). In his treatise *On the Origin of Language* Herder unfolds what he means by his understanding of reason as reflection upon the senses (namely as *Besonnenheit*). Reflection is coterminous with language, because it is connected with and yet abstracted away from the sphere of the senses: "Humanity as placed into the state of reflection (*Besonnenheit*) which is peculiar to it, has invented language; the latter is the free work of this reflection (*Besonnenheit*)."[48] The animal lives in the present. Its nonsymbolic language does not know of the gulf that lies between being and its conception.

According to Herder, humanity can only survive if it reflects upon and thus learns from the past. In Spinozist terms one could describe his notion of reflection as the *conatus* that is specific to humanity. Indeed Herder mentions self-preservation as raison d'être of existence his late *Metakritik*.[49] By interpreting mental work as part of humanity's material or existential condition, Herder enmeshes the mind into the sphere of nature and the environment at large.

Yet Herder does not uncritically sing the praises of the mind. Humanity's cerebral advantage can also be its destruction. "Humans," as Terry Eagleton has recently put it, "are more destructive than tigers because, among other things, our symbolic powers of abstraction allow us to override sensuous inhibitions on intra-specific killing."[50] Symbolic Language reflects upon the senses but it is removed from their immediate range of influence. This distance prevents the instinct driven violence of tigers but it is also capable of hugely increasing our destructive capacities, precisely because of its removal from instinctual inhibitions. Eagleton tangibly and perceptively illustrates this point as follows:

> If I tried to strangle you with my bare hands I would probably succeed only in being sick, which would be unpleasant for you but hardly lethal. But language allows me to destroy you at long range, where physical inhibitions no longer apply. There is probably no hard-and-fast distinction between linguistic and other animals, but there is an immense abyss between ironic and other animals. Creatures whose symbolic life is rich enough to allow them to be ironic are in perpetual danger.[51]

What Eagleton means by irony here is the distance between sense and meaning as established by symbolic language. In his philosophy of both mind and history Herder focuses on the long range that has the capacity to reign in violence while at the same time hugely increasing its lethal radius.

---

48 Herder, *Frühe Schriften. 1764–1772*, p. 722.
49 Herder, *Schriften zur Literatur und Philosophie 1792–1800*, ed. by Hans Dieter Irmscher (Frankfurt: Deutscher Klassiker Verlag, 1998), p. 406.
50 Eagleton, *The Idea of Culture* (Oxford: Blackwell, 2000), p. 98.
51 Ibid.

Like Spinoza, Herder encourages us to be mindful of the mind. Humanity can kill like no other animal species by dint of its distancing powers of the mind:

> No animal devours its own kind out of indulgence; no animal cold-bloodedly kills its kin on account of a command issued by a third party. No animal has the kind of language which humanity has and far less writing, tradition, religion and arbitrary laws and rights.[52]

Clearly Herder links cultural achievements (such as literature and religion) to the darker side of our civilized world. What connects culture's bright aspect with its destructive one is the issue of arbitrariness. Herder seems to be saying that our laws and rights are as arbitrary as the sign system that governs our diverse languages. Culture has become our second nature. This transmutation is significant, because our cultural setup is not as predictable and necessary as that of the animals. Herder sees necessity and certainty in the life of the animals and this is what is lacking in the human sphere: "it is only we who have chosen not necessity but arbitrariness as our deity."[53] What is arbitrary is precisely humanity's second nature which is culture. Culture is unevenly situated between the bodily and the cerebral, shifting both away from their respective center while rendering them unstable entities.[54] This instability is another word for mobility. Without the sure instinct of the animals we have to shift from the bodily to the cerebral. It is this mobility that compensates for the loss of sure instinct.

In his essay *On the Origin of Language* Herder implicitly identifies humanity's mobile capacities with its reflective ones. He argues that it is precisely the work of reflection which compensates for the loss of instinct: "If the human should *not be an instinctive animal*, it *had to be a reflective creature* by dint of the non-binding activity and positive power of the soul."[55] Humanity needs to reflect upon its loss of sense. It has to reckon with its instinctive failures by way of reflection.

---

52 Herder, *Werke Vol III/1. Ideen*, p. 102.
53 Ibid.
54 Eagleton has brilliantly described the term culture as double refusal of natural determinism and cerebral autonomy: "The idea of culture, then, signifies a double refusal: of organic determinism on the one hand, and of autonomy of spirit on the other. It is a rebuff to both naturalism and idealism, insisting against the former that there is that within nature which exceeds and undoes it, and against idealism that even the most high-minded human agency has its humble roots in our biology and natural environment." Eagleton, *The Idea of Culture*, pp. 4–5.
55 Herder, *Frühe Schriften. 1764–1772*, p. 719.

3. Historiography as Reflection upon the Senses

Crucially, historiography compensates for humanity's instinctual shortcomings. The empirical data that the study of history provides bear an intriguing resemblance to the sensual complexities of animal life. Herder's philosophy of the factual does not, however, turn positivistic. The assembly of historical documents is not enough. Rather humanity has to learn from its mistakes in both the present and the past. What the animal does via sensual instinct, the human needs to perform via the reflective activity of cultural critique. Yet reflection does not operate in an ethereal realm. Rather its work relies on empirical data. This is why Herder calls reflection *Besonnenheit*.

The term *Besonnenheit* describes the mind's dependence on the senses. Herder deliberately uses this term, because it combines the bodily with the rational and the sensuous with the intellectual. He makes clear that it is in the semantic field of this word *Besonnenheit* that "oppositions cancel each other out" (*wo Entgegensetzungen einander aufheben*).[56] Taking issue with the scholarly consensus it is worth emphasizing that Herder's notion *Besonnenheit* is Spinozist rather than merely a translation of Locke's term "reflection."[57] His term certainly refers to Locke's notion of reflection but Locke's "reflection" does not incorporate a reference to the senses and the body as does Herder's *Besonnenheit*. Beiser sees *Besonnenheit* as merely a borrowing from Locke. What is crucial here is that Herder's coinage is not merely cerebral. Herein consists its Spinozist slant: it is a word that literally does not exclude the senses because it depicts the workings of the mind as idea of the body: the corporal and the bodily lose their respective demarcations and as such they traverse back and forth between their respective centers of gravity.[58]

Already in his *Journal of My Voyage in the Year 1769* Herder focuses on Spinoza's understanding of the mind as the idea of the body. As with Spinoza, Herder stresses the interdependence of reflection and action. Extending and developing Spinoza's critique of a Cartesian mind body dualism, Herder

---

56 Ibid., p. 719.

57 Beiser, *The Fate of Reason: German Philosophy from Kant to Fichte* (Cambridge, MA: Harvard University Press, 1987), p. 134.

58 In this context it is worth mentioning that Arnold Gehlen has appropriated Herder's depiction of humanity as lacking the sensual accuracy of the animal. There are, however, important differences between Gehlen and Herder's account. Indeed they reach different conclusions: Herder finds this lack of sensual accuracy problematic, whereas Gehlen celebrates it as humanity's intellectual superiority over the animal world. Gelhen belittles the animal's small universe as environment (*Umwelt*) and uncritically extols humanity's world (*Welt*): "es hat 'Umwelt', nicht Welt." Gehlen, *Der Mensch. Seine Natur und seine Stellung in der Welt* (Wiesbaden: Aula Verlag, 1986), p. 175.

advances a philosophy of the senses. He does so not only by taking issue with the predominance of the cerebral over the corporeal but also by excoriating a hierarchy of sensual perception. The mind interacts with the body in a way similar in which the senses interact amongst themselves:

> Moreover we have to make use of all our senses. The sense of touch, for example is dormant in our time, and the eye takes its place, though often only very inadequately. [. . .] In general there is no axiom more noteworthy, and almost more often forgotten, than this: without the body, our mind will not function; if the senses are crippled, the mind is crippled too; if the senses are used vigorously and in proper measure, the mind, too, is invigorated.[59]

The parallelism of the expression "in action" or "in use" (*im Gebrauch*) gets lost in English translation. The mind cannot act without a body. Likewise corporal action (*Gebrauch*) invigorates cerebral activity. Herder thus emphasizes the interdependence of various bodily and mental performances. Without the sense of touch, human perception becomes impoverished. Here Herder implicitly introduces an historical aspect into Spinoza's critique of the mind/body dualism.

How does history enter into this philosophical topic? Through his historical approach Herder naturalizes human creations: they are not eternal; instead they participate in a natural process of decay. This is Herder's genetic approach (which J. G. Fichte transforms into his science of knowing)[60]: it de-eternalizes human achievements and it removes contemporary preferences and predilections from the central position they might otherwise occupy in the formation of judgments on the aesthetic value and moral accomplishment of a given product or character.[61] Around the time at which Herder embarked on his journey of 1769, he started work on his treatise *Sculpture* (*Plastik*). In this essay he develops his genetic approach when he discusses how the antique sense of touch made room for the philosophical sense of sight within modernity. As with poetry, sculpture belongs to a past that cannot replace the present.

---

59 Herder, *Herder on Social and Political Culture*, Barnard, F. M. (ed.), p. 83. Herder, *Journal meiner Reise im Jahr 1769*, ed. Katharina Mommsen (Stuttgart: Reclam, 1983), p. 143.

60 Even though Fichte is heavily indebted to Herder's genetic approach, he radically changes the meaning of the term genetic. Fichte makes the term genetic coterminous with the production of thinking. The genetic transcends the factual sphere of observation to reach a new or "higher" sphere of the factual that of "knowing": "In this way we will ascend from factual terms to genetic ones. These genetic elements can themselves become factical in *another* perspective, in which case we would be compelled again in connection with this new *facticity* to ascend genetically, until we arrive at the *absolute source*, the source of the science of knowing." Fichte, *The Science of Knowing. J. G. Fichte's 1894 Lectures on the Wissenschaftslehre* (Albany: State University of New York Press, 2005), p. 51.

61 Beiser rightly emphasizes the naturalizing approach of Herder's historical or genetic method. Beiser, *The Fate of Reason*, p. 142.

Herder argues that our relationship to Greek sculpture should be one of friendship rather than one of idolatry. As moderns we must be wary of submitting to an idolatrous and thus mindless worship of the past which would destroy our distinctive particularity.[62] The study of what has been forgotten establishes both proximity and distance. The sense of touch belongs to a distant age. In the excerpt quoted above, Herder appreciates the cognitive value of this neglected sense.

The tactile sense has been marginalized due to the progression made by the non-tactile rational sciences (philosophy is a case in point). Herder, however, argues that the senses are not distinct from reason. Following Spinoza, he perceives of the mind as the idea of the body and this is why reason reasons about the senses. Reflection is this form of reasoning: it is precisely what Herder's notion *Besonnenheit* denotes. As Howard Caygill has pointed out, Herder develops an all-inclusive notion of reflection, one that embraces the lowly faculty of touch: "In place of discrete faculties or capacities for thinking, willing, and language, he proposes a totality of human powers which structures itself through 'reflection'."[63] In order to present an accurate account of reflection, Herder has to attend to the intellectual powers of a haptic perception. From the inception of the age of philosophical inquiry onwards, which according to Herder is one-sidedly based on the sense of sight, the capacity of touch has been marginalized and almost completely forgotten. By retrieving this lost sense, Herder in fact revolutionizes the emerging "modern" discipline of aesthetics:

> Instead of reducing aesthetics to taste (*Geschmack*) by legislating judgement, Herder emphasizes the productive discrimination of *tasten*. He points to an alignment of beauty, production, and autonomy in the production of proportion which synthesized a view of beauty as embodiment with a notion of culture as the self-cultivation of freedom through reflective judgement. With this position, the epoch of beauty and the police-state is theoretically superseded.[64]

In this quote Caygill delineates the groundbreaking effect of Herder's fascination with an almost forgotten relic of the past: with the sense of touch which modern society has deemed insignificant. Caygill clearly shows how this transformation of aesthetics has important political ramification: by dissolving

---

62 "We should treat them [i.e. Greek sculptures] as friends, not idols. Instead of subjugating ourselves to them, we should treat them, as the name suggests, as *exemplars* that present to us in bodily form the truth of ancient times, making us aware of the proximity and distance between their form of life and our own." Herder, *Sculpture. Some Observations on Shape and Form from Pygmalion's Creative Dream*, ed. and trans. by Jason Gaiger (Chicago: University of Chicago Press, 2002), p. 61.

63 Howard Caygill, *Art of Judgement* (Oxford: Blackwell, 1989), p. 177.

64 Ibid., p. 183.

the divide between the cerebral and the corporal,[65] Herder also undermines
the hierarchical societal structure that has been advocated by German political
theorists of the police state from Samuel Pufendorf (1632–94) to Christian
Wolff (1679–1754).

In this way the retrieval of the lost sense of touch has the capacity to revo-
lutionize modern aesthetics as well as politics. Herder's historical imagination
is therefore not of antiquarian interest only. By dint of the historical imagination, the distant past can be rendered relevant for an accurate understanding
of contemporary concerns. As long as this proximity does not destroy an
awareness of the present the so conceived closeness of the past still remains
distant. Herder establishes a fine balance between the ancients and the moderns as well as between the corporeal and the cerebral. He thus does not play
off touch against eyesight. Rather, he argues for a combination of both senses,
which in turn would enhance rather diminish the life of the mind. Like Greek
antiquity the sense of touch belongs to a premodern age that is analogous to
the ontogenetic stage of childhood.

The difference between child and adulthood might indicate the construction of an hierarchy in which one is inferior to the other. This is, however, not
Herder's point. Rather he wants to bring about the anamnesis of what has
been forgotten and repressed.[66] In a way similar to which the divergence
between body and mind establishes their mutual interdependence, the present
cannot properly function without being cognizant of the past. Here it is worth
emphasizing the immense impact of Herder's thought. Heidegger would later
focus on this issue of the exclusion of the past in his critique of *das Man* in
Being and Time. Heidegger contrasts his notion of decision (*Entschlossenheit*)
with the exclusionary reserve or taciturnity (*Verschlossenheit*) of the contemporary public (*das Man*). Heidegger's decision is one toward being (*Sein*) in its
nonexclusive entirety and he characterizes being by historicity and therefore,
by what has been marginalized; i.e. death, guilt and decay: "*The general public
(Man) on the other hand is essentially reserved in all situations*. It only recognizes the '*general state*' and loses itself in the next '*opportunities*' and carries
through existence by means of the adding up of 'accidents' which it illusorily
takes and proclaims as its own achievements."[67]

---

65 As Frederick Beiser has shown, Herder's notion of force (*Kraft*) describes this
    isomorphism of mind and body: "Herder's theory postulates a single principle, a
    single concept to unite our notions of mind and body: the concept of power (*Kraft*).
    The essence of power is defined as self-generating, self-organizing activity, activity
    that gradually develops from simpler to higher degrees of organization. The differ-
    ence between mind and body is not a difference in kind, then, but only one in
    degree: the body is amorphous power, the mind organized power." Beiser, *The Fate
    of Reason*, p. 146.

66 For a discussion of this point see Inka Mülder-Bach, "Eine 'neue Logik für
    Liebhaber': Herders Theorie der Plastik," in Hans Jürgen Schings (ed.), *Der ganze
    Mensch: Anthropologie und Literatur im 18. Jahrhundert* (DFG Symposion 1992)
    (Stuttgart: J. B. Metzler, 1994), p. 360.

67 Heidegger, *Sein und Zeit* (Tübingen: Niemeyer, 1976), p. 300.

Without the rather condemnatory tone of the preceding quote from Heidegger's *Being and Time*, Herder neither devalues natural or historical data that constitute the empirical body of knowledge. In his *Journal of my Voyage in the Year 1769*, however, he dismisses as romantic any belief in the immediacy of the past:

> In every age—though in each in a different way—the human race has had happiness as its objective; we in our own times are misled if, like Rousseau, we extol ages which no longer, exist and never did exist, if we make ourselves miserable by painting romantic pictures of these ages to the disparagement of our own, instead of finding enjoyment in the present. Seek then even in biblical times only that religion and virtue, those examples, those forms of happiness, which are appropriate to us: become a preacher of virtue *of your age!*[68]

Herder anticipates Nietzsche's critique of historicism in the essay "The Uses and Abuses of History" that is part of the book *Untimely Observations* (1873–76).[69] Crucially, Herder advances this analysis while questioning Rousseau's one-sided depiction of the "noble savage". This assessment of pre-modern culture constructs a radical divide between past and present. While acknowledging the difference between the bygone and the contemporary, Herder attempts to save what has passed from being forgotten and dead. He does not advocate an uncritical study of history. Rather, he tries to focus on those elements which are relevant for problem solving in the present. In this way the study of history always already requires the mediation of the present and, possibly, the future. Contrary to the common perception of Herder as a romantic, he in fact clearly articulates that humanity cannot find enjoyment in an immediate manner.[70] The senses depend on the reflection of the mind in the same way as the reflection of the mind depends on the work of the senses. Sustainable enjoyment can only be attained through the interaction between these two disparate faculties.

The study of both natural and human history thus enables survival of the senses within the here and now. In his essay *On the Origin of Language* Herder

---

68 Herder, *Herder on Social and Political Culture*, p. 89. Herder, *Journal meiner Reise im Jahr 1769*, 30–31.

69 For an insightful discussion of this essay see Samuel Weber's *Targets of Opportunity: On the Militarization of Thinking* (New York: Fordham University Press, 2005), pp. 42–43.

70 Norton characterizers Herder as an Enlightenment thinker but he argues that Herder derives the Cartesian ideal of certainty from sensuous immediacy. Norton rightly points out that Herder reverses Descartes. This reversal is, however, a parody. In parody something of the original is lost while something else is retained. What is lost is Descartes' ideal of certainty. In similar manner, the immediate is itself mediated through reflection, through what Herder calls *Besonnheit*: it is mediation of sensuous experience in and through the workings of the mind. Norton, *Herder's Aesthetics and the European Enlightenment* (Ithaca, NY: Cornell University Press, 1991), p. 42.

dialectically affirms that the present incorporates the non-presence of the past. In the same way as it cannot immediately live in the sensory realm of the body alone, humanity equally cannot do without the reflection on its history, if it wants to survive within the present. Like Spinoza, Herder is concerned not with ideals but with the immanence and the physicality of the *conatus*. Here, however, life's ongoing self-preservation (*conatus*) pertains not only to the materiality of nature but also to the remnants of the human past. The past represents a cynosure by which humanity can orient itself on its journey into the future.

The diversity of human cultures that the study of history presents is not an end in itself for Herder. On the contrary reflection upon bygone viz. divergent ways of dealing with problematic issues holds out the key for human survival. The animal has instinct as a sure guide for its life within the present. Humanity, however, needs to co-ordinate not only mind and body but also its historical ramifications into a diverse unity. The diverse flourishes on the abyssal ground that separates being from its conception. We cannot grasp being in an immediate manner, according to Herder. Neither can we resuscitate what has ceased to exist. As has been intimated above, Herder clearly realizes that the past cannot be repeated.

This realization characterizes the realist foundations of Herder's historicism. Herder distinguishes between the human and the animal by referring to this loss of wholeness and instinctual unity. He first does so in his award winning essay *On the Origin of Language*. This work extends Spinoza's focus on the immanent sphere of nature to linguistic inquiry. He refutes Johann Peter Süssmilch and Johann Georg Hamann's thesis about the divine origin of human language.[71] He argues instead that "*even as an animal man has language.*"[72] This is the opening sentence of the essay. Later on Herder revises this statement, when he discusses historical developments. It is history that introduces the gulf between the wholeness of being and the specialization of thought. This historical process of fragmentation establishes the difference between the animal and the human, even though both share a common existential ground. In this way difference does not amount to opposition or, worse still, enmity.

Rather than preparing the ground for hostility, history sows the seeds of diversity. History therefore forms an aspect of being. It introduces change over time not by founding new substances. Rather as a temporal entity it transmogrifies Spinozist ontology. It introduces a quasi-Kantian "ought" into Spinoza's one substance theory. This metamorphosis unfolds via spin-offs. What is spun off is exactly diversity. Over time (i.e., in history), the one substance "being" generates an infinite amount of divergent and diverse subsets of existence.

---

71 Frederick Beiser has vividly described Hamann's high expectations of the essay and his ensuing disappointment about its naturalism: Beiser, *The Fate of Reason*, p. 136.

72 Herder, *Herder on Social and Political Culture*, p. 117. *Schon als Tier, hat der Mensch Sprache*. Herder, *Frühe Schriften 1764–1772*, 697.

The diverse subset only turns violent if it loses sight of its dependence on a common existential situation, which it shares with the whole body of natural diversity. The human thus differentiates itself from the animalistic without actually abandoning the ground of being which it has still in common with the animal.

Significantly, Herder describes this evolutionary differentiation of the human out of the animalistic with a particular view to the wider perspective on existential interrelatedness. In contrast to Kant, Herder argues that humanity cannot overcome its reliance on its animal nature. In his essay *On the Origin of Language* Herder even goes so far to say that: "It is certain that man is vastly inferior to the animals in the power and the reliability of his instinct; it may even be said that we do not possess at all what in many species of animals we call inborn capacities and natural attitudes."[73] Herder underlines this statement in the German original in order to emphasize the actual drawbacks of progression. The sense that Herder emphasizes the artistic talents of the animal gets lost in English translation. What the human lacks are not only the animal's "inborn capacities and natural attitudes" but also its "congenial aesthetic capacities" (*Kunstfähigkeiten*) and its "artistic-creatvie drives" (*Kunsttriebe*).[74]

Yet Humanity's loss also resembles its gain. Here we encounter an instance of what I call Herder's historical law of compensation. Significantly, in his *Ideas for the Philosophy of Humanity* he clearly formulates this concept while discussing the physiological composition of animals. As has been intimated above, Herder refers to "nature's compensation" (*Compensation der Natur*) in order to explain how certain animals that are lacking either "sensitive nerves" or "rigorous muscles" are all the more richly endowed with a "tenacious attraction."[75] Herder's law of compensation renders lack a gain and gain a lack and Eliot's *Daniel Deronda* centers on precisely such Herderian dialectic of gain and loss as will be discussed in Chapter 8. It outdoes the dualism between absence and presence and concomitantly it questions the assumed divide between humanity and the exteriority of nature.

In contrast to Vico, with whom he is often compared, Herder does not establish a dualism between human history and nature.[76] Rather than constituting

---

73 Herder, *Herder on Social and Political Culture*, p. 127. Herder, *Frühe Schriften 1764–1772*, ed. by Ulrich Gaier (Frankfurt: Deutscher Klassikerverlag, 1985), p. 711.

74 Michael N. Forster's recent translation of the Treatise provides an accurate translation of *Kunstfähigkeiten*: "*That the human being is inferior to the animal in strength and sureness of instinct, indeed that he quite lacks what in the case of so many animal species we call innate abilities for and drives to art,* is certain." Johann Gottfried Herder, *Philosophical Writings*, ed. and translated by Michael N. Forster (Cambridge: Cambridge University Press, 2002), pp. 77–78.

75 Herder, , *Werke Vol III/1. Ideen*, p. 90.

76 As Isaiah Berlin has shown Vico was a dualist: Berlin, *Three Enemies of the Enlightenment: Vico, Hamann, Herder*, ed. by Henry Hardy, (London: Pimlico, 2000), 145–46.

a separate entity, humanity, with both its advantages and disadvantages forms part of the natural whole:

> every creature is a numerator contributing to the huge denominator, which is nature itself, because humanity too is after all only a fraction of the whole, a proportion of forces, which should build itself into a whole in this and in no other organization through the communal help of its members.[77]

Herder here illustrates with an arithmetic image what precisely he means by the term "nature's compensation". The sphere of numbers harks back to his discussion of a scattering of human qualities in *This Too*.

Humanity's distinctive gifts compensate for the weaknesses that distinctively appertain to the animal and humanity learns to balance out its lack by studying zoology and biology. Not only does Herder submerge philosophy into anthropology; he also broadens the scope of anthropological studies in his *Ideas* when he says that we can only fully understand human achievements by studying humanity's biotope or its vegetative and animalistic environment. "Enjoy your position, humanity," writes Herder and he goes to qualify this statement by saying that this position is one of interdependence and so he encourages the reader "to study yourself, as noble creature of the middle (*Mittelgeschöpf*) in everything that is living around you."[78] Humanity's environment is, however, that of the animal.

4. Herder's Non-uniform Universalism

The animal's artistic capabilities are limited to a circumscribed sphere of activity. Their intensity declines in inverse proportion to the special radius of their potential influence. Human artistic capabilities, in contrast, have a universal perspective. It is this universal perspective of humanity which Heidegger, following Herder, will call human openness to toward the world (*in-der-Welt-sein*) in *Being and Time*. Whereas the animal does what it does with skillful and thorough dedication, its sphere of knowledge and activity is limited. Compared with the human, the animal has a narrow horizon: "Man", on the other hand, "has no such uniform and narrow sphere in which only one operation is to be performed; a world of activities and purposes surrounds him."[79] Here Herder characterizes humanity by its sensitivity to diversity: it thrives in a plural universe of activities (*Geschäften*) and purposes (*Bestimmungen*). The human does not differentiate itself from the animalistic through the overcoming of sensual activity. On the contrary, what distinguishes humanity from the animal is an extension of an animalistic sense perception:

---

77 Herder, *Vol III/1. Ideen*, p. 99.
78 Ibid., p. 69.
79 Herder, *Herder on Social and Political Culture*, p. 128. Herder, *Frühe Schriften 1764–1772*, p. 713.

His (i.e. "Man's") senses and his organization are not adapted to one single thing; his senses have to serve all his purposes, and hence for each individual thing they are weaker and duller. The power of his mind embraces the whole world; hence his imagination is not focused on one single thing. Consequently, he has no instincts, no native skills—and, which is more pertinent to our case— no instinctive language.[80]

This important quote from the *Treatise on the Origin of Language* is an elaboration of the excerpt on the artistic drives quoted previously. Herder describes the birth of humanity as the beginning of a transnational consciousness. Whereas the animal is tied to a specific locality, the human is a truly universal creature, precisely because of its lack of a specific instinctual strength. Its strength is written in the plural. These strengths are less intense but the same absence of intensity is compensated through a larger assembly of qualities which are scattered throughout the universe in the form of humanity's diversity.

The English translation is rather misleading, since it gives rise to the impression that the human lacks "instincts" and "native skills". This is not what Herder says in the German original. Indeed, he underlines the singular form of "no artistic drive" (*kein Kunsttrieb*), "no artistic capacity" (*keine Kunstfertigkeit*) and "no animal language" (*keine Tiersprache*) in order to emphasize the absence of any singular and monolithic disposition within the human constitution. Herder does not say that the human lacks a relation to animal language as this would of course contradict the sentence with which he opens his essay *On the Origin of Language* (*Schon als Tier, hat der Mensch Sprache*). Rather, Herder argues against a monolithic conception of humanity. Indeed he characterizes the human by the inability to focus on one specific issue or one specific place. Accordingly the human is the creature of both divergence and diversity: "His senses and his organization are not sharpened on One thing (*Eins*); his senses are oriented onto everything and of course he has therefore weaker and duller senses if seen from the perspective of one single issue."[81] He denies that humanity can be narrowed down to one sphere of activity, language and purpose. He thus takes issue with a somewhat uniform conception of universality. He instead upholds the notion of a concrete universal that instantiates plurality.

While embracing the whole world, humanity faces the danger of losing touch with the real as a singular entity. Worse still, it might establish an identity between any given aspect of its particular formation and the whole that lies "out there." While celebrating the human as creature of the middle, Herder emphasizes that this position of intra-human diversity is itself part and parcel to (rather than opposed to) nature's plurality. In order to avoid the logical fallacy which equates the human with the universe or god (which of course amounts to what Spinoza has criticized as anthropomorphism), Herder opens

---

80 Herder, *Herder on Social and Political Culture*, p. 128. Herder, *Frühe Schriften 1764–1772*, p. 713.
81 Herder, *Frühe Schriften 1764–1772*, p. 713.

his *magnum opus*, the *Ideen*, with the discussion of the planets and the extra human cosmos. This cosmic view does, however, not subject global expansiveness to the order of thought.

Herder argues for not only a zoological/biological but also cosmological approach to anthropology, "because our habitat, the earth, is nothing in itself, but receives its constitution and form as well as its capabilities for the organization and sustainability of its creatures from wonderful forces which cover the cosmos at large."[82] The opening pages of the *Ideen* discuss the planets, however, without attempting to fathom the laws that make up their existence. Herder does not deny the epistemological lawfulness of cosmic being. In Spinozist fashion he refuses, however, to equate an ideational construct with the laws of nature. In doing so he avoids trimming down natural diversity into a uniform concept that fits a would be universality but which in actual fact only pertains to the subjective stance of an "I think" (i.e. a *cogito*).

In this way Herder avoids Greek *logocentrism* precisely because he refuses to equate physical reality with cognition. In an important book Alain Badiou has recently analyzed the Greek philosophical tradition as an epistemological will to fathom the mechanics of the cosmos. According to Badiou Greek "wisdom consists in appropriating the fixed order of the world, in the matching of logos to cosmos."[83] Spinoza, in contradiction, critiques various categorizations (most prominently those of good and evil) in order to question an identification of the cosmos with logos. As has been discussed in this chapter, Herder's philosophy of the mind focuses on reflection as mode of mindfulness vis-à-vis various discrepancies that separate being from the arbitrary statutes of culture.

Rather than bemoaning the divergence between ideational constructs and the embodied world, Herder celebrates this non-identity as the site of anthropological diversity. According to Badiou, the main tenants within the Greek philosophical tradition are, in contrast, totalitarian:

> Greek discourse is *cosmic*, deploying the subject within the reason of a natural totality. Greek discourse is essentially the discourse of totality, insofar as it upholds the *sophia* (wisdom as internal state) of a knowledge of *phusis* (nature as ordered and accomplished deployment of being).[84]

Although having a global and even cosmic perspective, Herder's thought does not turn totalitarian precisely because he maintains that the laws of the cosmos cannot be grasped by human epistemologies: as he emphasizes at the planetary opening of the *Ideen*, the laws of the cosmos are invisible (*unsichtbaren Gesetze*).[85] Herder underlines Spinoza's schooling in the Hebrew Bible

---

82 Herder, *Vol III/1 Ideen*, p. 17.
83 Badiou, *Saint Paul: The Foundation of Universalism*, trans. by Ray Brassier (Stanford, CA: Stanford University Press, 2003), p. 41.
84 Ibid.
85 J. G. Herder, *Werke Vol III/1. Ideen*, p. 19.

and its Jewish Medieval commentaries in order to distinguish his intellectual background from the more Greek and Christian training of Descartes. Indeed he depicts this refusal to engage in logical fallacy as a Jewish achievement in his Spinoza dialogues *Gott*. In the manuscript version of these dialogues, Herder contrasts Descartes *cogito ergo sum* with the *eyeh asher eyeh*, "the I am who I am (or who I will be)" of the Hebrew Bible.[86]

In order to better understand the motivations that drive Herder's critique of an absolutist epistemology, the following two chapters discuss his restless educational itinerary. This restlessness almost performs his conception of human reflection as mobile entity that cannot stay tied to one place. How does this appreciation of mobility and diversity square with the common characterization of Herder as godfather of nationalism? Did his upbringing predispose Herder to nationalistic ways of thought? The following chapter attempts to address these questions.

---

86 See *Herder Werke Vol. II. Herder und die Anthropologie der Aufklärung*, ed. by W. Pross (Munich: Hanser, 1987), pp. 1086–1087.

CHAPTER 4

FROM THE DISSECTION THEATRE TO POPULAR PHILOSOPHY OR HERDER'S SPINOZIST THEOLOGY

From the German Idealists onwards, culture comes to assume something of its modern meaning of a distinctive way of life. For Herder, this is a conscious assault on the universalism of the Enlightenment. Culture, he insists, means not some grand, unilinear narrative of universal humanity, but a diversity of specific life-forms, each with its own peculiar law of evolution.

Terry Eagleton, The Idea of Culture 12

1. Friedrich Meinecke's Critique of Herder's Romanticism

As has been intimated in the preceding chapter, the significance of Herder's revision of Spinoza's thought consists in his onto-anthropological critique of Kantian moral philosophy. Yet the relationship between Herder and Spinoza has been largely ignored and belittled.[1]

Rather than focusing on a detailed discussion of various seventeenth and eighteenth century influences on Herder,[2] this book attempts to show why Herder is relevant for contemporary debates about homogeneity and universalism. Until now critics have focused on Spinoza's influence on the work of Moses Mendelssohn, G. E. Lessing, Goethe and Heine.[3] These writers and thinkers hold a firmly established place in the pantheon of Enlightenment culture. Herder, in contrast, has struck readers as somewhat odd.[4] He has been

---

1 A notable exception is David Bell's *Spinoza in Germany from 1670 to the Age of Goethe*, [Bithell Series of Dissertations. Volume Seven] (London: University of London/Institute of Germanic Studies, 1984). Bell, however, sides with Jacobi's and Kant's combined critique of Herder's Spinoza interpretation: Bell, *Spinoza*, p. 133.

2 See, for example, Robert S. Mayo's study *Herder and the Beginnings of Comparative Literature* (Chapel Hill: The University of North Carolina Press, 1969).

3 For a brilliant discussion of Spinoza's influence on Lessing, Mendelssohn and Heine see Willi Goetschel's excellent study *Spinoza's Modernity. Mendelssohn, Lessing, and Heine* (Madison: The University of Wisconsin Press, 2004).

4 Alexander Gillies excludes Herder from the pantheon of German classical thinkers: Gilles, *Herder* (Oxford: Basil Blackwell, 1945), p. 114. Michael Morgan refers to the "very protean quality of" Herder's "genius that, at least until relatively recently, has probably done as much as anything else to block the emergence of a more widespread and informed appreciation, not simply of his importance in a general sense, but of what precisely this importance consists in." Morgan, *Herder and the Poetics of Thought: Unity and Diversity in On Diligence in Several Languages* (University Park, Pennsylvania: Pennsylvania State University Press, 1989), p. 1. Berlin emphasizes,

castigated as the founder of nationalism and romanticism.[5] His philosophy seems suspect because it raises the suspicion of relativism. Herder indeed combines idealistic conceptions with the recognition of their relativity.

Questioning Beiser's assessment of Herder as an unproblematic Enlightenment thinker, Sonia Sikka has recently argued that "he [i.e. Herder] nonetheless can legitimately be described as a kind of relativist."[6] Beiser is, however, right when he maintains that the target of Herder's critical and sometimes polemical writing "is not the *Aufklärung* per se but those elitist *Aufklärer* who believed that philosophers know what is good for the people."[7] According to Beiser, Herder opposes "the value of cultural diversity" to "cosmopolitan uniformity."[8] It is, however, important to emphasize that Herder does not sacrifice universalism (universalism is of course different from uniformity) to cultural diversity. Indeed he attempts to reconcile the diverse with the universal.

Universalism allows for idealism, while cultural diversity questions the value of monolithic and absolute ideas. This peculiar commingling of a weak idealism—weak is the appropriate word here, because, as we have seen in the preceding chapter, Herder defines humanity in terms of weakness rather than strength—with a weak relativism is the outcome of his espousal (rather than rejection) of various divergences (i.e. between word and thing, being and concept etc.) as the site of diversity. In this context Sikka has pointed out that Herder's ideal of *Humanität* is always already open to pluralist revisions: "Herder sees human history as a progressive struggle towards a regime of

---

however, the nonnationalistic outlook of Herder's thought: "Patriotism was one thing, nationalism another: an innocent attachment to family, language, one's own city, one's own country, its traditions, is not to be condemned. But he goes on to say that aggressive nationalism is detestable in all its manifestations, and war are mere crimes. This is so because all large wars are a from of abominable fratricide." Berlin, *Three Enemies of the Enlightenment*, 181. See also Wilhelm Dobbek's "Johann Gottfried Herders Haltung im politischen Leben seiner Zeit," *Zeitschrift für Ostforschung*, Vol. 8 (1959): 321–387. Frederick Beiser has redressed this one-sided assessment of Herder as an anti-Enlightenment thinker and has argued that Herder's critique of the Enlightenment is "essentially internal: it criticizes the *Aufklärung* strictly in the light of its own ideals." Beiser, *Enlightenment, Revolution, and Romanticism: The Genesis of Modern Political Thought, 1790–1800* (Cambridge, MA, 1992), p. 204. Whereas Beiser strongly grounds Herder's Enlightenment thought in a Kantian tradition, John H. Zammito has recently argued that he offers an alternative to Kant's transcendental philosophy: Zammito, *Kant, Herder, and the Birth of Anthropology* (Chicago: The University of Chicago Press, 2002), p. 8.

5 Robert Reinhold Ergang labels Herder a nationalist. Nevertheless he is careful to point out the non-militaristic and humanitarian character of Herder's work: Ergang, *Herder and the Foundations of German Nationalism* (New York: Octagon Books, 1966) [originally published by Columbia University Press in 1931], p. 263.

6 Sonia Sikka, "Enlightenment Relativism. The Case of Herder," *Philosophy & Social Criticism* 31 (no. 3 2005): 309–341 (310).

7 Beiser, *Enlightenment, Revolution, and Romanticism*, p. 197.

8 Ibid., p. 195.

peaceful diversity, free of the religious persecution he particularly despises, expressing in manifold ways the ideal of *Humanität*, and he combines this ideal, but still plural, vision of humanity with a relativist appreciation of the diverse cultures and peoples that the good earth has supported."[9] Sikka's notion of "enlightened relativism" takes issue with Isaiah Berlin who seems to detect in Herder's thought a Romantic and anti-Enlightenment "denial of unity," and "denial of the compatibility of ideas."[10] Herder as relativist who denies unity is quite akin to being the godfather of romantic tribalism and modern nationalism.

In the first part of the twentieth century, in contrast, critics faulted Herder for his lack of German chauvinism and for his hostility to Prussian militarism. His romanticism was associated with his rejection of militant nationalism and his disgust with racist accounts of human difference. Friedrich Meinecke thus argued that Herder's unsympathetic approach to "Frederick the Great's enlightened despotism and militarism"[11] foreclosed insight into the workings of both history and the modern state: "This was not the frame of mind in which to understand the State as an individual and self-developing structure. Thus Herder was unable to do justice to its tremendous power in the interplay of historical forces."[12] Meinecke saw in Herder's abhorrence of war "a relapse into the old conceptions based upon Natural Law and universal reason."[13]

Strikingly, in Meinecke's influential account an inclusive universalism coincides with the "reactionary" forces of romanticism. Herder as godfather of romanticism sharply contrasts with the rationalism of Kant. According to Meinecke, Kant's rationalism, however, upholds the notion of race, which divides humanity into separate and isolated identities. As we shall see (in Chapter 6), Kant indeed took issue with Herder's universal conception of humanity, which refused to take on board concepts of European racial superiority. Meinecke clearly sides with Kant, when he blames Herder's "romantic" universalism for his repugnance at the modern Kantian notion of race:

> But he [Herder] adopted a much more critical attitude to the now emerging concept of race, which had recently (1775) been broached in the first instance by Kant. His ideal of humanity revolted against this idea, for he regarded it as likely to drag humanity down again to a purely animal level, though in so doing it must be admitted that he failed to reckon with the causal significance of race. It seemed to Herder to be ignoble even to speak of races among mankind. He held that all the racial colors run together, and in the end were left with nothing but different shades in one great picture.[14]

---

9 Sikka, "Enlightened Relativism," p. 331.

10 Berlin, *The Roots of Romanticism*, ed. by Henry Hardy (London: Pimlico), p. 67.

11 Meinecke, *Historism. The Rise of a New Historical Outlook*, trans. by J. E. Anderson with a Foreword by Sir Isaiah Berlin (London: Routledge & Kegan Paul, 1972), p. 341.

12 Ibid.

13 Meinecke, *Historism*, p. 353.

14 Meinecke, *Historism*, p. 357–358.

On this view, Kant is progressive insofar as he includes the ranking of different human races into his understanding of universalism. Why is Kant's endorsement of a racial account of humanity progressive? Because it helps confirm the truth value of history's unilinear development: here European progress triumphs over non-European backwardness. The notion of race serves to endow this narrative of history's progression with quasi-scientific objectivity.[15]

2. Herder's Theology: Teleology that Outdoes Itself

What precisely is responsible for Herder's rejection of the idea of history's unilinear development? Here Meinecke pinpoints theology as the center of weakness in Herder's thought. Around this weak spot revolves his rejection of all those features that seem to account for Europe's developmental superiority over the non-Western world. According to Meinecke, his theological sensibility shapes Herder's "reactionary" outlook. It preconditions his understanding of history's tendency not only to progress toward scientific and artistic fulfillment but also to decline by diverging from an original revelation:

> This theological approach to the most ancient traditions again narrowed down Herder's developmental thinking in another respect. For what he depicted was nearly always the history of degeneration or disorderly growth in the midst of an endlessly rich development of the pure original revelation.[16]

Meinecke struggles to find a teleology of history in Herder's thought. When he appears to find it, it turns out to be a theological teleology. This kind of teleology, however, outdoes itself: it is inscrutable, because humanity, due to its epistemological limitations, cannot perceive its goal.

This raises the question as to how Herder's thought was received among theologians. Can one speak of a distinctive Herderian theology? From the publication of his essay *On the Origin of Language* (early 1770s) onwards Herder was at odds with the orthodox establishment. Largely due to the unorthodox views propounded in this essay, his application for a professorship in theology at the University of Göttingen was rejected in 1775. The advisors of King George III apparently argued against his acceptance as professor of theology:

> On October 3, 1775 King George III, presumably influenced by advisors in London, wrote to the Council in Hannover, whose functionary, Hofrat Brandes, had been carrying on the correspondence with Herder about such ultimate

---

15 As Wulf Koepke has pointed out the charge of being "unscientific" has haunted the reception of Herder's thought. Koepke, "Introduction" in Koepke (ed.), *Herder, Language, History, and the Enlightenment* (Columbia, SC: Camden House, 1990), pp. 1–8.

16 Meinecke, *Historism*, p. 320.

details such as salary and prerequisites: ". . . Now the Bückeburg Consistorial Councilor Herder, whom you have nominated for the accomplishments of this double purpose [i.e. professor and preacher], has been described to me as a man who, though he does not lack requisite learning, might possibly be criticized with respect to his orthodoxy and qualities of temper."[17]

Herder was unorthodox because he denied the divine authorship of the Bible, believed that revelation was not a prerequisite of the Christian faith but was rather scattered throughout all religions. He moreover did not propound a systematic theology which advanced a Christology or offered a dogmatic conception of sin. As Clark has succinctly put it, "the simple truth is that Herder's religion at this time [i.e. ca. 1764] lacked two important doctrines common to most Christian creeds: (1) a systematic doctrine of the nature of sin, and (2) the doctrine of the vicarious sacrifice of Jesus Christ."[18] Clark goes on to make clear that this state of affairs is by no means restricted to the year 1764: "although Herder was at no time an atheist or agnostic, he was likewise at no time after 1764 a believer in the majority of the doctrines of his church or any other."[19] This unorthodoxy would certainly have found strong support in the Socinianism which informs Spinoza's writings on Jesus' political and social impact rather than on the doctrinal core of Christian instruction (be that original sin or redemption through crucifixion).[20] Like Spinoza, Herder focuses on Jesus' humanity, on his *justitia* and on his *caritas*.[21] Herder's theological work was scandalous, because it was radically nondogmatic. The theologian Friedrich Wilhelm Kantzenbach has rightly emphasized Herder's heterodoxy. According to Kantzenbach Herder promotes the personal religion of Jesus which is quite different from the organized religion of Jesus Christ the redeemer.[22] In a highly idiosyncratic way Herder revised and, to an orthodox reader undermined, modern Christian thought along Spinozist lines.[23]

In an important essay about the *Sense of Feeling*, which was composed around 1770, that is to say, around the time in which he conceived the ideas of his controversial essay *On the Origins of Language*, Herder, without mentioning Spinoza's name, asserts God's immanence: "God thus belongs to

---

17   Robert T. Clark, *Herder: His Life and Thoughts* (Berkeley: University of California Press, 1955), p. 207.
18   Ibid., p. 210.
19   Ibid., p. 211.
20   I am greatly indebted to Jonathan Israel for an illuminating conversation about Spinoza's fascination with Jesus' politics consisting of *justitia* and *caritas*.
21   When Herder gave Goethe a copy of Spinoza's *Ethics*, he draws a parallel between Spinoza's and Jesus' teaching; See Bell, *Spinoza in Germany*, p. 98.
22   See Kantzenbach, *Herder* (Hamburg: Rowohlt, 1970), p. 104.
23   As Clark has pointed out Herder theology is very liberal compared to the orthodoxy of Kant's theological focus on original sin and the old Adam: Clark, *Herder*, 320. Bell has rightly argued that Herder's critique of Kant derives from his Spinozism: Bell, *Spinoza in Germany*, p. 143.

the world (*Gott gehört also zur Welt*)."[24] Wolfgang Pross compares the significance of this early essay to Goethe's Spinoza studies.[25] Why is this short piece
of writing so important? It commingles a theological sensibility with the
supposed atheism of Spinozist thought. As such it is closely linked to Herder's
critique of Moses Mendelssohn's attempt to prove the soul's immortality in his
celebrated book *Phaedon* (which established his European reputation as the
"German Socrates").

In what sense is the issue of the soul's immortality closely associated with
Herder's Spinozist revision of theology? In his essay about the *Sense of Feeling*
Herder applies Spinoza's conception of the mind as the idea of the body to
theology, saying that God is the idea of the world:

> In this way God feels and tastes, as it were, the whole world. So he hears the
> whole world. So he thinks the whole world, which is an idea of his which really
> exists. [. . .]. He is the idea, the force of the world.[26]

In his critique of Mendelssohn's *Phaedon* Herder denies that the soul can
live without the body—be that in this earthly life or in a transcendent afterlife.
In his important letter exchange of April 1769 with Mendelssohn, Herder
advances a highly unorthodox argument about God's immanence which he
derives from what he sees as Spinoza's break with Descartes mind-body divide.

Herder opens his critique of Mendelssohn's attempted proof of the soul's
immortality with a discussion of philosophy's general hostility to embodied
life on earth: "the liberation from sensuous notions and the totally spiritual
perfection are for you," Herder addresses Mendelssohn, "as well as for most
philosophers and theologians the first sources for the remunerations that await
us in a future state."[27] This future state is coeval with the death of the body.
Herder counters theological and philosophical pleas for a liberation from
the body by characterizing humanity as "a hybrid nature" (*eine vermischte
Natur*).[28] It is due to the mixed constitution of human life that it cannot do
without a body if it wants to cheat death.

In other words, Herder unmasks a secret death wish behind philosophy's
and theology's hostility toward the body. Hannah Arendt has made a similar
point apropos Plato's (to whom Mendelssohn's *Phaedo* is of course heavily
indebted) and Aristotle's praise of the contemplative life.[29] Herder, however,

---

24 Herder, *Werke Vol. II Herder und die Anthropologie der Aufklärung*, ed. by
    Wolfgang Pross (Munich: Hanser, 1987), p. 245.
25 See Pross' commentary on *Zum Sinn des Gefühls* in Herder *Werke. Vol II*,
    pp. 884–895.
26 Herder, *Werke. Vol II*, ed. by Pross, p. 245.
27 Moses Mendelssohn, *Briefwechsel, Vol. II, 1* ed. by Alexander Altmann (Stuttgart-
    Bad Cannstadt: Friedrich Frommann Verlag, 1976), p. 175.
28 Ibid.
29 See Arendt's, *The Human Condition*, with an Introduction by Margaret Canovan,
    2nd edition (Chicago: University of Chicago Press, 1998), p. 20.

goes a step further. He questions not only the philosophical-theological prioritization of the mind over the body, but he also maintains that we cannot find any form of hierarchical ranking—of which the prioritization of the mind over and above the body is a striking example—within life as such.

At this point Herder implicitly translates Spinoza's philosophy of nature into the realm of politics and history. He argues that instead of hierarchical progression towards perfection which discards anything deemed imperfect, history unfolds itself as cyclical spirals where every element sustains and enjoys its capacities and potentials. Like Spinoza, Herder does not reject goals and endeavors. What he questions is the ranking of goals that results in forms of exclusion. In his essay *On the Cognition and Sensation of the Human Soul* Herder ridicules the hierarchical division of capacities as follows: "Since with classes, rank, and modes of life, alas!, the abilities have separated as well; since there stands written on our chair 'what *he who sits there is supposed to be*.'"[30] Hierarchies work via nomenclatures; they force individuals into the performance of one exclusive task and define this individual exclusively by his role as worker. In a draft of the 1775 version of *On Cognition* Herder contrasts human hierarchical and categorical thought with God's rejection of any forms of exclusion: "Similarities, classes, orders, and levels are therefore only boarded walls of necessity or card-houses of play. The Creator of all things does not see as human beings see; He knows of no classes, each thing is only identical with itself."[31] This contrast between human ways of seeing and those of the Creator serves to question hierarchies and other ways of exclusion.

In a similar way Herder's critique of Mendelssohn's *Phaeton* focuses on the elevation of the mind over the body in the Platonic and orthodox Christian conception of immortality. Countering Plato's account of the immortality of the soul, Herder announces to Mendelssohn the Spinozist argument according to which everything is equally perfect:

> Moreover in this world everything is perfect; but from the perspective of the future world, nothing is perfect in this world. That is why humanity is diverse. Yes, to enjoy and act in this world [*zum Genuß dieser Welt*] they may all be good in their different ways: the Lapplander and the Hottentot, Newton and the orangutan—but as regards the training of a future world as well as the training of the soul's capacity no-one is good for anything.[32]

Herder defends human diversity while undermining the concept of a future absolute state of perfection. He does of course not deny the validity of human prospects but he questions whether they should be narrowed down to one issue or aspect (be it the soul, or one particular nation or group). Humanity and nature are diverse because we cannot find in this world a concentration of strength within one single point. Instead, perfection is scattered throughout

---

30 Herder, *Philosophical Writings*, p. 226.
31 Ibid., p. 231, footnote 67.
32 Mendelssohn, *Briefwechsel*, Vol. II,1, 178.

the universe. The philosophical-theological hope for a non-bodily and thus perfect life after death is misconceived, because we cannot conceive of perfection beyond our powers of embodied joy and action (i.e. *Genuß*).

As I have shown elsewhere, Mendelssohn was one of the most pronounced philosophers of human diversity in the eighteenth century.[33] Not surprisingly, he responded sympathetically to Herder's critique. Mendelssohn was of course sympathetic to Herder's Spinozist thought. Later, in 1785 the late Mendelssohn was deeply shaken by Jacobi's *On the Doctrine of Spinoza*. As Willi Goetschel has recently argued, "Spinoza the Jew poses less of a problem for Mendelssohn than it does for Jacobi's form of Christianity. For Mendelssohn, Spinoza's metaphysics does not present any problem for, but is fully compatible with, Judaism."[34] Mendelssohn made clear that he agreed with Herder's appreciation of embodied diversity. He argued that Herder misunderstood him, writing that "our thoughts about the human soul are not as distant to each other, as you seem to maintain."[35] Indeed Mendelssohn, who attempted to make Spinoza's philosophy socially acceptable by relating it to Leibniz' rationalism,[36] responded to Herder's plea for the implicit perfection of embodied life by concurring that "the sensuousness of human nature is the flower of its perfection."[37] While Herder could receive a flowery response from the Jewish Enlightenment philosopher Mendelssohn, his Spinozist approach was, however, bound to scandalize Christian orthodoxy.

3. From Medicine to Theology and Philosophy

So why does Herder offend orthodoxy by maintaining that God is the idea of the world? He was after all trained as a theologian and was thus aware of the scandalous nature of his theological arguments. So why did Herder consciously and conscientiously challenge the religious establishment of his time? This question brings us to the reasons that motivated him to study theology in the first place. In contrast to other eighteenth-century German thinkers with a protestant background—Friedrich Hölderlin is a famous example of an adolescent intellectual who was obliged to study theology with a view of earning a living as a pastor, (which he finally refused to become)—theological studies were not forced upon the young Herder. In fact he began his University studies by reading medicine. It was his discomfort with his medical training that opened up Herder's interest in theology. What precisely made Herder turn away from his initial scholarly pursuit? Medicine has a strong practical component and it

---

33 For discussion of Mendelssohn as a philosopher of human diversity see Mack's *German Idealism and the Jew*, pp. 79–97.
34 Goetschel, *Spinoza's Modernity*, p. 178.
35 Mendelssohn, *Briefwechsel*, Vol. II, 1, p. 182.
36 See Goetschel's *Spinoza's Modernity*, p. 92.
37 Mendelssohn, *Briefwechsel*, Vol. II, 1, p. 183.

might well have been this balance between practice and theory that attracted Herder in the first place. What alienated him from the desired practical pursuits of a medical doctor was the confrontation with death. In 1762, during the dissection undertaken by a Russian field doctor at the University of Königsberg, Herder passed out in horror. As Simon Richter has put it:

> The sight of the dissected body was a painful *Reiz* for Herder; spontaneous contraction (*Zurückziehung*) occurred in the form of passing out. He became all body as his consciousness fled. Returning to consciousness, his repulsion for the body decided him once and for all for the study of theology and philosophy. Days later he began attending the lectures and seminars of Immanuel Kant.[38]

The dissection of the body lays bare its veiled but inherent decomposition. Becoming body uncannily instantiates a near death experience: the loss of consciousness seems to introduce the reign of corporeal life, which turns out to be death. On this view, Herder appears to subscribe to Descartes' mind-body divide. Rather than being the idea of the body, the mind escapes from the body's material entrapment in disease and decay: "What Herder is afraid of is the unavoidable presence of death in the material body. Once again confronted with the body, Herder passes out, and parts company altogether from the body, even as his own body slumps to the ground."[39] Richter thus offers an intriguing account of Herder's confrontation with the medical body.

This is, however, only one part of his educational itinerary. True, confronted with the decayed body, as so forcefully presented in the dissection theatre, Herder abandoned his medical training and took up the study of theology and philosophy under Kant's generous mentorship. What attracted him immensely to the precritical Kant was independence of thought as well as the all-inclusive quest for truth. Even after having taken issue with Kantian transcendental philosophy, the mature Herder of the *Letters toward the Advancement of Humanity* praised Kant as an inspiring teacher:

> no intrigue, no sect, no advantage, no nomenclatural ambition (*Namen-Ehrgeiz*) ever held out for him the least attraction (*Reiz*) compared to the expansion and enlightenment of truth. He encouraged and pleasantly extorted *independent thinking* (*Selbstdenken*); despotism was not part of his personality (*Gemüt*).[40]

When Herder took issue with what he perceived to be the dogmatism of Kant's transcendental philosophy, he might well have believed himself to act according to the teachings of his former mentor. His critique of the post-1769

38　Richter, *Laocoon's Body and the Aesthetics of Pain. Winkelmann, Lessing, Herder, Moritz, Goethe* (Detroit: Wayne State University Press, 1992), p. 106.

39　Ibid., p. 127.

40　Herder, *Briefe zu Beförderung der Humanität*, ed. by Hans Dietrich Irmscher (Frankfurt a. M: Deutscher Klassiker Verlag, 1991), p. 424.

Kant thus enacted the instructions of the pre-1769 Kant: namely, independent thinking and the nonexclusive quest for enlightenment.

Yet this enthusiastic search for truth opens up an abyss of lifelessness which in a perturbing way resembles Herder's traumatic experience in the dissection theatre. In 1764 Herder finished his theological and philosophical studies in Königsberg and left for the Baltic city Riga where he worked as a writer, priest and teacher. From this far-off and rather marginal place Herder established himself as an outstanding German literary critic. Herder, the son of a lower-class family, became a prominent public figure by dint of his work as a writer. Neither his lowly origins nor the marginality of the place in which he wrote dampens the appeal of his literary output. Here he is clearly the pupil of Kant: diffidence about his economic and class background does not deter him from gaining recognition of his intellectual achievements.

Why does Herder nevertheless feel uncomfortable as a writer? He enters a space that seems to be free of domination. Jürgen Habermas has famously called this space the "public sphere". Here different arguments compete for prominence on purely rational grounds, regardless of the social and economic status of its participants: "The 'domination' of the public, according to its own idea, was an order in which domination itself was dissolved; *veritas non auctoritas facit legem*."[41] On this view, the emerging eighteenth-century public sphere subjects domination to the powers of reason. This explains why Herder could achieve public prominence through his *Fragments about New German Literature*. It does, however, not account for the widespread appeal of his work as a literary critic.

The fact that Herder developed his popular philosophy as a critic of literature seems to substantiate Habermas' thesis according to which the public sphere originates in the literary world and then expands into a wider political realm. A Cartesian mind-body divide underlines Habermas' evolutionary understanding of rationality. Jonathan M. Hess has recently questioned this opposition between the literary-representational body politic (which belongs to the age of absolutism) and the purely rational discourse of the fully developed bourgeois public sphere.[42] Hess counters Habermas' argumentation by pointing out that the seventeenth and eighteenth-century absolutism of the French and German monarchies "claimed its own form of political rationality"

---

41 Habermas, *The Structural Transformation of the Public Sphere. An Inquiry into a Category of Bourgeois Society*, trans. by Thomas Burger with the assistance of Frederick Lawrence (Cambridge, MA: Massachusetts Institute for Technology Press, 1989), p. 82.

42 For a critique of the Marxist provenance of Habermas' understanding of the public sphere see Benjamin W. Redekop's *Enlightenment and Community. Lessing, Abt, Herder and the Quest for a German Public* (Montreal & Kingston: McGill-Queens University Press, 2000), 3–28. See also Craig Calhoun's (ed.), *Habermas and the Public Sphere* (Cambridge, MA: Massachusetts Institute of Technology Press, 1992).

and that therefore the Habermasean separation between the rational, on the one hand, and, the body politic, on the other, was not historically water tight.[43]

Hess' critique of Habermas' understanding of the eighteenth-century public sphere helps explain Herder's ambiguous attitude toward literature. Herder was concerned that the world of letters falls prey to paralysis. He feared that the world of letters would deaden rather than enliven its participants. In order to avoid the potentially paralyzing effect of literary production and consumption Herder attempted to link the work of intellectual inquiry to the sphere of both the body and the body politic. In his work as a literary critic Herder attempted to connect the apparently irrational sphere of the corporeal with the workings of the mind.

4. Herder's Critique of Leibniz's and Kant's Academic Philosophy (Schulphilosophie)

Literature held out the promise of refashioning philosophy as anthropology. This was precisely the aim of popular philosophy, which set itself apart from the academism of philosophical inquiry. When, in the 1760s, Herder abandoned his medical studies, he embraced the philosophy of the precritical Kant. The young Kant (pre-1769) was caught in, and perhaps to some extent, confused by the battle between *Schulphilosophie* and popular philosophy (*Popularphilosophie*).

The conflict between these two philosophical factions touches upon an issue on which Spinoza focused his attention toward the end of the seventeenth century.[44] In what ways do highly refined systems of ideation lose touch with the empirical constitution of the social and the natural world? This question provided the driving force that helped establish the public validity of *Popularphilosophie*. Christian Thomasius was the intellectual father of popular philosophy. He made philosophical inquiry relevant for the solving of political and social problems. In this way he advocated the abolition of torture and witch burnings which were still practiced at the end of the seventeenth and the beginning of the eighteenth century. The school philosophers, in contrast, abstained from addressing political and social questions.[45]

The pre-critical Kant kept a critical distance from the metaphysical and concomitant nonpublic leanings of the *Schulphilosophie*. He attempted to make philosophy useful for the women and men on the street.[46] Herder not

---

43 Hess, *Reconstituting the Body Politic. Enlightenment, Public Culture and the Invention of Aesthetic Autonomy* (Detroit: Wayne State University Press, 1999), p. 145.

44 See Montag's *Bodies, Masses, Power*.

45 See F. M. Barnard's, *Self-Direction and Political Legitimacy: Rousseau and Herder* (Oxford: Clarendon Press, 1988), p. 128.

46 Cf. Nicolao Merker, *Die Aufklärung in Deutschland* (Munich: Beck, 1982), p. 90.

only enthused about the analytical skills of his mentor but he also endorsed his public commitments. His *Observations on the Feelings of the Beautiful and the Sublime*, as John H. Zammito has ingeniously put it, "thrust Kant to the forefront of 'popular philosophy' at the time" and "made him an exemplary *reflektierende* [sic] *Schriftsteller.*"[47] The critical Kant did not abandon this concern with the public sphere. Although he theoretically interdicted any philosophical questioning of the established order, he nevertheless formulated a moral philosophy that at the same time resembled a political philosophy. In the following, I will discuss how Herder detected in the work of the post-1769 Kant an academicism, which he had previously critiqued in the work of Leibniz. What Herder criticized in both Leibniz and the critical Kant was the hierarchical vision that characterizes *Schulphilosophie*.

In both his ethics and his work on epistemology, the critical Kant advised individuals and social groups not to fight for an amelioration of their material conditions. Rationality precisely prescribes an independence from any reliance on physical and thus contingent factors. It thus proscribes social conflict.[48] Herder opposed this demotion of bodily and sensuous needs. Concomitantly, his politics was more egalitarian and democratic than that of his former mentor.[49] It is this Spinozist vision of a non-hierarchical society that explains Herder's break with the critical Kant. Herder collected folk poetry of a variety of peoples not in order to announce an ethnocentric vision. Rather he took an intense interest in popular culture (i.e. folk songs etc.) with a view to establishing the realm of the literary as a diverse field which includes all classes and all cultural identities. Herder prepared the ground for Goethe's *Sturm and Drang* period by developing a democratic concept of literary production and consumption. Herder's mentorship was significant for the young Goethe, because it introduced him—via Spinoza and Shakespeare—to a non-hierarchical understanding of the arts, one that is not the exclusive realm of aristocrats and academics: "Poetry is not the 'private inheritance' of a few noblemen or academicians, but is a physiological, psychological, and social attribute of the least educated, least socially advanced human beings, as well as the highest, since it is original with language itself."[50] Herder does not separate poetry from quotidian life. Poetry participates in language, which is the common threat that interconnects humanity in its entirety.

In contrast to Herder, Kant attributes little importance to linguistic issues and focuses instead on morality and questions of epistemology. In true academic

---

47 Zammito, *Kant, Herder*, p. 106.

48 For a detailed discussion of the interrelation between Kant's moral and political philosophy see, Mack, *German Idealism and the Jew*, pp. 23–41.

49 Overturning the image of Herder as "conservative demagogue," Frederick Beiser is justified in characterizing Herder as a radical democratic thinker: Beiser, *Enlightenment, Revolution, and Romanticism*, p. 190.

50 Clark, *Herder*, p. 136. For a detailed discussion of Goethe's critique of an exclusive notion of literature see Benjamin Bennett's *Goethe as a Woman: The Undoing of Literature* (Detroit: Wayne State University Press, 2001).

fashion the mature Kant did not pay much attention to the material cravings of "the masses." Herder's anthropological focus on the diversity of bodily and spiritual needs, by contrast, preconditioned his democratic political outlook. He remained a popular and literary philosopher throughout his life, but he never turned into a demagogue. Isaiah Berlin emphasizes Herder's distance to any form of demagogy. He thus differentiates Herder's approach from that of Mazzini, Michelet and Sismondi and associates it with a non-hierarchical vision peculiar to writers and thinkers such as Spinoza, Ruskin, Lamennais or William Morris:

> He [Herder] celebrates German beginnings because they are part of, and illumi-
> nate, his own civilisation, not because German civilisation ranks higher than that
> of others on some cosmic scale. "In the works of imagination and feeling the
> entire soul of the nation reveals itself most freely." This was developed by
> Sismondi, Michelet and Mazzini into a full-scale political-cultural doctrine; but
> Herder stands even closer to the outlook of Ruskin or Lamennais or William
> Morris, to populists and Christian socialists, and to all of those who, in the
> present day, are opposed to hierarchies of status and power, or to the influence
> of manipulators of any kind.[51]

Kant, on the other hand, became increasingly concerned with establishing the authority of philosophy as a master discourse that should prove capable of regulating the ways of thought within other academic disciplines in particular, as well as within the larger population in general. Berlin emphasizes the difference in Kant's and Herder's respective political outlook. He points out that Herder is "indignant about Kant's proposition that 'man is an animal who needs a master'; he replies 'Turn the sentence around: the man who needs a master is an animal; as soon as he becomes human, he no longer needs a master.'"[52] Berlin goes so far to see in Herder's questioning of both Kant's political philosophy and his philosophy of history the "true beginnings" of "the perception that cruel and sinister implications are contained in any doctrine that preaches the sacrifice of individuals on the altar of vast abstractions—the human species, society, civilization, progress (later thinkers were to say race, State, class and the chosen élite)."[53] Herder has however not received the credit he deserves for his critique of hierarchical structures within society. Why is this so?

As Robert Clark and Emil Adler have rightly pointed out, at the end of the nineteenth century Herder's contribution to philosophy and to other disciplines was unfortunately judged by neo-Kantians.[54] Rudolf Haym,[55] Moritz

---

51 Berlin, *Three Critics of the Enlightenment: Vico, Hamann, Herder* (ed.), Henry Hardy, London: Pimlico, 2000, p. 206.

52 Ibid., p. 187.

53 Ibid.

54 See Clark's, *Herder*, 2 and Emil Adler's *Herder und die deutsche Aufklärung* (Vienna: Europa Verlag, 1968), p. 57.

Kronenberg,[56] and Eugen Kühnemann[57] found him wanting. They took Herder to task for not having followed Kant's critical turn. This harsh and unfair assessment of Herder's work has shaped much of twentieth-century scholarship. Herder's realism resulted in his questioning stance toward a uniform conception of humanity, which he associated with Kantian moral philosophy. In contrast to the critical Kant, Herder advocated a philosophy of the factual. He paid his respect to empirical facts, by learning about cultural diversity from traveling throughout Eastern and Western Europe as well as from studying travel literature (Georg Forster's account of his journey to the South Pacific with Captain Cook, for example).

It is this Spinozist realism that distinguishes his appreciation of particularity from the school philosophical emphasis on generality as propounded by the mature Kant. Rather than labeling Herder as regressive or totalitarian, it is more apposite to focus on how his writings offer an intriguing glimpse into a new way of thinking about reason and its dependence on both the body and the multitude.[58] In this respect he might be of greater relevance to contemporary political and scientific questions than Kant's concern with the generality of the *a priori*.[59] Herder's critique of Kant's academicism might in fact be comparable to Spinoza's revision of Descartes' mind-body dualism in the previous century.

In a crucial sense the critical Kant revived certain rationalist assumptions (as propounded first by Hobbes and Descartes and then Leibniz) that underpinned the *Schulphilosophie*. Following a school philosophical tradition the critical Kant demoted the relevance of particularity. He characterized the pragmatic not as the particular but as the general. As Zammito has shown this emphasis on generality went hand in hand with sidelining the connection of soul to body, which Spinoza highlighted in his critique of Cartesian dualism:

> The emphatic sense of *pragmatic* in Kant's revision of his anthropology lectures was the repudiation of somatic/physiological considerations. The connection of soul to body was simply not something to be elucidated further, even though it was obviously not to be denied. Instead, Kant stressed theory of action and the self-consciousness of choice. Kant from the outset concerned himself with self-consciousness as the unique mark of the human.[60]

In contrast to Spinoza's critique of a monolithic epistemology, "Kant did not propose to *discover* human nature through a consideration of human variety."[61]

---

55 Haym, *Herder nach seinem Leben und seinen Werken* (Berlin: Aufbau, 1880).

56 Kronenberg, *Herders Philosophie nach ihrem Entwicklungsgang und ihrer historischen Stellung* (Heidelberg: Carl Winter, 1889).

57 Kühnemann, *Herders Persönlichkeit in seiner Weltanschauung* (Berlin, 1893).

58 For a brilliant discussion of Spinoza and the multitude see Montag's *Bodies, Masses, Power*.

59 Zammito has refuted H. B. Nisbet's Kantian dismissal of Herder as unscientific: See Zammito's, *Kant, Herder*, pp. 323–324.

60 Ibid., p. 297.

61 Ibid., p. 299.

Instead, he "proposed to *derive* it from a metaphysical—'transcendental'—argument about the 'fundamental grounds of the possibility [of] human nature.'"[62] In this way the mature Kant positioned his understanding of humanity within a decidedly school philosophical context. Zammito sums up Kant's view of anthropology as follows:

> In short, if we consider the manner in which Kant introduced his new "science" of anthropology to his students over the course of the some thirty years he taught it, what emerges is an increasingly dogmatic and antiempirical posture, and a more marked academicism within a putatively worldly project.[63]

Although his philosophy had both a political and anthropological focus, Kant defined both politics and anthropology in terms of generality (viz. pragmatics). The logical procedure by which he arrived at such characterization was deductive and thus affirmed the transcendental validity of the *a priori*.[64] He took up a strictly rationalist line of argument as first promulgated by Hobbes and Descartes and then theologically revised by Leibniz.

In this way the mature Kant stood in a school philosophical tradition. Herder, in contrast, would refuse to take a turn toward this level of generality. The abstraction away from empirical particularity to logical uniformity characterizes a narrowly conceived rationalism. It cannot be emphasized enough that the school philosophers followed Leibniz's rationalist approach. At the end of the seventeenth and the beginning of the eighteenth century Leibniz set out to combine a strong theological stance with the mechanical philosophy as most vigorously formulated by Descartes. Leibniz characterized his approach as the "middle path":

> In my opinion it is best to take the middle path, which satisfies both religion and science: I accept that all corporeal phenomena can be traced back to mechanical efficient causes, but those mechanical laws as a whole must be understood as themselves deriving from higher reasons.[65]

---

62 Ibid.
63 Ibid., p. 301.
64 Leibniz was searching for an objective standard by which a perfect state of generality could be generated. He tried to find this standard linguistically by endeavoring to develop a universal language. Recently Peter Fenves has compared Mendelssohn's conception of language as fluid and context specific with the notion of a general language as propounded by Leibniz: Fenves, *Arresting: Language. From Leibniz to Benjamin* (Stanford: Stanford University Press, 2001), p. 89. Susan Neiman has drawn attention to the desired state of translucency implicit in Leibniz notion of a general viz. universal calculus: Neiman, *Evil in Modern Thought: An Alternative History of Philosophy* (Princeton: Princeton University Press, 2002), p. 25.
65 G. W. Leibniz, *Philosophical Texts*. Translated and edited by R. S. Woolhouse and Richard Francks (Oxford: Oxford University Press, 1998), p. 163.

Descartes made clear that his philosophy helped to strengthen the doctrinal core of the Catholic Church (see Chapter 1). He emphasized, however, the self-sufficient mode of his scientific and philosophical inquiries. Philosophy might support religion rather than undermine it, but it certainly does its work as a separate and autonomous entity.

According to Descartes, philosophy independently arrives at the eternal truths that constitute Christian dogma. Leibniz held that the metaphysics of the latter were part of the logical inquiries of the former. He thus argued that the philosopher had to turn to God in order to fully understand the mechanism that governed nature. Leibniz thereby affirmed the inseparable link between the immanent as well as mathematical laws of mechanics, on the one hand, and metaphysics that make up various theological systems, on the other. While he did not separate the body from the mind in a manner as stark as Descartes and Hobbes did, he nevertheless proclaimed the superiority of the cerebral over the corporeal. In this way the final causes that he associated with his notion of the soul as monad were closely tied to the efficient causes that characterize the Cartesian mechanics of the body.

This union between body and soul describes Leibniz's notion of the pre-established harmony. The seemingly indifferent work perpetrated by mechanical operations emerges as being enfolded within the care of providential reason. Yet Leibniz's preestablished harmony still enshrines a mind-body dualism. The body does not know what it does. The factual viz. empirical aspect of life (rather than an interaction with the mind) governs bodily functions. Mind and body therefore coexist in two separate spheres of activity. The harmony between them is preestablished. It thus does not result from actual interaction.

Yet the harmonious balance between the two entities might strike one as non-dualist. Panjotis Kondylis has argued that Leibniz undermines Descartes' mind body dualism precisely by relating the physical to the metaphysical. This is to some extent true. However, Leibniz clearly leaves the mechanical system of Descartes intact. He only embeds it within a strong theological context. Kondylis interpretation forms an integral part of his revisionist interpretation of the Enlightenment. His central thesis is that Enlightenment thinkers reacted against Cartesian thought. This thesis is quite thought provoking and innovative. It is clearly pertinent for an accurate interpretation of Herder's version of the Enlightenment. Whether it does full justice to the rationalist agenda of Leibniz's philosophy is another question.[66]

Concurring with Panjotis Kondylis's analysis, Jonathan I. Israel has recently argued that Leibniz's theory of the monad offers a way out of Cartesian dualism. According to Israel, his preestablished harmony is thus akin to Spinoza's one substance theory.[67] In the middle of the eighteenth century, Moses

---

66 See Kondylis' *Die Aufklärung im Rahmen des neuzeitlichen Rationalismus* (Stuttgart: Klett-Cotta, 1981), pp. 177–178.

67 Israel, *Radical Enlightenment: Philosophy and the Making of Modernity 1650–1750* (Oxford: Oxford University Press, 2001), pp. 512–513.

Mendelssohn already analyzed points of convergence between Leibniz's and Spinoza's respective philosophies. Indeed Mendelssohn maintained that Leibniz was heavily indebted to Spinoza's monism in his formulation of the preestablished harmony. From the perspective of intellectual history, Mendelssohn's reading of Leibniz is a key moment because it introduced Spinoza into intellectual discussions not in the commonly received form of a bugbear threatening immorality and atheism but rather as a thinker capable of addressing important philosophical issues (such as the mechanistic mind body divide) that lay at the heart of the eighteenth century's self perception as "modernity." By positing an intellectual debt that Leibniz presumably owed to Spinoza, Mendelssohn thus made Spinoza's thought socially acceptable.

The imputed philosophical congruence between the two thinkers is, however, not clearly borne out by textual evidence. Leibniz thus often accused Spinoza of atheism. In his essay "Nature itself; or, the Inherent Force and Activity of Created Things—confirming and illustrating the author's dynamics" (1698), Leibniz discusses the one substance theory as "a doctrine of very ill repute which an irreligious, though admittedly clever, author has recently introduced to the world (or at least revised)."[68] Elsewhere he writes that "it is evident that Spinoza denies God intelligence and free will."[69] While pointing out similarities between Leibniz's notion of the monad and Spinoza's monism, Israel in the end underlines the theological difference that makes their thought diverge into opposite directions:

> Spinoza, Leibniz remarks in his *Théodicée*, was right to "oppose an absolute power of determination that is without any grounds; it does not belong even to God"; his mistake was to push this insight to the point of insisting on the universal validity of absolute necessity. The superiority of his own system over those of Descartes, Malebranche, and Bayle, as well as that of Spinoza, and its special aptness for defending religion, morality, and authority both political and ecclesiastical, he believed, lay precisely in his having "sufficiently proved that neither the foreknowledge nor Providence of God can impair either His justice or goodness, or our freedom."[70]

This divergence between Spinoza and Leibniz, therefore, does not only have a theological but it also has a broader political and philosophical dimension. In contrast to Spinoza who described the mind as the idea of the body, Leibniz opposed the empirical viz. bodily to the rational in the *Monadology* as follows: "There are also two kinds of *truth*: those of reasoning and those of *fact*. Truths of reasoning are necessary, and their opposite is impossible; those of fact are contingent, and their opposite is possible."[71] On this view, the rational

---

68 Leibniz, *Philosophical Texts*, trans. and ed. by R. S. Woodhouse and Richard Francks (Oxford: Oxford University Press, 1998), p. 214.

69 Leibniz, "Remarks on Spinoza's Philosophy," in Wayne I Boucher (ed.), *Spinoza: Eighteenth and Nineteenth Century Discussion. Volum1 1700–1800* (Bristol: Thoemmes Press, 1999), p. 99.

70 Israel, *Radical Enlightenment*, p. 514.

coincides with the necessary as well as with the eternal and sharply contrasts with the factual which is contingent. Leibniz in fact takes issue with the Spinozist idea of the mind as the idea of the body in his "Remarks on Spinoza's Philosophy." Here he emphasizes his disagreement with the argument according to which "mind and body are the same thing:"[72] "With this," Leibniz writes, "I disagree. Mind and body," according to Leibniz, "are no more the same, than the principle of action, and the principle of passion."[73] In this way he clearly establishes a hierarchical divide between the body, which he demotes to passivity, and the mind, which he elevates to the sphere of action. Herder, in contrast, stresses the interdependence of the cerebral and the corporal. He sees this Spinozist monism at work at the conception of biblical narratives.

In his treatise *Archeology of the Orient* (1769) Herder argues that Leibniz' idealism has little in common with the world of the Hebrew Bible. In an ironic mode he plays the Leibnizian Monad off against the Biblical Moses:

> But now, be it the *immateriality* and *spirituality* and *simplicity* and *immortality* of the soul—and please nothing but the soul, the *singular* monad, which, as a philosopher knows, always spins around in a circle and is midway riddled with holes at the point from where it is hanging—dear people search for this in your metaphysics, in your Socrates' of the eighteenth century but not in Job and not in Moses![74]

The Monad which Herder contrasts with Moses of course refers to Leibniz and the reference to a plurality of Socrates' has its singular instance in Moses Mendelssohn. (As has been intimated above, Mendelssohn earned the title "the German Socrates" through his attempt to prove the immortality of the soul in his *Phädon*.)

Countering an exclusive focus on the soul's immortality and immateriality Herder maintains that both Hebrew and Greek antiquity are Spinozist (and thus centered on ontology) rather than the metaphysical. In other words, the world of the ancients incorporates ethics into the physical realm and does not oppose the latter to an absolute norm that exists in a separate metaphysical sphere as propounded by what Herder sees as the orthodoxy of the eighteenth century (Leibniz, Warburton[75] and Grundling): "Like Moses, Job, Pythagoras,

---

71 Leibniz, *Philosophical Texts*, p. 272.

72 Wayne I Boucher (ed.), *Spinoza. Eighteenth and Nineteenth Century Discussion. Volum1 1700–1800*, 97.

73 Ibid.

74 Herder, *Sämtliche Werke*, Vol 6, ed. by Bernhard Suphan (Berlin: Weidmannsche Buchhandlung, 1883), p. 444.

75 In contrast to Robert Lowth's interpretation of the Hebrew Bible as both prophetic and poetic, William Warburton insisted in his *Divine Legislation of Moses* (1738–1740) on the unprophetic and allegorical rather than metaphorical nature of biblical writing. For a discussion of Warburton's metaphysical approach to scripture see Jonathan Sheehan's *Enlightenment Bible: Translation, Scholarship, Culture* (Princeton, NJ: Princeton University Press, 2005), 161–162.

Plato and God in his words (in his words because he does not demonstrate
what he means via *methodo mathematica*) I prefer to be an atheist, pantheist
and the first *Spinoza ante Spinozam* to being Warburton, Grundling and the
most orthodox metaphysicians of the century."[76] Here Herder relates Spinoza's
assumed atheism to both Jewish (Moses and Job) and Greek (Pythagoras and
Plato) antiquity. He distinguishes this Spinozist understanding of the Bible,
which emphasizes the materiality of the letter,[77] from what he perceives to be
eighteenth-century orthodox theology (i.e. Warburton and Grundling).

Similarly, in his *Spinoza Dialogues* or *Gott* Herder argues that rather than
being indebted to the Cabbala as Johann Georg Wachter (1673–1757) has
claimed in *Der Spinozimus im Jüdentuhumb* (1699), Spinoza's conception of
God relates to the Hebrew Bible in general and to the Mosaic conception of
God as "I am what I am" (*ehyeh asher ehyeh*) in particular. Herder cites this
conception and relates it to Spinoza's one substance theory while contrasting
it with what he understands as the Cabbalistic theory of divine emanations:
"'*I am what I am and will be what I will be.*' This notion incorporates
the highest and completely incomparable existence as much as it excludes all
emanations. Spinoza held onto this high and singular notion; that is why he is
dear to me."[78] The biblical unity of God founds the interconnectedness of
difference in the secular domain of nature and history, whereas Leibniz's
Monad, in Herder's view, makes difference absolute while not recognizing
that the universal is itself particular and the particular is itself universal.

In his 1800 version of the Spinoza Dialogues Herder goes a step further: he
argues that Spinoza introduces a Jewish element into Cartesian rationalism.
More importantly, Herder sees in Spinoza's Jewish heritage a challenge to the
dualism that informs and shapes both Descartes' and Leibniz' philosophy.
One could in fact read Spinoza's central notion of *conatus*—at least my interpretation of it—as being congruent with the basic ethical teachings of rabbinical Judaism. As Warren Montag has clearly shown, as a child and adolescent
Spinoza went to one of Europe's finest Jewish schools and this early and excellent training might well have informed the conception of Spinoza's ethics.
Spinoza's idiosyncratic take on the *conatus* as not only the preservation of the
self but also and concomitantly that of the other may indeed have a foundation in basic rabbinical teaching—in particular, Hillel the Elder's: "If I am not
for myself, who will be for me? And when I am for myself, what am 'I'? And
if not now, when?" (*Pirkei* Avot 1:14).[79]

In the 1800 version of his Spinoza dialogues Herder indeed differentiates
Cabbala from what he understands as the "proper" Jewish heritage of the
Torah (the five books of Moses). He characterizes Spinoza as "an antipode of
the Cabbala" and then goes on to say that this hostility is only "natural" for

---

76 Herder, *Sämtliche Werke*, Vol. 6, 445.
77 See Montag's *Bodies, Masses, Power*, pp. 1–26.
78 Herder, *Herder und die Anthropologie der Aufklärung*, 810–11.
79 Here and throughout this entire book I am deeply indebted to longstanding con-
    versations with Paul Mendes-Flohr.

someone who "has been brought up as a Jew" and who "has introduced a Jewish perspective into the Cartesian philosophy."[80] Herder's dismissive attitude to cabbalistic writings is certainly narrow-minded. Yet it cannot be overlooked that this hostility to the cabbala, in particular, and to mysticism, in general, is part and parcel of Herder's Enlightenment outlook (it is due to this rationalist condemnation of the cabbala that it was only rediscovered by Gershom Scholem at the beginning of the twentieth century, that is, after the influence of Romanticism in the nineteenth century).

What is crucial here is that Herder denies that there is any relation between Spinoza's philosophy and Cabbalistic thought in order to critique Friedrich Heinrich Jacobi's assessment of the Dutch-Jewish philosopher's close relationship to the Cabbala. In the work which provoked the famous Spinoza controversy of 1785 Jacobi claims that Spinoza's nihilism is the offspring of cabbalistic influences: "*a nihilo nihil fit*; which Spinoza, according to frequently used notions, just as the philosophizing cabbalists and others before him, considered."[81] According to Jacobi Spinoza's denial that God created the world out of nothingness is proof positive of his nihilism and atheism. Jacobi attempts to disqualify Spinoza by arguing that Spinozist thought, as the most explicit form of nihilism, is nothing original but a clarified and crystallized version of the cabbala (rather than the Bible): "The Cabbalist Philosophy, as much as is open to critical scrutiny—and according to its best commentators, the younger von Helmont, and Wachter—is nothing other, as philosophy, but undeveloped, or newly confused Spinozism."[82] Rather than following cabbalistic influences, Herder argues against Jacobi that Spinoza signals his proximity to the *ehyeh asher ehyeh* conception of the Divine by "opening" his *Ethics* "with the essential notion of God."[83]

Herder proceeds to connect his understanding of Spinoza's appreciation of the *Torah* to the seventeenth and eighteenth-century context of Descartes' and Leibniz' respective mind-body divides. Herder thus singles out the Jewish background within Spinoza's thought as that element that explains his departure from Descartes' dualism between the cerebral and the corporeal, writing that Spinoza's "philosophy does not derive from the Cartesian *I think, therefore I am*; but from the holy name of his fathers *I am what I am and will be what I will be*."[84] By affiliating Spinoza with the Jewish biblical tradition, Herder separates Spinoza from what he sees as the orthodox viz. one-dimensional rationalism of Hobbes, Descartes and Leibniz. Herder's Spinoza interpretation, however, does not only undermine the rationalism of the Enlightenment but also questions religious orthodoxy, because his conception of the biblical God is Spinozist—rather than referring to an otherworldly realm it denotes

---

80 Herder, *Herder und die Anthropologie der Aufklärung*, 1086.
81 F. H. Jacobi, *Über die Lehre des Spinoza in Briefen an den Herrn Moses Mendelssohn* (Breslau: Gottlieb Löwe, 1785), p. 14.
82 Ibid., p. 171.
83 Herder, *Herder und die Anthropologie der Aufklärung*, p. 1086.
84 Ibid., p. 1087.

Spinoza's one Substance theory. The perfection of the Divine does not reside in a supramundane sphere; be that Descartes's *cogito* or Leibniz's preestablished harmony. On the contrary, it cannot be separated from the contingency and thus imperfection of the factual.

Herder's philosophy of the factual implicitly critiques Leibniz as the intellectual predecessor of Kantian metaphysics. Rather than seeing Herder as an imitator of Leibnizian thought, as is commonly done in the critical literature,[85] it would be more accurate to see him as a creative developer of Spinoza's naturalism. Spinoza argues for a principle of necessity but he does not distinguish the necessary from the natural and therefore factual (see Chapter 1). Rather he combines in his definition of necessity the cerebral with the corporal. This is made abundantly clear in Spinoza's conception of the mind as the idea of the body. Leibniz's opposition between the contingency of nature and the timeless truth of reason, in contrast, relates back to Descartes' mind body dualism.

In his critical period Kant took up Cartesian elements within Leibniz's thought. He did so when he formulated the distinctions between the noumenal and the phenomenal, between the realms of nature and freedom. Herder, on the other hand, advocated a philosophy of the factual. Which elements exactly distinguish Herder's Spinozan thought from the Cartesian and Leibnizian dualism between the rational and the factual? When he was still a pupil of the precritical Kant, Herder wrote a couple of essays on Leibniz as well as on two important philosophers who were disciples of Leibniz: Christian Wolf and Alexander Baumgarten both shaped the German philosophical culture in the early eighteenth century and Baumgarten "invented" the discipline of aesthetics.

The young Herder excoriates Baumgarten's 1750 book *Aesthetica* for not enacting what its title announces. He points out that aesthetics means "the teaching of sensibility" (*eine Lehre des Gefühls*)[86] and this is precisely what the Leibnizian Baumgarten fails to present. What he offers instead is speculation. Herder takes issue with the deductive, *a priori* and thus highly ethereal (*wie aus der Luft*)[87] method of Baumgarten's approach which harks back to both Descartes' and Leibniz's definition of reason. The critical Kant would develop

---

85　Thus Seigel has recently depicted Herder's philosophy as heavily indebted to both Leibniz and the French enlightenment: Seigel, *The Idea of the Self. Thought and Experience in Western Europe since the Seventeenth Century* (Cambridge: Cambridge University Press, 2005), 334. Seigel goes on to argue that Herder follows Leibniz's metaphysical concerns when he theologized the materialism of a French sensualist like Diderot: Seigel, *The Idea of the Self*, p. 336. Herder's writing on forces within nature does not refer to Leibniz's preestablished harmony. Instead it develops and deepens Spinoza's conception of the *conatus*. Similar to the *conatus*, Herder's notion of forces denotes those elements within nature that ensure its sustainability.

86　Herder, *Werke. Vol. II*, ed. by W. Pross, p. 30.

87　J. G. Herder, *Werke. Vol. II. Herder und die Anthropologie der Aufklärung*, p. 29.

and radicalize this notion of reason's *a priori* constitution. Terry Eagleton concurs with Herder's critique of the emerging discipline of aesthetics: "If Baumgarten's *Aesthetica* (1750) opens up in an innovative gesture the whole terrain of sensation," writes Eagleton, "what it opens it up to is in effect the colonization of reason."[88] In his critique of Leibniz, Herder attempts to reverse this colonization of reason. He argues for a combination of the rational with the inclinational (the former is general, while the latter is particular). The particularity of one's inclinations can be reconciled with rational rules as long as one does not oppose reason to inclination: "The instinct is, however, always present and leads us, without rationalization to that which reason wants. It does so while we walk, eat and do what gives us pleasure."[89] Here we see how the young Herder attempts to combine ethics with ontology. The "ought" partakes of being. Reason interacts with the emotions. The instinctive does not undermine the workings of rational consideration.

Significantly Herder proves capable of combining the emotive with the intellectual, precisely because he sees enjoyment and happiness as the motive force behind both activities. This non-exclusive approach to the mind-body problematic certainly refers back to Spinoza's eudemonistic definition of ethics and sharply contrasts with the critical Kant according to whom knowledge "of the connection between happiness and virtue is not only metaphysically impossible but morally disastrous."[90] How can we best understand the preconditions for Herder's critique of Kant?

So far criticism has focused on establishing what exactly Herder read.[91] Did Herder beg to differ from what he read? This crucial but often neglected question will be discussed here. The influence of the French Enlightenment on Herder has been well documented. The question of Leibniz's impact on his intellectual development is likewise beyond doubt. What has so far not been sufficiently investigated is how Herder undermined Leibniz's understanding of reason. The irony implicit in the title "Truths out of Leibniz's Philosophy" (*Wahrheiten aus Leibniz*) has not been noticed. It has been characterized as a summary of Leibniz's thought rather than as a subtle critique of it.[92]

If Herder summarizes Leibniz' philosophy then he does so by way of inversion. His mode of writing can thus be described as ironic. Benjamin Bennett

---

88 Eagleton, *The Ideology of the Aesthetic* (Oxford: Blackwell, 1990), p. 15.
89 Herder, *Werke. Vol. II*, p. 43.
90 Neiman, *Evil in Modern Thought*, p. 67.
91 German Herder scholarship has largely focused on tracing various influences on Herder, while not analyzing what this reception history may mean for a better understanding of Herder's thought. John H. Zammitto's groundbreaking book *Kant, Herder, and the Birth of Anthropology* offers a refreshing contrast to the influence studies tradition.
92 Wolfgang Pross thus characterizes Wahrheiten aus Leibniz as a "Zusammenfassung" of Leiniz's philosophy. Herder, *Werke. Vol.II*, p. 863.

rightly detects irony as the defining trope of Herder's way of thought. Bennett's approach is exceptional in that he focuses not on congruencies between Leibniz and Herder's work but on crucial points where they differed:

> Excessive theorizing (or in Goethe's terms, failure to theorize with irony) is what Herder holds against Leibniz when he rejects the idea of "egoistic monads" or of the dreaming monad that *could think entirely without words*, that is the individual who attempts to think beyond the limits of the world of experience in which his words inevitably place him.[93]

Significantly Herder criticizes in both Leibniz and Kant's academic approach to thought a disregard to its linguistics foundations. According to Herder, thought reflects upon sense experience and it is this reflection that operates in the workings of language (see the discussion of *Besonnenheit* in the preceding chapter).

Most importantly Herder reverses Leibniz's demotion of the senses. In a tongue in cheek manner he postulates that the senses are the basis for the workings of the soul as truth derived from Leibnizian thought: "The soul is nothing without the senses" (*Nichts ist die Seele, was nicht durch die Sinne*).[94] This statement turns upside down Leibniz's notion of substance as independent from the influence of sensuous experience. In his famous *Discourse on Metaphysics* (1686), Leibniz maintains that the soul remains impervious to any influences from the external world. It is determined by God's directions alone: "But in whatever form we take it, it is always false to say that all our notions come from the senses that are called external. [...] Now in strict metaphysical truth there is no external cause which acts on us except God alone, and he alone communicates himself to us directly in virtue of our continual dependence."[95] In his commentary on Leibniz, Herder belittles God's central role and he thus questions the theocentric approach of Leibniz's *Discourse on Metaphysics*. Herder replaces this theological element with the immanence of the senses.

How can we explain this shift from theology to sensuality? That this permutation occurs in Herder might strike one as especially odd. For was he not a trained theologian? Herder does not only attack high levels of ideation within narrowly defined philosophical undertakings. He also undermines the ideational basis of theological doctrine. Developing and radicalizing Spinoza's critique of anthropomorphism and anthropocentrism, he is a critic of both theology and philosophy. Herder castigates absolutist assumptions within philosophical thought. What he objects to in philosophy is precisely its tendency to assume the voice of an omniscient deity.

---

93 Bennett, *Beyond Theory: Eighteenth-Century German Literature and the Poetics of Irony* (Ithaca, NY: Cornell University Press, 1993), 251.

94 Herder, *Werke. Vol. II*, p. 46.

95 Leibniz, "Discourse on Metaphysics" in Leibniz, *Philosophical Texts*, pp. 53–93, p.79.

As he makes clear in *Yet Another Philosophy of History* teleological thought constitutes nothing else but an anthropomorphic theology: "Generally," Herder writes,

> the philosopher is most an *animal* when he would wish to be most reliably a God—thus also in the confident calculation of the *perfection* of the world. Of course, if only it were true that everything proceeded prettily *in a straight line* and that every *succeeding human being* and *every succeeding race* got *perfected* according to *his* ideal in *beautiful progression* for which he alone knew the *exponent* of virtue and happiness.[96]

In a highly ironical tone Herder here reverses the hierarchical divide between the intellectual and the animalistic sphere: the philosopher who attempts to overcome nature turns out to be an animal (*Tier*), that is to say, that which teleological thought seeks to leave behind emerges as its "proper" sphere of activity. Herder goes on to unmask the anthropomorphism that makes the philosopher "always the *ratio ultima*, the last, the highest link in the chain of being, the very culmination of it all."[97] Leibniz's writings on the preestablished harmony are the target of the spoof on the philosopher who "pronounces on the perfection of the world."

At the same time Herder here makes Spinoza's critique of theology as anthropomorphism relevant for a new understanding of history. The quasi-omniscient view into God's laboratory gives rise to various teleologies of history, either in a religious or a secular form. Herder contrasts the straight line of the philosopher qua theologian with a literary thinker *à la* Lawrence Sterne.[98] The straight line in the excerpt quoted above refers to Sterne's *Life and Opinions of Tristram Shandy*. The novel substitutes "the omniscient, omnipotent narrator humorously deployed by Fielding," with "the vague half-knowledge and frustrated impotence of Tristram."[99] At the beginning of Vol VIII, Tristram refers to "all that has been said upon *straight lines* in sundry pages of my book [. . .]."[100] He thus emphasizes the central role of digression and the lack of omniscience on his part. As narrator he pays attention to that which is other than himself. He therefore has to digress. In the excerpt quoted above Herder implicitly argues that digression resembles the constitutive principle of dialogical thinking. The philosopher who fabricates straight lines

---

96 Herder, *Philosophical Writings*, p. 334. Herder, *Herder und der Sturm und Drang*, p. 658.

97 Herder, *J. G. Herder on Social and Political Culture*, p. 214, Herder, *Herder und der Sturm und Drang*, p. 658.

98 Robert S. Mayo and Rudolf Haym have clearly established the influence of Sterne on Herder's thought in the Riga period (when he composed *Yet Another philosophy of history*): Mayo, *Herder and the beginnings of Comparative Literature*, 58.

99 Chirstopher Ricks, "Introduction," in Sterne, *The Life and Opinions of Tristram Shandy*, ed. by Graham Petrie (Harmondsworth: Penguin, 1985), pp. 7–28, p. 13.

100 Sterne, *The Life and Opinions of Tristram Shandy*, p. 515.

gives an account of his ideas and ideals alone and he refuses to engage with the divergent reality of the world. He thus remains stuck in the self-enclosed academic sphere of *Schulphilosophie*. In a vein similar to Spinioza's critique of theology as anthropomorphism Herder uncovers the anthropomorphic nature of ideational constructions.

This is the programmatic aim of Herder's Riga essay on *How Philosophy can become more universal and useful in serving the best interests of the people*. Here he emphasizes Spinoza's primacy of action and deplores that the rational perfection of philosophical discourse induces passivity. What Herder critiques is not the contemplative nature of thought, but rather that it tends to lose touch with the non-ideational realities in which an active life is inevitably enmeshed. Philosophy "elevates us towards *thought*" but in doing so it de-habituates us from action: "because if any muse loves peace and quiet (*Ruhe*), then it is the goddess of philosophy."[101] Herder fears that the passivity of thought as encountered in the *Schulphilosophie* of the eighteenth century could be consubstantial with the restiveness of a lifeless body. In order to avoid the replication of the dissection theatre within the world of letters, Herder advocates thinking in action. How can reflection be connected to action? The following chapter will address this question.

---

101 "Wenn jene [i.e. philosophy] uns *zum Denken* erhübe, so verlernten wir das Handeln; denn wenn irgend eine Muse die Ruhe liebt, so ists die Göttin der Philosophie." Herder, *Frühe Schriften 1764–1772*, ed. by Ulrich Gaier (Frankfurt a. M.: Deutscher Klassiker Verlag, 1985), 113.

Chapter 5

From the National to the Transnational

It does not seem to me, Austerlitz added, that we understand the laws governing the return of the past, but I feel more and more as if time did not exist at all, only various spaces interlocking according to the rules of a higher form of stereometry, between which the living and the dead can move back and forth as they like, and the longer I think about it the more it seems to me that we who are still alive are unreal in the eyes of the dead, that only occasionally, in certain lights and atmospheric conditions, do we appear in their field of vision.

Sebald, Austerlitz, p. 261

1. *Herder's Ironic Usage of Prejudice in* This Too a Philosophy of History

How does Herder extend and enrich Spinoza's critique of an epistemology become absolutist? In order to accurately address this question it is worth providing a brief review of Herder's intellectual background. This chapter will continue the preceding discussion as to the ways in which Herder diverges from those thinkers who have until now been portrayed as mayor influences on his work. In the previous chapter I have analyzed Herder's critique of Leibniz' hierarchical divide between the factual and the rational and here I will show how his critique of a mind/body dualism in the thought of Condillac, Rousseau, Descartes at the beginning of his intellectual career (when he was a pupil of the pre-critical Kant), laid the ground for his questioning approach to Kantian transcendental philosophy. Herder's response to the French Sensualist tradition shaped his interpretation of Spinoza's thought. How does Spinoza's work on self-preservation and self-destruction and his dimissal of various epistemological constructions relate to the political and social problems that haunt an increasingly global age? In the eighteenth century Herder addressed these issues by shifting the emphasis of critical inquiry away from academic uniformity to an appreciation of anthropological diversity.

The previous chapter has discussed Herder's unease with philosophical academicism (i.e. Schulphilosophie). Herder perceived in such philosophy a hierarchical divide that separates the everyday world of action from the academic realm of reflection. He took issue with highly developed types of ideation in the thought of Descartes, Leibniz and the mature Kant with a view towards establishing a Spinozist viz. non-hierarchical vision of philosophy. Reflection and action were not to be separated into different entities which contrast with one another in terms of superiority and inferiority. Rather they were to be conceived as interdependent. Here we reach the point where it becomes apparent that Herder's reference to the Volk (the people) results from his fear of a somewhat dead form of book learning, one that is disconnected from the social and political world of action.

Herder has often been called the "godfather of nationalism," because in a curious manner he attempted to relate thinking to the societal sphere of action.[1] This of course begs the question as to why the world of letters requires the concept of the nation in order to become socially relevant. Herder was well aware of this question. He in fact critiqued a narrow concern with one particular nation. The national perspective is myopic and it is precisely for its intrinsic imperfection that Herder proclaims its exemplary perfection. True, he praised the ancient Hebrews for their patriotism, but he also argued that this patriotic zeal was part of a larger perspective. He does not vilify the, in Slavoj Žižek's words, "most precious elements of Jewish spirituality itself," namely its "focus on a unique collective experience."[2] As F. M. Ballard has shown in quite some detail, Herder in fact grounded his appreciation of a particular group identity in precisely this "unique collective experience."[3] In his *Journal of my Voyage in the Year 1769* he refers to his "inclination (*Neigung*) toward the Hebrews considered as people."[4] By accentuating the communal element Herder differentiated his approach from other eighteenth-century philosophers such as Voltaire and Kant who praised "exceptional" viz. "philosophical" Jews and differentiated between them and the Jewish community as whole. In this way Voltaire denies the existence of philosophy as an essential part of Jewish communal existence: "You ask, what was the philosophy of the Hebrews? The answer will be a short one—they had none."[5] In an important study

---

1   This interpretative trend was initiated by Robert Reinhold Ergang who, in the first half of the twentieth century, characterized Herder as the philosopher of nationalism: Ergang, *Herder and the Foundation of German Nationalism* (New York: Columbia University Press, 1931), p. 50. However, Ergang emphasizes Herder's "humanitarian nationalism" that is far removed from "violent, militaristic nationalism." Ergang, *Herder and the Foundations of German Nationalism*, p. 266. Recently this nuanced view of putative nationalistic elements in Herder's thought has given way to the simplistic and rather mind boggling equation of Herder with Hitler. In his attempt to redeem Heidegger from any association with Nazism, James Phillips has thus found an easy scapegoat for Nazi ideology in the work of the eighteenth-century 'liberal' and enlightenment philosopher. According to this account Heidegger critiqued Nazism for its intrinsic "Herderian liberalism": Phillips, *Heidegger's Volk: Between National Socialism and Poetry* (Stanford: Stanford University Press, 2005), p. 44.

2   Žižek, *The Puppet and the Dwarf: The Perverse Core of Christianity* (Cambridge, MA: Massachusetts Institute of Technology Press, 2003), p. 8.

3   See Barnard's "The Hebraic Roots of Herder's Nationalism," in Barnard, *Herder on Nationality, Humanity, and History* (Montreal and Kingston: McGill-Queen's University Press, 2003), pp. 17–37.

4   Herder, *Journal meiner Reise im Jahr 1769*, p. 124.

5   Frances-Marie Arouet (Voltaire), "Jews (1756), in Paul Mendes-Flohr and Jehuda Reinharz (eds), *The Jew in the Modern World: A Documentary History* (Oxford: Oxford University Press, 1995), pp. 30–305, p. 304. For a discussion of Kant see Mack's *German Idealism and the Jew*, pp. 23–41.

Jonathan M. Hess has elucidated how Herder—in striking contrast to most of his contemporaries (like Kant and the philologist Johann David Michaelis)— "in his reflections on Jewish history, explicitly identifies modern Jews with biblical Judaism, stressing what one might call in contemporary terms the continuity of Jewish memory."[6] As Herder put it in his *Fragments* apropos Jewish national identity "patriotism pours flames into the veins of each people as part of its initial formation (*Bildung*)."[7] This, however, is only a first step.

The focus on one's own traditions enables the formation of a particular identity. The latter, however, is not only particular but at the same time universal. In his *Journal of my Journey in the Year 1769* Herder delineates the plan of a universal history, which does not exclude any type of communal or individual identity. This book would embrace: "All spaces! All times! All peoples! All forces! All hybrid identities!"[8] This book would later materialize as the *Ideas toward a Philosophy of Human History*, which is arguable Herder's magnum opus.

The concept of a transnational history was of course not new in the eighteenth century: Bishop Bossuet had prominently expounded this idea in his 1681 *Discours sur l' Histoire Universelle*. In contrast to Bossuet, however, Herder does not conceive of the universal from a specific theological-doctrinal perspective. Neither does he attempt to emulate Voltaire and Iselin and write the triumphal story of civilization's progress toward rationality. As Berlin has ingenuously put it:

> There is *Fortgang*, but this is not the same as the notion of progress enunciated by, say, Turgot or Condorcet, or, in particular, by Voltaire (for example, in *La Philosophie d' histoire par feu l'abbé Bazin*), against whom, together with the Swiss philosopher of history Iselin, Herder's thunderbolts are specifically directed.[9]

From Herder's point of view, history does not so much resemble the straight line of a teleological narrative as disintegrate into different but equally valid tableaus. Historical time thus gives way to historical space, which presents the view of not one single nation but a plurality of nations. Does this argument about the specialization of history not conflict with the common image of Herder as the originator of a temporal understanding of human cultures?[10]

Herder certainly emphasizes temporality but he does not proclaim the progress of history. Instead he depicts human existence in fluid and ceaselessly

---

6 Hess, *Germans, Jews and the Claims of Modernity* (New Haven, CT: Yale University Press, 2002), p. 67.

7 Herder, *Frühe Schriften 1764-1772*, ed. by Ulrich Gaier (Frankfurt a. M.: Deutscher Klassiker Verlag, 1985), p. 280.

8 Herder, *Journal meiner Reise im Jahr 1769*, p. 17.

9 Berlin, *Three Enemies of the Enlightenment*, pp. 215–216.

10 This emphasis on the temporal in Herder's thought accounts for his prominence in Meinecke's (who is otherwise quite critical of Herders repugnance of state power) book on *Historism*: Meinecke, *Historism*, p. 309.

changing terms in order to upend rather than uphold essentialist notions of one nation's superiority over another. Every national achievement is bound to disintegrate with the flow of time. Neither Greece, nor Rome nor Egypt's high point of civilization lasts forever. They thus have to refer to each other across temporal and geographical boundaries. "Neither Egyptians, not Romans, nor Greeks were *at all times* the same,"[11] Herder writes in *This Too a Philosophy of History*. This implies that he does not abandon space while appreciating the forces of time. He attempts to rescue both the past and those non-Western communities that are associated with it, from being judged by the absolute value standard of either classical Greece or contemporaneous Europe. While emphasizing the passing of time, Herder's historical perspective is therefore not espousing a notion of "improvement through development." This is why it is not only temporal but also spatial: the focus on one specific time and one specific nation broadens into a sight of transnational and trans-temporal inter-connectedness through both space and time. Each entity is not sufficient in itself. Humanity therefore needs to establish pathways between periodical and national borders in its search for different recompenses that compensate for its singular insufficiencies.

Herder's *This Too a Philosophy of History* (1774) vibrates in this tension between the national and the transnational (the title of this essay of course has an ironic relation to Voltaire who first coined the notion "philosophy of history"). Critics have faulted the work for its hybrid style that commingles satire with serious philosophical inquiry.[12] This criticism misses Herder's point: he sets out to illustrate that one can only engage with philosophy by involving its opposite: the "lowly" realm of satire and literary irony.[13] The hybrid character of its composition performs the content which *This Too* depicts: it sets out to prove the absurdity of trying to arrive at the truth in a one-dimensional, uni-linear manner. Contrary to Voltaire and Iselin's teleological thought, Herder argues that history does not unfold in terms of a straight line (see previous chapter). The crucial point here is that oppositions are codependent on each other. Humanity stays alive not because of its supposed linear progression toward ethical perfection. On the contrary, human history moves through dif-ferent stages that mutually oppose each other in order to make up for their

---

11 Herder, *Herder und der Sturm und Drang 1764–1774*, p. 613.

12 See Clark, *Herder*, pp. 187–206.

13 Benjamin Bennett has recently discussed Herder in the context of irony as a domi-nant characteristic of eighteenth-century writing and thought. Herder's writings are contradictory and ironic, because they attempt to avoid the closure implied in the construction of a philosophical system such as that developed by Kant. Accord-ing to Bennett eighteenth-century literature resists the Kantian move toward a sys-tem: Bennett, *Beyond Theory: Eighteenth-Century German Literature and the Poetics of Irony* (Ithaca, NY: Cornell University Press, 1993), 162. Bennett argues that Herder uses contradiction in a strategic way in order to avoid being trapped in the one-dimensionality of one particular discipline or one particular system: Ibid., p. 252.

intrinsic lack; for their various points of strengths which are at the same time insufficiencies.

It is this void that gives rise to the desire for action. It is only through Herder's account of human lack that we can do justice to his seemingly paradoxical identification of the national with the transnational. How does this copresence of the transnational within the national square with the common image of Herder as godfather of nationalism and ethno-centric romanticism? In a startling way Herder seems to praise native prejudices:

> Prejudice is *good* at the appropriate time, because it makes one *happy*: it pushes peoples (*Völker*) to their respective *centers of gravity* (*Mittelpunkte*), it makes them more solid on their trunk, more blossoming in their specific type, more fervent and therefore more blissful in their *inclinations* and *aims*.[14]

What has so far been overlooked is that this laudatory approach is itself ironic. Herder credits prejudice only within the context of one particular stage ("at the appropriate time"). He employs the notion of happiness in order to describe those elements that are life affirming in an otherwise precarious and fragile existence (revealingly he refers to the tiny image of blossoms on a trunk while metaphorically delineating the formation of social identity).

This initial stage is necessary for the establishment of a specific identity but it has to incorporate what opposes it if it is not to fall prey to the destructive and self-destructive forces of anti-intellectualism and bigotry. Yet without prejudice there would not be identity formation, which is paradoxically the *sine qua non* of universality. One does justice to Herder's appraisal of prejudice if one reads it in the light of Hegel's notion of the *concrete universal* (which the latter might well have derived from the work of the former). As Žižek has put it, "the true Hegelian 'concrete universality' is the very movement of negativity which splits universality from within, reducing it to one of the particular elements, one of its own species."[15] A similar form of splitting occurs in Herder's understanding of prejudice. Herder emphasizes the temporal element within this split. He does so by radically refashioning the Enlightenment idea of historical progress.

Rather than moving toward perfection, history changes its course, precisely because each of its stages is insufficient as an independent entity. Each particular community and each historical period embodies a lack that necessitates the copresence of what is its opposite. Anticipating Walter Benjamin's famous thesis according to which there "is no document of culture which is not at the same time a document of barbarism,"[16] Herder argues that

> It was precisely the machine that made *far-reaching vices* possible which also *raised virtues* so *high*, *spread efficacy* so far and wide. Is humanity capable of

---

14 Herder, *Herder und der Sturm und Drang 1764–1774*, p. 618.
15 Žižek, *The Puppet and the Dwarf*, p. 87.
16 Michael Löwy, *Fire Alarm: Reading Walter Benjamin's 'On the Concept of History'*, trans. by Chris Turner (London: Verson, 2005), p. 47.

pure *perfection* in a single [*in Einem*] present condition at all? Peak borders on valley. About noble *Spartans* there dwell inhumanly treated *Helots*. The Roman *victor* dyed with *red dye of the gods* is invisibly also *daubed* with *blood; plunder, wickedness*, and *lusts* surround his chariot; before him goes *oppression*, in his train follows *misery* and *poverty*. – Hence in this sense too *shortcomings* and *virtue* always dwell together in one human hut.[17]

This copresence of shortcomings and virtue may well have a point of reference in what, as Manfred Walther has intriguingly put it, is Spinoza's insight into humanity's "necessary false consciousness" (*notwendiges falsches Bewustsein*).[18] Spinoza does of course not want to increase or aid false consciousness. He foregrounds the shortcomings of our mind (in other words consciousness) so that we are more aware of them and are thus better able to avoid taking these false mental constructs as a true representation of the world. Similarly, Herder does not dismiss prejudice as something we can easily overcome simply because it is false. He argues that prejudice is necessary because it is an inevitable part of our faulty mental constitution. An awareness of this falsity helps not taking ideological distortions for a true assessment of what is actually the case. Here again Herder adapts Spinoza's philosophy of the mind to the sphere of the social sciences (i.e. anthropology, history and sociology). Radicalizing Spinoza, Herder argues that prejudice or, in other words, false consciousness is one of the driving forces behind human diversity.

Human history unfolds along the trajectory not of a single line but of infinitely diverse threads, which intersect with each other. Attention to one instance distorts rather than does justice to the communal work that characterizes humanity. Philosophy, therefore, does not stay put. If it wants to remain in touch with the frequently contradictory reality of the factual it has to traverse different spaces and different times. Both anthropology and philosophy are mobile sciences. The philosopher transmogrifies into a traveler. The traveling philosopher becomes sensitive to the presence of change and difference: the harmful can have beneficial uses and what is beneficial can turn harmful.

In this way the vice of prejudice gives birth to universality. Herder identifies the universal with the failure of a myopic viz. prejudicial vision. In other words, the limitation of life necessitates the espousal of prejudice as the stepping-stone toward recognition of how the particular does not coincide with itself. By recognizing itself as prejudicial, particularity realizes universality as the foundation of its own existence. Following Spinoza, Herder identifies intellect not with the will (as Descartes does) but with the faculty of understanding. In the previous chapter we have seen how he defines reflection as thought about the senses and emotions: as *Besonnenheit*. Herder's notion of prejudice

---

17 Herder, *Philosophical Writings*, p. 295. Herder, *Werke. Vol. 1. Herder und der Sturm und Drang*, p. 616.

18 I am most grateful to Manfred Walther for a detailed and very helpful discussion about Spinoza's political philosophy.

incorporates a reflective moment: both prejudice and at the same time the reflection upon what is prejudicial.

A skeptical reader might object that this appraisal of prejudice gives rise to relativism. Following Max Rouché,[19] many critics have accused Herder of cultural relativism.[20] This chapter shows why it is a mistake to discuss Herder's work as either relativist or universalistic. He clearly affirms a universal idea of humanity. Rather than being a relativist Herder develops and creatively extends Spinoza's realism to the global context that has prominently emerged since the middle of the eighteenth century. Although he argues for a radical perspectivism, Herder is not a relativist who fails to recognize the value of ideas and concepts. What he questions are monolithic ideas that prohibit the flourishing of competing conceptions of the good life. As Žižek has recently argued, the conscious embrace of prejudice, viz. of a certain limited point of view, does not amount to a denial of truth: "everything is not relative—but this truth is the truth of the perspectival distortion as such, not the truth distorted by the partial view from a one-sided perspective."[21] It is this "truth of the distortion" on which Herder focuses when he scandalously extols prejudice. The truth in question here is distortion's reflection upon itself: its self-consciousness or self-awareness—its mindfulness of itself.

What conditions Herder's appraisal of prejudice is the identification of insight with failure. According to Herder the truth of sacred scripture is its failed and therefore imperfect human foundation. The identification of failure with achievement characterizes humanity and divinity alike. From his early writings of the Sturm und Drang period to his mature work of Weimar Classicism, Herder conceived of the human as a hybrid entity (a "hybrid thing"— *Mittelding*—as he put it in *This Too* and a "hybrid creature"—*Mittelgeschöpf*— as he put in the *Ideen*).[22] Not a single nation and not a single historical period avoids the confrontation with its own void. In this way the virtue of the Spartans cancels itself out when one takes into account that slavery forms the basis of their civilization. Virtues and vices are therefore scattered throughout the plurality of different national identities.

---

19 See Max Rouché's introduction to Herder's *This Too* in J. G. Herder, *Une autre philosophie de l'histoire*, bilingual edn., trans. Max Rouché (Aubier: "Éditions Montaigne, 1943), p. 74. Cultural relativism, in turn, has been closely associated with Nazism: Sikka, "Enlightened Relativism: The Case of Herder," *Philosophy & Social Criticism* 31 (2005): 309–341 (309). In this way Karl Popper accused Herder of relativism in *The Open Society and its Enemies* (London: Routledge, 1952). See also R. G. Collingwood's *The Idea of History* (Oxford: Clarendon Press, 1946) and H. S. Reiss' *The Political Thought of the German Romantics* (Oxford: Clarendon Press, 1955).

20 See Patrick Gardiner's, "German Philosophy and the Rise of Relativism," *Monist* 64 (1981): 138–154 and Brian J. Whitton's "Herder's Critique of the Enlightenment: Cultural Community versus Cosmopolitan Rationalism," *History & Theory* 27 (1988): 146–168.

21 Žižek, *The Puppet and the Dwarf*, p. 79.

22 Herder, *Ideen zu Philosophie der Geschichte der Menschheit*, Wolfgang Pross (ed.), Darmstadt: Wissenschaftliche Buchgesellschaft, 2002, p. 69.

Each nation is insufficient as an independent entity. Precisely through immersing itself into its imperfect foundations the myopic national perspective reveals a transnational horizon. There is no such thing as a self-contained entity. Herder announces the bursting of the vessel: "Human nature to wit is not a vessel, which contains a single, absolute independent immutable happiness, as the philosopher defines it: it attracts, however everywhere as much happiness as it is capable of."[23] The philosopher, who attempts to isolate the good into a single unit, diverges from the real.

The real, according to Herder, is an infinitely fractured unity that is scattered throughout the universe in a chaotic and unsystematic manner. Worse still the attempted distillation of virtue within an autonomous quintessence may give rise to nationalism and colonialism, because it theorizes otherness as the repetition of sameness. Herder thus takes issue with the homogenous tendencies within the self-proclaimed philanthropy of eighteenth-century thought:

> And the *universal, philosophical, human-friendly tone of our century* grants so gladly to each distant nation, each oldest age, in the world "our own ideal" in *virtue* and in *happiness*? Is such a unique judge as to *pass judgment on, condemn,* or beautifully *fictionalize* their ethics according to its own measure alone? Is not the good on the earth *strewn about*? Because one form of humanity and one region could not grasp it, it got distributed into a thousand forms, it roams forth—an eternal Proteus!—through all parts of the world and all centuries.[24]

Critiquing this uniform conception of humanity, Herder develops his notion of national identity. The universal is scattered into a plurality of diverse entities which make up humanity's unity. The crucial point here is that the nation is not an independent unit. It is rather part of the bursting of the vessel that transnationally contains the plural good of humanity. Each identity has a center in itself, which is itself de-centered. "Prejudice" is therefore "good" only "at the appropriate time"; when it "pushes nations (*Völker*) to converge upon their center."[25] This center, however, is only a small part of an infinitely fractured unity and Herder appraises prejudices while developing his theory of diversity. The center only comes into being in order to split apart into new kernels of identity. Different national prejudices make up the transnational body of diverse identities.

Yet if one nation takes itself to be the center of the universe, it falls prey to dementia. Having succumbed to what Spinoza criticizes as the anthropomorphic conception of God, it takes itself as a quasi-divine absolute and thus loses touch with its own limitations. Indeed it has then disconnected with its surroundings; it has lost a sense of reality. In the last part of *This Too* Herder makes clear that his usage of the term prejudice is not only affirmative but

---

23 Herder, *Werke. Herder und der Sturm und Drang 1764–1774*, p. 617.
24 Herder, *Philosophical Writings*, pp. 297–298. Herder, *Werke. Herder und der Sturm und Drang 1764-1774*, p. 618.
25 Herder, *Werke. Herder und der Sturm und Drang 1764–1774*, p. 618.

also ironic. A view from a broader perspective reveals the madness of the particular that assumes the position of the universe. It is such presumption of completeness that does violence to loving-kindness, not prejudice which knows itself as what it truly is:

> The chain of almighty, all-wise goodness is entwined one part *into* and *through* the other a thousandfold—but each member in the chain is in its place a *member*—hangs on the chain and does not see *where in the end the chain hangs*. Each in its delusion [*Wahne*] feels itself to be the *central point*, in its delusion feels everything *around itself only to the extent* that it pours rays or waves on this point—beautiful delusion![26]

Here Herder introduces the traditional image of the chain of being into the sphere of national and international politics.[27] Nationalist politicians are as deluded as pre-Copernican scientists and philosophers who conceive of the earth as the center of the universe. The allusion to the rays of the sun is clearly a reference to the premodern conception of the cosmos.

Herder is, however, critical of how far the modern universe has progressed ethically and politically. In this way he argues that the formal abolition of slavery has introduced a new form of mercantile colonialism:

> In Europe slavery has been abolished because it has been calculated how much more these slaves would cost and how much less they would bring in than free people. Only one thing have we permitted ourselves: to *use as slaves*, to *trade*, to *exile* into silver mines and sugar mills, *three parts of the world*—but those are not *Europeans*, not *Christians*, and in return we receive silver and gemstones, spices, sugar.[28]

The abolition of slavery makes place for a new kind of slavery. This new form is as ethno-centric and bigoted as the old form has been: it exploits non-Christians and non-Europeans while reveling in the profits reaped from such exploitation. Herder goes on to detect behind the idealism of European philanthropy the economic "ideal" of profit maximization. He coins the term *Preisideal* as a pun on the ideal of commerce: the German word *Preis* connotes both commercial price as well as moral or intellectual praise.[29]

Herder reveals the ethics of his century as labeling "indeed *honorable* and *glorious*" the "*robber of houses, chambers, and beds.*"[30] As a colonialist the

---

26 Herder, *Philosophical Writings*, p. 335. Herder, *Werke. Herder und der Sturm und Drang 1764–1774*, pp. 659–660.

27 See Arthur O. Lovejoy's masterly study *The Great Chain of Being: A Study of the History of an Idea. The William James Lectures Delivered at Harvard University 1933* (Cambridge, MA: Harvard University Press, 1936).

28 Herder, *Philosophical Writings*, p. 328.

29 See Ibid., p. 332 footnote 110.

30 Herder, Ibid., p. 333.

thief gets "*paid* by the state."[31] Herder gives this thrift short shrift. He
maintains that reward for robbery is not a sustainable source of income.
As Spinozist Herder reads the self's exploitation and destruction of the other
as nothing but self-destruction.

Over time the boomerang will return to the one who set it on its course:

> The more we Europeans invent *means* and *tools* to subjugate, to deceive, and to
> plunder you other parts of the world . . . Perhaps it will one day be precisely your
> turn to *triumph*! We affix chains with which *you* will pull *us*; the *inverted pyra-*
> *mids of* our constitutions will turn *upright* on your ground; *with us you will* . . .
> Enough, it is evident that everything is tending *to a large whole*![32]

This quote is filled with self-interest: Herder seems to be concerned about
how Europeans will suffer injustices that are equal to the wrongs they have
inflicted on non-Europeans. This type of calculated and calculating thinking,
is, however ethical rather than un-ethical, because it conceptualizes the self
not as an isolated self-righteous unity but, on the contrary, as intrinsically and
intimately tied to others. Herder has learned from Spinoza that true self-
preservation looks out for both the self and its environment. A triumphal
and absolutist or god-like self-image has deleterious effects for oneself.

Herder unmasks the uniform conception of universalism as nothing but the
inflated representation of exclusive selfhood. He first takes issue with the uniform standard of one exclusive conception of either philosophical or theological truth. *Mutatis mutandis*, this questioning of the homogeneity of certain
strands within Enlightenment thought (i.e. Voiltaire's teleological philosophy
of history) is then closely connected to his critique of the delusion that elevates
one nation to the center of the universe and institutes it as the arbiter of what
other nations should look like.

Herder's move is one of irony: rather than establishing a single standard of
judgment, he sheds light on what such standard misses. Ironic meaning derives
its validity from that which is missing. Herder draws attention to this lack that
constitutes what we perceive to be knowledge. He employs the image of the
chain not in order to fathom human nature. Instead he questions whether we
can ever see its endpoint: where does the chain end, he asks (*wohin die Kette
reicht?*).[33] Not seeing the endpoint, we turn our own limited world into the
vastness of the cosmos.

This delusion has political and social consequences. Those who are thus
deluded think that they can use the chain, which is the world, as an instrumen-
talist device by means of which they can enchain ("We affix chains with which
you will pull *us*";)[34] "*three parts of the world*."[35] Ironically, nations take their

---

31 Ibid.
32 Herder, Ibid., p. 352.
33 Herder, *Herder und der Sturm und Drang*, p. 683.
34 Herder, *Philosophical Writings*, p. 352.
35 Ibid., p. 328.

"anthill" (*Ameisenhaufe*) to be the "globe" (*Weltall*).[36] Recognition of prejudice means the realization of limits. The study of history reveals such limits. History, in Herder's view, shows that the center does not hold. The national center is the starting point for the recognition of transnational interdependence.

That is why according to Herder, national literature gives birth to transnational writing. Is this not a paradox? Not really, if we take into account Herder's monogenetic understanding of humanity. As we shall see Herder rejected a polygenetic account of human genesis (see following chapter). According to Herder humanity has a common denominator: the particular is always already the universal and the universal is always already the particular. His concern with particularity therefore evolves from his universalism. Herder transposes Spinoza's monist understanding of nature into the sphere of cultural history.

According to Spinoza there is not one single "natural" body that can rationally claim reason as its exclusive possession. Rather, it forms part of the whole of humanity in every aspect of its diversity. Spinoza's notion of the mind's eternal nature introduces a novel conception of what it means to be a unity. As unified form, Spinoza's eternity of the mind at the same time constitutes a plurality. This is why, as Žižek has recently pointed out, "Spinoza, the philosopher of the multitude, is quite logically, also the ultimate monist, the philosopher of the One."[37] Herder introduces a historical dimension into this Spinozist account of human and natural interconnectedness: once one historical/literary/artistic phase disappears, its heritage remains alive as part of the diverse forms of identity that traverse the scene of the present. Herder's particularistic unity thus inhabits plurality. Herder asks us to shed the illusion or delusion of being unified selves:

> Do you in the whole universe, as it weaves its work dead and alive *all at once*, find *yourself* the exclusive central point towards which everything operates?, or do not *you* yourself cooperate (*where?*, *how?*, and *when?*—who asked you about this?) in the service of a *higher* purpose *unknown* to you![38]

Herder questions his audience. His question is itself riddled with questions and it is this uncertainty of the questioner that calls into question the certain knowledge promulgated by the *cogito* ("*unknown* to you!").

2. Herder's Spinozist Journeys to France

The sense of confusion that arises from a seemingly endless string of questions illustrates Herder's sense of humanity's opaqueness. We are a question to ourselves. Opposites crisscross each other so that the particular turns out to be

---

36 Herder, *Herder und der Sturm und Drang*, p. 682.
37 Žižek, *The Puppet and the Dwarf*, p. 24.
38 Herder, *Philosophical Writings*, p. 336.

universal while the universal is constituted by a plurality of particulars. The same crisscrossing structure shapes the relationship between the cosmopolitan and the republican. Without cosmopolitanism, republicanism would be deprived of continuity.

Herder's understanding of continuity does not replicate Leibniz' idea of the preestablished harmony; it is instead a historicist substitution of Spinoza's notion of the eternal mind. Without being universal, the particular republican body politic would fall prey to the forces of decay and would thus resemble the lifeless body from which Herder retreated in the medical dissection theater. The turn from medicine toward the world of letters is one towards life. Yet, writing needs a body if it wants to cheat death. And the body in question is that of a skewed vision: it is at once particular and plural. It is the material body (medicine) but at the same time it resembles spiritual/intellectual (what the German denotes as *geistig*) corporeality (the subject matter of Herder's understanding of theology and philosophy).

In this way Herder does not escape from the dissection theatre to find peace and quiet in the book learning of philosophy and theology. He is as disturbed by theological and philosophical inquiry as he is by the anatomical sight into the lifeless medical body. What explains Herder's unceasing uneasiness within different academic faculties (i.e. those of the humanities—philosophy and theology—and those of the sciences—medicine) and, relatedly, why does he provocatively appraise prejudice and thus offend those to whom he belongs (i.e. Enlightenment intellectuals)? Herder composed *This Too* in his Bückeburg period, that is to say after his studies with Kant in Königsberg and after his work in Riga which he left for a cosmopolitan journey throughout Europe. This journey would lead him to France where he seemed to turn rather prejudicial. Yet his usage of "prejudice" (as we have seen in the preceding section) is ironic: it denotes not the fullness of knowledge but the lack of a limited sphere of identity. The self-consciousness of the prejudicial is thus a humbling experience. Here the self calls itself into question and thereby furthers what Žižek has recently defined as love:

> In other words, the point of the claim that, even if I were to possess all knowledge, without love, I would be nothing, is not simply that *with* love, I am "something"—in love, *I am also nothing*, but, as it were, a Nothing humbly aware of itself, a Nothing paradoxically made rich through the awareness of its lack.[39]

Could it be that Herder's appraisal of prejudice and his restless switching from one academic discipline to another are related on account of their respective motivation, which arises from a startling awareness of lack and mortality?

His persistent perturbation is driven by the fear of death. The study of philosophy and other humanistic disciplines, which he pursued in Königsberg, confronted him with another form of deadness: that of the word. His uneasiness

---

39 Žižek, *The Puppet and the Dwarf*, p. 115.

grew so intense that he abandoned his successful work as a literary critic, teacher and priest in Riga: in June 1769 he sold all of his books and set sail to a journey first through the North Sea and then through France. What he bemoans in his work as a writer and educator is the disconnection between the worlds of letters and the public at large: "We have already lost the public (*Publikum*)", he writes in one of his Riga essays, "since time immemorial; the people (*Volk*) of the burgers and the people (*Volk*) of scholarship."[40] The paratactic juxtaposition of the bourgeois sphere and the scholarly world underscores a lack of monism. Herder is clearly interested in addressing a united but pluralistic *Volk*. Does this notion of the people nevertheless give rise to totalitarianism? His concept of *Volk* does definitely not have racist connotations. As the quotation above indicates it is instead grounded within the world of letters: he sees it as his task to connect the *Volk* of the burgers with the *Volk* of the scholars, but not to submerge the identity of the former with that of the latter.

Anthony La Vopa has emphasized the way in which Herder identifies national aspirations with the literary public sphere. In order to change society at large, literature has to become a pluralistic and at the same time unified public space. Once again ancient Israel offers the blueprint for the intellectual life of the present:

> The originality of Herder's view lay in his heightened awareness that a language itself, as encoded medium for social interaction, could form a regime, corrupt and unbending in its enforcement of invidious social distinctions. In the face of this linguistic regime, Herder developed his ideal of a unitary "public language" (*Publikum der Sprache*). His historical example was the Hebrew society of the Old Testament, whose language had molded a *Volk* into a single "moral being" and, in its organic unity across generations, a "*genetic individual*." He drew the lesson that a "nation" is *cultivated* (gebildet), and becomes orderly, honorable, "moral," and "powerful," through its language. Under the guidance of its literary clerisy, Germany might develop a modern variant on the Hebrew "public of language"; but only if the language of a "neighboring nation" was not allowed to "completely exterminate" its own.[41]

Searching for this unitary public of language Herder paradoxically abandons his commitment to the republicanism of Riga and leaves for a cosmopolitan journey throughout Europe. His *Journal of my Voyage in the Year 1769* opens with his misgivings about the narrow republicanism that characterized life in Riga. "I did not like myself," he reminisces about his life in the Baltic city, "neither as a companion in the society in which I moved, nor in the exclusiveness (*Ausslieẞung*), which I had brought upon myself."[42] He feels uneasy in the hierarchical society of a provincial town.

---

40 Herder, *Frühe Schriften 1764–1772*, p. 134.
41 La Vopa, "Herder's *Publikum*: Language, Print, and Sociability in Eighteenth-Century Germany," *Eighteenth Century Studies* 29.1 (1996): 5–24, 11.
42 Herder, *Journal meiner Reise im Jahr 1769*, p. 7.

In Riga, however, he was not consigned to a lowly working class sphere. He instead belonged to the higher, educated middle class. It was this exclusion from other, "lowlier" spheres of life, which causes his self-dislike:

> I did not like myself as schoolteacher, this sphere was too narrow [*zu eng*], too strange [*zu fremd*] and too inadequate [*zu unpassend*] for me and I was too wide [*zu weit*], too strange and too active [*zu beschäftigt*] for the sphere I moved in.[43]

A chiasm of strangeness and inadequacy connects Herder's personal sphere and the society into which he refuses to fit. What he disliked about his life in Riga was the demotion of an active life: the chiastic equivalent of the "too inadequate" in the first part of the sentence is the "too active" at its end. Action seems to associate the burger too much with what lies below his/her sphere: the menial activity of the working classes. "I did not like myself as burgher," Herder writes reflecting on his uneasiness with bourgeois society, "because my domestic way of life involved the following: restrictions, only a few productive outcomes and a rotten often disgusting calmness (*eine faule, oft eckle Ruhe*)."[44] He then goes to emphasize that "everything then was revolting" to him in Riga.[45]

On leaving Riga, Herder particularly regrets having neglected his French language studies: "Above all, I should have concentrated far more on the French language."[46] This linguistic exercise would not have been an end in itself. Rather it would have facilitated a better understanding of contemporary French thought.[47] Why was Herder so keen to delve into the writings of the French Enlightenment? The latter held out the hope of a non-hierarchical vision of society. He hoped to find in France a public sphere that somewhat resembled the inclusiveness which he associated with the societal structure of ancient Israel. What he encountered instead was what he perceived as the social exclusivity of France's intellectual class. As a result of this disappointment with French intellectual and social life, Herder set out to differentiate his thought from that of the French Sensualists. An understanding of Herder's divergence from the French enlightenment helps us understand why Herder (later) detected in Kant's critical philosophy the presumptions of "complete" knowledge that lies beyond the limited sphere of "prejudice."

Spinoza's critique of an absolutist epistemology assisted Herder in formulating his response to transcendental philosophy as developed by the mature Kant. Herder's inflection of Spinoza's thought is, however, itself inflected by his reading of the French materialist and Sensualist philosophers such as La

---

43 Ibid.
44 Herder, *Journal meiner Reise im Jahr 1769*, 7.
45 Ibid.
46 Herder, *J. G. Herder on Social and Political Culture*, p. 63. Herder, *Journal meiner Reise im Jahr 1769*, 8.
47 Ibid., p. 63.

Mettrie (1709–51), Denis Diderot (1713–1784), Etienne Bonnot de Condillac (1715–80) and, most importantly, Jean-Jacques Rousseau (1712–78). As has been intimated above, Herder was not disinterested in French social and intellectual life. Far from being narrow-minded, he left republican Riga in order to broaden his knowledge of different cultures.

Clearly Riga was not cosmopolitan enough for Herder. His constant uneasiness with one specific academic discipline and with one given identity brings to the fore his rather unstable intellectual outlook. It is this shifty sense of belonging that caused his creative deviation from various sources that he was studying. In this way he turned away from the academic, "schoolmasterly" republicanism of the German community in Riga and immersed himself into contemporary French philosophy.[48] He above all did so in order to find support for his questioning of a hierarchical divide between the world of the academy and the sphere of every day life. Throughout his writings Herder attempts to undermine various measurements by which we divide humanity and the world at large into a superior and inferior sphere. In *This Too* he takes issue with the exclusivity of a single perspective: "If you hold your face close up to the image, carve at this silver, pick up at that little lump of pigment, you never see the *whole image*—you see anything but an *image!*"[49] Exclusivity of sight causes blindness or delusion.

The delusion of a single-minded perspective amounts to a loss of reality. As we have seen in the preceding section, in his essay *Cognition and Sensation* (1775) Herder differentiates between each individual's capacity and the regulations and class restrictions imposed by the symbolic social order. The supposition to be a clearly defined member of a social class cuts both ways: it either enhances or restricts a given person's capacity for action. Social hierarchies thus limit individual achievements. Significantly, Herder detects behind these forms of social rankings what Spinoza has criticized as theology's anthropocentricism and anthropomorphism. Herder, in turn, refers to a theological discourse in order to critique the symbolic order of his society. In this context B. A. Gerrish has established an intriguing comparison between Heine's and Herder's Spinozism:

> According to Herder, we can no longer think of God as a being who acts from outside the world on other beings, nor can we represent the divine activity as arbitrary. Rather, God is precisely the luminous, rational necessity that discovers itself within nature to scientific inquiry. But Herder was not merely interested in a sounder philosophical concept of God. Like Heine afterward, he was concerned about what he took to be the defects of conventional Christian piety;

---

48 Harold Mah has rightly argued that French philosophy attracted the young Herder due to its refinement that seemed an adequate preparation for life in the world at large: Mah, *Enlightenment Phantasies: Cultural Identity in France and Germany 1750–1914* (Ithaca, NY: Cornell University Press, 2003), p. 40.

49 Herder, *Philosophical Writings*, p. 293.

only, for Herder, the main problem lay not in Christian spiritualism but in a naïve geocentricism that wanted a deity at human disposal.[50]

As this important quotation makes clear, Herder's questioning of social hierarchies is not only part of a political but also of a theological endeavor. By critiquing ranks and classes Herder of course is at odds with the Christian and Neo-platonic tradition. As Walter Burkert has pointed out, "hierarchy is a term introduced by the most influential work of Christian Neoplatonism, Pseudo-Dionysus Areopagita, in the fifth century A.D."[51] Like Heine afterward, Herder reads Christianity against the grain.[52] Heine attempts to redeem the realm of bodily/sensuous enjoyment. He blames the Judeo-Christian tradition for having equated the corporeal with the sinful.[53] This demotion of the sensuous is, however, part of a hierarchical construction of the world where spirit reigns supreme. As we will see in the following paragraphs Herder (like Heine) is attracted by the French sensualist tradition, because of its attempt to think mind and matter together.

Indeed, Herder's starting point for his critique of both Descartes' dualism and Leibniz's rationalism is the hylozoism (or "thinking matter") of the French Sensualist tradition. Zammito has brilliantly shown the confluence of Spinozism and hylozoism in French Sensualism: "'Thinking matter'—hylozoism—became the physical-metaphysical possibility of the day. This was the *positive* sense of the term *Spinozism*, especially after the middle of the eighteenth century. Denis Diderot gave brilliant expression to the impact of these ideas in *D'Alembert's Dream*."[54] Clearly Diderot and Condillac had an immense influence on Herder's philosophical development. Here again, however, his intellectual affiliation proved to be rather unstable.

It is this unceasing uneasiness with one particular way of thought and with one particular social group that has rightly alerted Harold Mah, Robert S. Leventhal and Karl Menges to Herder's closeness to a postmodern sensibility.[55] What precisely differentiates Herder's thought from that of his French intellectual predecessors? The study of influence only minimally touches upon

50 B. A. Gerrish, *Continuing the Reformation: Essays on Modern Religious Thought* (Chicago: University of Chicago Press, 1993), p. 120.

51 Walter Burkert, *Creation of the Sacred: Tracks of Biology in Early Religions* (Cambridge, MA: Harvard University Press, 1996), p. 85.

52 Burkert argues that from the fifth century A.D. onwards Neoplatonism shaped the reading of the New Testament: Ibid., p. 85.

53 For a detailed discussion of this point see Mack, *German Idealism and the Jew*, pp. 89–97.

54 Zammito, *Kant, Herder*, p. 231.

55 See the following: Mah, *Enlightenment fantasies*, 44; "Erkenntnis und Sprache. Herder und die Krise der Philosophie im späten achtzehnten Jahrhundert," in Wulf Koepke (ed.), *Herder: Language, History, and the Enlightenment* (Columbia, SC: Camden House, 1990): 47–69; Leventhal. *The Disciplines of Interpretation: Lessing, Herder, Schlegel and Hermeneutics in Germany 1750–1800* (Berlin: de Gruyter, 1994), p. 231.

this question.[56] How can we differentiate Herder's approach from that of John Locke and the French Sensualist Enlightenment? Jerrold Seigel has recently analyzed how Condillac on epistemological grounds disintegrated a Spinozistic isomorphism of body and mind: Condillac's "thinking provides little scope for an organic integration between reflection and the other dimensions."[57] Seigel makes Condillac's "need to affirm strongly materialist and spiritualist positions at the same time" responsible for this "absence of such integration."[58] This disconnection between materialism and an equally strongly maintained spiritualism is not peculiar to Condillac's thought. In this way Seigel goes on to say that "we shall find similar configurations in his compatriots, beginning with Diderot and Rousseau."[59] The corporeal and the cerebral do not meet either in Condillac's work, in particular, or in the French enlightenment tradition, in general. This juxtaposition of both entities eventuates in the postulation of the mind's priority over the body. It is this hierarchical divide between the lowly sphere of bodily action and the higher realm of intellectual inquiry that caused Herder's uneasiness with prerevolutionary French society. According to Condillac, the attainment of freedom depends on a completely "non-material"[60] understanding of self-hood.

Does Rousseau subscribe to a similar prioritization of the mind over the body? In an important study Richard Velkley has recently shown how Rousseau's predominantly cerebral understanding of freedom helped shape the critical philosophy of Kant. Significantly the precritical Kant introduced Herder to Rousseau's work.[61] Herder would later shape and sharpen Spinozist elements within Rousseau's thought in order to question the *a priorism* of Kant's critical philosophy. Herder none the less embraced a critical attitude to Rousseau and the French sensualists.

How can we pinpoint Rousseau's Spinozist point of departure? His as well as Diderot's naturalism derives from Spinoza: "As with Diderot—and Spinoza, whose work he undoubtedly knew—Rousseau's starting point is that man must live according to Nature."[62] Herder's focus on nature has usually been traced to Rousseau rather than Spinoza.[63] In Spinozist fashion Rousseau indeed characterizes natural right as establishing a balance between the concerns for the self and those for the other. There are "two principles," he writes

---

56 See Pross's "Herder und die Anthropologie der Aufklärung" in Pross (ed.), *J.G. Herder Werke. Vol. II* (Munich: Hanser, 1987), pp. 1128–1216 and Robert E. Norton's *Herder's Aesthetics and the European Enlightenment* (Ithaca, NY: Cornell University Press, 1991), pp. 82–118.

57 Seigel, *The Idea of the Self*, p. 187.

58 Ibid.

59 Ibid.

60 Ibid., p. 186.

61 See Friedrich Wilhelm Katzenbach's *Herder* , pp. 15–23.

62 Israel, *Radical Enlightenment*, p. 718.

63 Velkley, *Being after Rousseau: Philosophy and Culture in Question* (Chicago: University of Chicago Press, 2002), p. 16.

in the Preface to the *Discourse on the Origin of Inequality*, "that are prior to reason, of which one makes us ardently interested in our well-being and our self-preservation, and the other inspires in us a natural repugnance to seeing any sentient being, especially our fellow man, perish or suffer."[64] The qualification about the state of nature as being prior to reason is, however, important, because it establishes a divide between the rational and the natural that does not occur within Spinoza's *Ethics*. Rousseau deepens this dualism between reason and nature, when he upholds the Cartesian separation between mind and body:

> Like Descartes, Rousseau argues that one of the substances in man is indissoluble and immortal, namely the soul. From this he was able to argue for a form of reward and punishment in the hereafter and the absolute quality of good and evil.[65]

This Cartesian element within Rousseau's thought assisted Kant in the formulation of his critical turn. An opposition between mind and body as well as between nature and reason supports teleological thought.

How can this be? Nature comes to be seen as a purposeless entity which contrasts with reason as that element in which purposive action originates. As Velkley has astutely put it, "Kant had been disturbed in the early 1760s by the lack of satisfactory teleology in earlier modern accounts of human reason and action."[66] According to the critical Kant, reason denoted the purposive autonomy of the mind. He opposed the teleological capacity of the cerebral to the arbitrariness of the corporal. Herder refused to demote bodily activity as inferior to that of the mind. He thus broke with an ideational tradition that Kant derived from Plato, Descartes and Leibniz. While still being a disciple of the precritical Kant, Herder undermined Leibniz's rationalism by inflecting it through his Spinozist critique of the French Enlightenment. Herder's critique of Rousseau, Condillac, Voltaire and other representatives of the French enlightenment goes hand in hand with his questioning of Leibniz' hierarchical divide between the factual and the rational (see previous chapter). These respective critiques prepared the ground for Herder's critical engagement with Kant's rationalism.

It is important to delineate differences between Herder and his various intellectual mentors if we want to do justice to this rather marginalized eighteenth-century philosopher. He was a thinker who was not only well read but also a critical reader and an original writer. His originality has to do with his application of Spinozist ethics to the realms of history, literature and politics. His writings on France and on French philosophy are so outstanding

---

64 Rousseau, *The Basic Political Writings*, trans. and ed. by Donald A. Cress (Indianapolis: Hackett, 1987), p. 35.
65 Israel, *Radical Enlightenment*, p. 719.
66 Velkley, *Being after Rousseau*, p. 99.

because here he advocates the embrace of what has so far been considered "marginal." His critique of French intellectuals is thus not anti-intellectual. On the contrary, it sets out to widen and diversify the sphere of rational inquiry.

Herder's radically democratic stance is a case in point: he took issue with the type of enlightenment intellectual who did not tolerate the presence of the uneducated.[67] In France Herder found an identity that coincided or at least tried to coincide with itself: the scholarly class affirmed its superiority by differentiating itself from the minor sphere of "the people." This state of affairs resembled the linguistic dichotomy in Germany between French as the language of the educated aristocracy and German, the usage of which was restricted to the demoted sphere of ordinary life: "The German language was relegated to the common people and its use considered vulgar."[68] In early eighteenth-century Germany, German was therefore still a minor language. French was the language of scholarly and academic discussion (Leibniz, for example, composed almost all of his writings in Latin and French).

Herder's plea for a national language is, however, not nationalistic. Rather it is part of his attempt to establish a unity that does not coincide with itself, a unity that is truly plural. One language that is common to both the scholar and the burger dismantles homogeneity rather than reinforcing it. In France there was of course one unified linguistic system. For Herder, it was, however, unified to the point that it turned homogenous. What astounded Herder in France was that a philosophical idiom colonized French society at large, eradicating the difference between a philosopher and a merchant. Countering this homogenizing trend, he attempted to unite both spheres in such way that neither assumed a stable identity. If each retained its respective differences, each would be cognizant of the fact that, as an isolated entity, it is "prejudicial" and thus not truly self-sufficient.

The world of the burger and the world of letters had to be codependent on each other so that each balances the singular force of its counterpart. One dimensional commitment either to anti-intellectualism or to hostility toward religion and other forms of popular culture precludes an awareness of human interdependence. Herder takes issue with the prioritization of one entity over another; be it spirit over matter or the educated over the so-called uneducated masses. According to Herder, hylozoism does not mean that the material dissolves in the spiritual or vice versa; on the contrary, the thinking together of matter and spirit leaves each substance intact so that each can complement what the other lacks. The obverse side of such interdependence is the identity of radical opposites: forms of radical opposition are in fact not opposites of each other but identical with what is so violently opposed.

Herder exemplifies this point through an analysis of the opposition between the fervently religious and the fervently anti-religious. In his *Travel Diary of 1769* Herder detects a common thread between religious fundamentalism and

---

67 See Beiser's *Enlightenment, Revolution, and Romanticism*, p. 190.
68 Ergang, *Herder and the Foundations of German Nationalism*, p. 20.

Enlightenment dogmatism. Both aim at a unitary form that is so pure and autonomous that it does not allow for any element that makes it look awry:

> What of all our erudition and learning, our printing presses, our libraries, and so on? One general calamity, one inundation of barbarians—even a Moravian spirit (*Geist*) in the pulpits, which makes learning a sin and a want of religion, and philosophy the source of ruin—can bring in the spirit (*kann einführen*) which burns libraries and printing presses, abandons the regions of learning and becomes ignorant for piety's sake. So with our deism, with our philosophizing about religion, with our too refined cultivation of reason itself, we are working ourselves to ruin. But this is inevitable in the very nature of things. The same material that gives us strength and turns our cartilage to bone ends by turning to bone even that which should remain cartilage; and the same refinement which makes the populace civilized eventually makes it old, weak and useless.[69]

By destroying what it deems minor, the enlightenment in fact destroys itself. A society that consists only of book learning loses its *esprit*. This was the curious state of affairs, which according to Herder shaped late eighteenth-century French society. France clearly did not resemble the plural unity of ancient Israel. Instead, contemporary French society seemed distressingly close to speculative and hierarchical tendencies, which, in Herder's view, caused the downfall of ancient Greece. Herder perceives in both societies a somewhat refined spirit that presumes its inevitably limited sphere of influence to be the center of the world. It is this presumptive attitude that results in death which is nothing else but the absence of creative originality: "The genuine achievements abate: that a people through its refinement of spirit, turns all the deeper into confusion once it has set foot on erroneous pathways, has been demonstrated by the incomparable Montesquieu in his work about the ancient Greeks. These delved more and more deeply into speculations about religion. Precisely by dint of their fine heads they thus overturned their foundations (*Gebäude*)."[70] The reference to Montesquieu is significant because it was Montesquieu who undermined the idea of sovereignty. Sovereignty is the exclusive power of one person or group. The principle of sovereignty thus precludes seeing the world from another's point of view.

As Hannah Arendt has pointed out, Montesquieu's theory of the separation of powers is closely related to his sober attitude toward reason and virtue:

> Montesquieu's famous insight that even virtue stands in need of limitation and that even an excess of reason is undesirable occurs in his discussion of power; to him, virtue and reason were powers rather than mere faculties, so that their preservation and increase had to be subject to the same conditions which rule over the preservation and increase of power.[71]

---

69 Herder, *J.G. Herder on Social and Political Culture*, 101. Herder, *Journal meiner Reise im Jahr 1769*, p. 90.

70 Herder, *Journal meiner Reise im Jahr 1769*, p. 91.

71 Arendt, *On Revolution* (New York: Penguin, 1990), p. 152.

Arendt goes on to stress that it was certainly "not because he wanted less virtue and less reason that Montesquieu demanded their limitation."[72] On the contrary, he advocated a nonexclusive approach to rationality and morality precisely because he attempted to uphold the standards of rational society. A rational society thrives, however, on plurality rather than on homogeneity.

In this way intellectualist hostility toward popular forms of culture (such as religion) might have anti-intellectual consequences: an elitist type of thinking may give rise to the exclusivity of fundamentalist politics (the Moravian spirit that advocates book burning). The refined head then turns out to be "a void filled in by appearances"[73]: it conceals the nothingness that its contours hide. Herder takes issue with an intellectualist hierarchy that produces uniformity. In his view, contemporary French theatre consists of "uniform gallantries."[74]

This uniformity denotes absence of diversity and thus lifelessness. The intellectualist standard banishes everything that appears to be "lowly". Herder goes on to list these absences:

> the far too lowly sphere of kisses etc. is gone, the exaggeration of the eyes etc. is gone, genuine marital love is not performed; the true affect of bridal love is too vulgar—partly ignoble and despicable and partly exaggerated and ridiculous—so what remains?[75]

Herder finds missing in a hierarchical and uniform aesthetics a certain excess of life that counters death and stagnation. He deplores the absence of exaggeration (*das Übertriebene*).

Significantly, Herder's social and aesthetic critique of French classicism anticipates a psychoanalytical sensitivity to the life-enhancing characteristics of seemingly irrational, "senseless" or exorbitant ways of perceiving and interacting with the world.[76] Freud's death drive, as Žižek has recently pointed out, denotes the uncanny rationality of excess and exaggeration:

> The paradox of the Freudian death drive is therefore that it is Freud's name for its very opposite, for the way immortality appears within psychoanalysis, for an uncanny *excess* of life, for an "undead" urge that persists beyond the (biological) cycle of life and death, of generation and corruption.[77]

What Herder misses in the general and uniform (as founded by social standards which permeate society's fabric in the form of rank and status) is the psychological insight that sheds light on the way humans "are possessed by

---

72 Ibid.
73 Žižek, *The Puppet and the Dwarf*, p. 152.
74 Herder, *Journal meiner Reise im Jahr 1769*, p. 94.
75 Herder, *Journal meiner Reise im Jahr 1769*, p. 94.
76 For detailed discussion of Freud's appreciation of the seemingly irrational and senseless see Mack, *German Idealism and the Jew*, pp. 136–154.
77 Žižek, "A Plea for a Return to *Différance* (with a minor *Pro Domo Sua*)," *Critical Inquiry* 32 (Winter 2006): 226–249 (245).

the strange drive to enjoy life in excess, passionately attached to a surplus that sticks out and derails the ordinary run of things."[78] Uniformity and hierarchy dismiss what sticks out and which derails the normative standards of social interaction: the exaggeration of life disappears. By banishing all those things that the hierarchical nomenclature proscribes as "lowly," art society goes empty handed. Herder misses the non-hierarchical stage of Moliere: "Moliere does not exist any longer: one is ashamed to laugh heartily."[79] This perceived vanishing of Moliere's inclusive type of theatre from the French stage, in particular, and from French society, in general, has an analogue in Herder's analysis of the death of the public sphere in ancient Greece.

Herder is famous for having announced the radical break that divides the contemporary world from classical Greek and Roman antiquity. In his *This Too a Philosophy of History* he thus takes issue with Winckelmann's classicist standard:

> The best historian of the art of antiquity, Winckelmann, obviously only passed judgment on the artworks of the Egyptians according to a Greek criterion, hence depicted them very well negatively, but so little according to their own nature and manner that with almost every one of his sentences in this most important matter the obviously one-sided and sidewards-glancing aspect glares forth.[80]

In his *Letters toward the Advancement of Humanity* he goes a step further by announcing the deadness of ancient Greece and Rome: "It would be foolish to wish oneself placed back into the times of Greece and Rome; this youth of the world is over as is the iron age of Rome's empire."[81] The vanishing of classical antiquity does not, however, imply that the legacy of ancient cultures *per se* do not have extenuated validity within contemporary society.

Anticipating Heinrich Graetz and George Eliot's argument about the death of ancient Greece and the unceasing life of Jewish culture from antiquity to modernity (see Chapter 8), Herder differentiates between Hellas' absence from and Israel's presence within the contemporary public sphere. Whereas Greek and Roman antiquity is subject to the forces of decay and thus death, the heritage of Israel is alive: it continues to influence public life in the present.

Significantly, in his *Letter towards the Advancement of Humanity*, Herder asks two parallel questions. One he answers in the affirmative and the other in the negative: "Do we have the public (*Publikum*) of the Hebrews? I think each people have it through *their language*."[82] The public sphere of rabbinic Judaism serves as a model for a linguistic-cultural rather than militaristic-nationalistic sense of identity.[83] Whereas Jewish antiquity has a vital role to play in the

---

78 Ibid.
79 Herder, *Journal meiner Reise im Jahr 1769*, p. 94.
80 Herder, *Philosophical Writings*, p. 283. Herder, *Herder und der Sturm und Drang 1764–1774*, p. 603.
81 Herder, *Briefe zu Beförderung der Humanität*, p. 332.
82 Ibid., p. 304.

contemporary universe, ancient Greece does not have social validity for modern life. "Do we have the public (*Publikum*) of the Greeks," Herder asks and he emphatically replies: "No; and in many respects it is perhaps good that we do not have it."[84] According to Herder, the absence of an inclusive cultural sphere affiliates contemporary French culture with the hierarchical structure of Greek and Roman antiquity.

The classicism of France thus attempts to rejuvenate something that cannot be brought back to life without loss of life. Herder's uneasiness with French culture was thus part of his general critique of classical learning.[85] He set out to demote what has been extolled and to extol what has been demoted as minor. He did not, however, condemn any one aspect but instead argued for the combination of what is different. Neither could thus exist in isolation.

In this way the present needs the past for its survival: "*One can never wholly annul what has gone before (even by way of improvement) without sacrificing the present.*"[86] The soul does not coincide with itself. It needs the body:

> In general there is no axiom more noteworthy, and almost none more often forgotten, than this: without the body, our mind will not function; if the senses are crippled, the mind is crippled too; if all the senses are used vigorously (*muntern*) and in proper measure, the mind too is invigorated.[87]

A homogenous public sphere of scholars replicates the paralyzing state where a soul goes without a body and the present attempts to live without recognition of the past. Different times are thus related to each other and the same holds true for different spatial entities.

This Spinozan philosophy of a monist plurality in which different entities interlink has its prototype in the relationship between the body and the soul. In the 1774 version of *On Cognition and Sensation* Herder maintains that there exists "no recognition (*Erkennen*) without the sense of feeling (*Empfinden*)."[88]

---

83 For a brilliant discussion of how Israel's self-preservation in form of the study of its foundational texts served as an example for Goethe's and Herder's conception of a linguistic-cultural rather than militaristic-nationalistic conception of German identity see Aleida Assmann, *Arbeit am nationalen Gedächtnis. Eine kurze Geschichte der deutschen Bildungsidee* (Frankfurt am Main: Campus, 1993).

84 Herder, *Briefe zu Beförderung der Humanität*, p. 308.

85 Herder's critique of a classical standard by which one should judge nonclassical and modern cultures is of course a continuation of the *Querelle de Anciens et de Modernes*. For a discussion of Joachim Du Bellay's *La Deffence et Illustration de la Langue Françoyse* (1549) influence on Herder's linguistic patriotism see Robert S. Mayo's *Herder and the Birth of Comparative Literature* (Chapel Hill: The University of North Carolina, 1969), p. 12.

86 Herder, *J. G. Herder on Social and Political Culture*, p. 79. Herder, *Journal meiner Reise im Jahr 1769*, p. 138.

87 Herder, *J. G. Herder on Social and Political Culture*, p. 83. Herder, *Journal meiner Reise im Jahr 1769*, p. 143.

88 Herder, *Herder und die Anthropologie der Aufklärung*, p. 545.

Inversely, the death of the soul is tantamount to the death of the senses: "Suppose the soul does not have powers of recognition any longer (a state with which we are only partly familiar from the experience of fainting), then there is death: paralysis."[89] In this way the natural sciences (medicine) are dependent on the humanities (philosophy) and vice versa. Herder intricately links the cerebral to the bodily sphere. According to him intellect/spirit is an invisible force that enhances life:

> What precisely spirit/intellect (*Geist*) is cannot be described, nor drawn, nor painted. But it can be felt. It appears as words, as movements, as striving, as force and impact. In the sensuous world we distinguish intellect/spirit (*Geist*) from body and ascribe to the former that which enlivens the body in all its elemental parts, what incorporates life and what awakens life, what attracts forces and what procreates forces (*fortpflanzet*).[90]

One can read this quotation as a reflection of the mature Herder (the Herder of 1793 to 1797, who composed the *Letters toward the Advancement of Humanity*) on his youthful retreat from the dissection theatre to the philosophical class room of Immanuel Kant. As has been discussed in this and the previous chapter, Herder also felt uneasy in the intellectual/spiritual sphere of the humanities (i.e. philosophy and theology). He tried to make both spheres (that of the spirit/intellect and that of the body/nature) interdependent so that neither coincides with itself. The mind is far from being a pure entity and according to Herder it is a hybrid, having a dual "capacity for both recognizing and sensing."[91] He goes on to expound the paradox of a divided self: "Soul without body is fanaticism (*Schwärmerei*); each finds its truth in the other: the wholeness of humanity."[92] Paradoxically the whole is fragmented. The soul does not coincide with itself; neither does the body.[93]

Each entity finds its truth in that which is the other of itself. Herder focuses on difference but crucially differences are only minimal: the body differs from the soul and yet without the excessive copresence of its opposite each entity would fall prey to death/paralysis. Differences are thus connected with the common thread of sameness. By arguing that "each finds its truth in the other" Herder (in his 1774 version of *On Cognition and Sensation*) relates the presumed divide between the body and the soul to an interactive understanding of universalism. This topic will be the starting point for the discussion in the following chapter.

---

89 Ibid., p. 545.
90 Herder, *Briefe zu Beförderung der Humanität*, pp. 87–88.
91 Herder, *Herder und die Anthropologie der Aufklärung*, p. 587.
92 Ibid., p. 663.
93 See M. Bell, *The German Tradition of Psychology in Literature and Thought*, 60 and 208.

CHAPTER 6

UNIVERSALISM CONTESTED: HERDER, KANT AND RACE

Houston Stewart Chamberlain, another forerunner of National Socialism, was even more direct. He read Kant within the context, as he saw it, of millions of bestial Blacks preparing for a race war. The alternative facing society was to enter a higher stage of culture or to fall into an unprecedented barbarism in which artificially civilized but still superstitious races— "as dreamless as so many cattle" prospered. Whether Chamberlain's reference to cattle intentionally recalled "the happy cattle" to which Kant compared the Tahitians, Chamberlain shows where philosophies about the meaning of human existence can lead when they are posed within a context framed by the discordant ideas of permanently unequal races and of a cosmopolitan history. Robert Bernasconi:

Why do the happy inhabitants of Tahiti exist?

The previous chapter has discussed how Herder incorporates into his writing about temporal interdependence a plea for the conception of our particular, national identities as transnational. The past complements what the present lacks and vice versa. In the same way each nation is dependent on others, so that the national is in fact transnational. The discussion of the preceding chapters focused on how Herder arrives at this understanding of historical and transnational interdependence via a Spinozist critique of anthropomorphic conceptions of God which serve to endow societal constructions of rank with quasi-sacerdotal status. This Spinozist critique of anthropomorphic conceptions of divinity has political ramifications. It questions the political theology of sovereignty and hierarchy. Conversely Herder conceptualizes pluralism and democracy as forms of politics that avoid an anthropomorphic theology which equates a particular human position with God or nature.

According to Herder the good is not concentrated in one geographical point, or one time, or one nation, rather it is scattered throughout the universe. He makes it clear that a single absolute conception of human nature does violence to human diversity. As Herder put it in *This Too*:

> For if, again, human nature is no container of an *absolute, independent, unchangeable happiness* as the philosopher defines it, but it everywhere attracts *as much happiness as it can*, is a *flexible clay* for, in the most different situations, needs, and pressures, also *forming* itself differently, [and] even the image of happiness *changes* with each condition and region (for what is this image ever but the *sum* of "*satisfactions of wishes, achievements of purpose*, and *gentle overcomings of needs*," which though, all *shape* themselves according to *land, time*, and *place*?)—then at bottom all *comparison* proves to be *problematic*.[1]

---

1 Herder, *Philosophical Writings*, p. 296.

Herder here sets out to persuade us to abandon absolute and changeless standards of human behavior. Comparisons between different ethnic and religious
groups are problematic, because we have no right to extol one over the other.
We are diverse and can therefore only find happiness and fulfillment in different social and cultural formations.

Herder emphasizes, however, that human diversity does not amount to a
separation between differing communities. The diverse is interconnected. This
is why he speaks out against the conception of societies as independent entities. Rather than being independent, communities are interdependent. From
the omniscient perspective of God, diversity is unity: "it is only the Creator
who *thinks* the whole *unity of one, of all*, nations in all their *manifoldness*
without having the *unity* thereby fade for him."[2] The factum of human diversity does not mean that we are created unequally. Neither does it offer proof
positive that we are separated into different races that have little in common
with each other (as is proclaimed by theorists of polygenesis). Clearly Herder
agrees with monogenesis: however different and seemingly noncompatible
with each other, we are created by the same creator and from the perspective
of creation our differences are not absolute but contingent. From our limited
human perspective we should not dismiss contingency and diversity but rather
see it as the condition of our existence.

Contingency and an uneven distribution of capacities calls for what Seyla
Benhabib has recently described as—while referring to Herder's philosophy of
language—"interactive universalism."[3] Benhabib approaches universalism
and democracy not via general theories but via diverse narratives: "but I can
become aware of the *otherness of others*, of those aspects of their identity that
make them concrete others to me, only through their own narratives."[4] As will
be discussed in this chapter, it is such pluralistic and narrative perspective of
human society and human diversity which Kant dismissed as unscientific in
Herder's Spinozist anthropology. Not surprisingly Benhabib bases her understanding of an interactive universalism on Herder's anthropology.[5] Herder
clarifies the political and social ramifications of his anthropology in the second
part of his *Ideas*. Here he dismisses the concept of race which no one less than
Immanuel Kant has brought to the level of scientific dignity at the end of the
eighteenth century (and following Kant, Johann Friedrich Blumenbach, even
though in contrast to Kant "Blumenbach seems never to have departed from
his earlier view whereby races as permanent divisions 'ran into one another by
unnoticed passages and intermediate shades'").[6]

---

2 Ibid., p. 293.
3 Benhabib, *The Claims of Culture: Equality and Diversity in the Global Era*
   (Princeton, NJ: Princeton University Press, 2002), p. 15.
4 Ibid., p. 14.
5 Benhabib clearly emphasizes Herder's importance for her conception of an interactive universalism: Benhabib, *The Claims of Culture*, p. 55.
6 Robert Bernasconi, "Kant and Blumenbach's Polyps: Neglected Chapter in the
   History of the concept of race," in Sara Eigen and Mark Larrimore (eds), *The German
   Invention of Race* (Albany: State University of New York, 2006), pp. 73–90 (p. 86).

There is, however, considerable resistance to the idea of discussing Kant within the context of race. After all the German philosopher of the Enlightenment has come to epitomize all that is valuable within modern European history. It is time to ask whether this identification is not deeply fraught and flawed. It seems to be fraught, because Kant is one of the most prominent theorists of the modern concept of race. Recently J. Kameron Carter has presented a brilliant analysis of the racism within Kant's theological philosophy in the important book *Race: A Theological Account*.[7] As Robert Bernasconi and Tommy L. Lott have pointed out, Kant's seminal essay *Of the Different Human Races* (1775) "is widely recognized as the first attempt to give a scientific definition of race based on a clear distinction between race and space."[8] Race is not effected by environmental factors (such as space)[9] because it is immutable. By defining race as an entity that "once formed resists further remodeling,"[10] Kant divided humanity along the lines of permanent boundaries. Kant's review of Herder's *Ideas* is crucial because it is here that the concept of race figures prominently. Even if we neglect Kant's critique of Herder's rejection of humanity's division into immutable races, the issue of immutability looms large in another context: that of religion. I have attended to this sense of fixed religious divisions in a previous study.

German Idealism and the Jews analyzes the subterranean tremors and aftershocks of a certain Kantian ideational paradigm that not only incorporates prejudices widespread in the general public of a given time, but also shapes and sharpens these prejudices into a seemingly rational, systematic, self-consistent whole.[11] To embark on such an analysis, the critic has to historicize philosophy, an approach that has often been interpreted as a violation of philosophy as such. It is through such a departure from common practices in intellectual history that we are able to better understand the relation between ideas themselves and their impact on culture, society and politics at large. As Bernasconi has judiciously put it:

> We need to pursue more vigorously the task of understanding how in the West the philosophy of history lent new legitimacy to the idea that some lives are of more value than others, even to the point of tolerating genocide. To do so means departing from that habit of thought that prevails in most contemporary studies within the history of philosophy: namely, the practice of studiously isolating

---

7   (Oxford: Oxford University Press, 2008).

8   Bernasconi and Lott (ed.), *The Idea of Race* (Indianapolis/Cambridge: Hackett, 2000), p. 8.

9   See R. Berman's *Enlightenment or Empire: Colonial Discourse in German Culture* (Lincoln: University of Nebraska Press, 1998), p. 3.

10 Bernasconi, "Who invented the Concept of Race? Kant's Role in the Enlightenment Construction of Race," in Bernasconi (ed.), *Race* (Oxford: Blackwell, 2001), p. 11–30; 23.

11 In a related way Jonathan M. Hess has brilliantly shown how Kant cast his notion of reason in Christian terms and opposed it to Judaism and the Jews: Hess, *Germans, Jews and the Claims of Modernity*, p. 149.

ideas from their cultural implications and historical effects. To understand history we need to investigate how ideas that may not be in relations of entailment
still come to be bound together.[12]

Deviating from Kant's approach, Herder proposes a view on history that
is not philosophical in a strict ideational sense, because he allows for the
contingent and unpredictable. At the same time, however, he does not conceive
of contingency as an absolute that we have to embrace wherever and in whatever form we encounter it. Unlike Heidegger afterwards, Herder does not
idealize temporality and contingency (in his Freiburg seminar on "logic as the
question of the essence of language" of the summer 1934, Heidegger speaks of
"our membership in the *Volk*"[13] and concomitantly "our submission to contingent temporality"[14]).

Herder does not make absolute either the ideational or the contingent viz.
temporal. His thought does not oppose fact with idea nor does it establish an
identity between these two distinct, but not necessarily opposed, entities.
Instead he argues that we are not fully able to grasp the laws governing the
interaction between the normative sphere of ethics and the ontological realm
of contingent temporality.

Following Spinoza, Herder distinguishes between our incomplete and often
inadequate assessment of the world and the world itself whose laws are both
ethical and ontological. We have to distinguish between the ontological and
the ethical because of our epistemological limitations: we cannot figure out the
laws governing their interaction. As Hampshire has astutely put it:

> According to Spinoza, we know *a priori*, and can prove, that human knowledge
> must at all stages be limited and incomplete; otherwise it would cease to be
> human knowledge and would become divine knowledge. But equally we know
> *a priori* what ignorance is and what complete knowledge would be; for we could
> not otherwise distinguish, as we do, between adequate and inadequate knowl-
> edge; we are able to recognize the inadequacy of our present scientific knowledge
> in respect of human behaviour, and we can envisage the possibility of our knowl-
> edge becoming progressively less inadequate; and this is precisely what the
> philosopher is doing in maintaining the determinist thesis.[15]

As Hamphsire has brilliantly analyzed in this quote, Spinoza's so called
determinism is a rational type of holism. What strikes us as incongruent is

---

12 Bernasconi, "Why do the happy Inhabitants of Tahiti exist?" in John K. Roth (ed.),
    Genocide and Human Rights: A Philosophical Guide (New York: Palgrave
    Macmillan) 2005, p. 145.

13 Heidegger, *Gesamtausgabe II. Abteilung: Vorlesungen 1919–1944 Band 38 Logik
    als die Frage nach dem Wesen der Sprache*, p. 57.

14 Heidegger, *Gesamtausgabe Band 38 Logik als die Frage nach dem Wesen der
    Sprache*, p. 58.

15 Hampshire, *Spinoza and Spinozism*, p. 122.

actually congruent, if we could only see it, but we cannot because we are human and not divine.

Herder broadens Spinoza's holistic determinism when he applies it to a critique of Kant's philosophy of history. It is Spinoza's noncongruency between our cognition and the laws governing the universe that causes the gulf to open separating nature or history from the normative realm of ideas. It would be tantamount to anthropomorphism and anthropocentricism if we were to bridge this gulf via the imposition of a particular theory onto what appears to us as the contingency of nature and history. Herder was troubled by the anthropocentric tendency in Kant's attempt to turn philosophy into a master narrative that polices historical and scientific investigations.

From Kant's perspective, philosophy *qua* philosophy seems to reside in a realm removed from the contingencies of historical events. From Herder's perspective, it is important to understand, however, that this enforced separation from the unpredictability of various historical realities sets the stage for the violent imposition of predictable, therefore "rational," schemata onto the infinite diversity of both individual actors and anthropological communities.

Philosophy often seems unwilling, if not unable, to bear the thought of what could potentially unhinge the pure, stable, and unchangeable order established by reason. The diverse changes brought about by history seem to shake philosophical cohesion at its foundations. As Berel Lang has pointed out,

> the image of philosophical thought as atemporal and undramatic, as itself nonrepresentational, has been very much taken for granted in the historiography of philosophy since the nineteenth century; it has in certain respects been part of the profession of philosophy since its origins.[16]

Lang focuses on both time and drama as elements that run counter to philosophy's self-understanding.

Meanwhile, up to the eighteenth century *historia* was concerned with the representation and explanation of particular events as they unfold with the passing of time, endlessly generating the emergence of new, varied social and cultural formations. What consternated Herder, however, was that philosophers increasingly turned to history not to historicize their thinking but rather to differentiate thought from the contingencies of historical time. As this philosophical project unfolded, philosophy attempted to free history of unpredictability through a process of assimilation. The previous chapters have traced the ways in which Herder resisted such assimilation. He did so by dissolving philosophy in the natural and social sciences. Here history does not become assimilated to an ideational paradigm but rather philosophy observes historical and natural phenomena in order to be transformed through them.

---

16 Berel Lang, *The Anatomy of Philosophical Style: Literary Philosophy and the Philosophy of Literature* (Oxford: Blackwell, 1990), p. 22.

What Herder understands by anthropology is this submergence of philosophical inquiry into the infinite diversity of the natural and historical world.

The philosophical destruction of the historical and its contingencies, in contrast, coincided with the birth of a philosophy of history; the *cognitio philosophica* made history commensurable with philosophy. Kant's essay "Idea for a Universal History from a Cosmopolitan Point of View" is crucial in this context. Kant here argues that it is only via philosophy that we can discover the purpose of history. The philosophy of history would transmogrify the natural waste of the historical into the refined end product of reason, because the rational is consubstantial with the teleological: "Reason is a faculty of widening the rules and purposes of the use of all its powers far beyond natural instinct; it acknowledges no limits to its projects."[17] The telos of philosophy overcomes natural restrictions. As John H. Zammito has shown, Kant "undertook to formulate his theory of the 'supersensible'"[18] in the wake of the Spinoza controversy (exactly the time of the publication of the first two volumes of Herder's *Ideas*). Kant's theory of the supersensible aims to rebut Spinoza's critique of teleology as anthropomorphism:

> Kant had not only scientific but also metaphysical positions to defend: the traditional notion of a transcendent, intelligent Deity who created the world, and the notion of individual moral freedom and responsibility. As he saw it, the trends in science and cosmology, "materialist" and "pantheistic," threatened these positions. Above all, the renaissance of the philosophy of Spinoza in Germany seemed to Kant to portend atheism in the form of materialistic determinism.[19]

Kant saw in Herder the prime target of Spinozistic atheism: "The context, by 1787, of Spinozism and pantheism, with Herder as their prime exponent raised profound dangers for the Aufklärung, in Kant's view."[20] The Spinozist critique of teleology was perhaps the most threatening issue for Kant during the Spinoza controversy in the late 80s of the eighteenth century. Following Spinoza, Herder argues that teleological reason comes close to assuming the omniscience that has traditionally been the provenience of God. Spinoza has warned against such conflation of the teleological with the theological in his critique of anthropomorphism.

A skeptical reader might object that Kant is the philosopher not of the limitless but of the limit. Transcendental philosophy indeed detects and delineates the boundaries between the empirical and the conceptual so that concepts can do their work in their own sphere without taking cognizance of what lie

---

17 Kant, *On History*, edited with an introduction by Lewis White Beck, trans. by Lewis White Beck, Robert E. Anchor and Emil L. Fackenheim (Indianapolis: Bobbs-Merrill Company, 1963), p. 13

18 Zanmito, *The Genesis of Kant's Critique of Judgment* (Chicago: University of Chicago Press, 1992), p. 6.

19 Zammito, *The Genesis of Kant's Critique of Judgment*, p. 191.

20 Ibid., p. 187.

beyond their modus operandi. It is this critical act of delineation that allows for the unlimited activity of philosophy's purpose. Philosophy's purpose is categorical in two senses: it does its work via categories—distinguished and separated from existential facts—and it coincides with the demands of the categorical imperative. The latter transforms transcendental philosophy, in fact, into theology.[21] It is in this context that Derrida has recently characterized Kant's moral philosophy as being so fervently Christian that it is actually evangelical. Derrida argues that:

> the idea of a morality that is pure but non-Christian would be absurd; it would exceed both understanding and reason, it would be a contradiction in terms. The unconditional universality of the categorical imperative is evangelical. The moral law inscribes itself at the bottom of our hearts like a memory of the Passion. When it addresses us, it speaks the idiom of the Christian—or is silent.[22]

The universality of the categorical imperative operates through the appeal of a promise: it promises our transfiguration into pure morality where we have overcome natural or sinful limitations—similar to the way in which Christ's passion takes away the sins of the world. The categorical imperative holds out the universal promise of leaving behind moral-practical limitations.

Here philosophy's telos consists in the blurring of the boundaries between human cognition and the divine as Kant makes clear in the *Opus postumum*: "The categorical imperative realizes the concept of God, but only in moral-practical respect, not with regard to natural objects."[23] Kant clearly differentiates between the moral and the natural. Within the moral sphere the purpose of the categorical imperative is to transform us into divinity. Paul W. Franks has recently described this transformation from the limited sphere of nature to that of freedom as follows:

> First, I pass from mere consciousness of the moral law to actual will-determination. Second, I pass from practically necessary but doubtful belief in freedom to practically necessary and well-grounded cognition of freedom. It is true that the idea of the moral law and the idea of practical freedom form a circle of mutual entailment. But if I trace that circle in the way Kant wants, I do not end up back where I started. *For I am transformed along the way* [italics in Franks' original].[24]

---

21 In a detailed study Paul W. Franks has recently argued that German Idealism from Kant onwards is "in some recognizable sense, theological." Frank, *All or Nothing. Systematicity, Transcendental Arguments, and Skepticism in German Idealism* (Cambridge, MA: Harvard University Press, 2005), p. 389.

22 Derrida, "Faith and Knowledge: the two sources of 'Religion' at the Limits of Reason Alone," in Derrida and Vattimo (eds), *Religion* (Cambridge: Polity, 1998), pp. 1–78 (p. 11).

23 Kant, *Opus postumum*, edited, with an introduction and notes, by Eckart Förster; trans. by E. Förster and Michael Rosen (Cambridge: Cambridge University Press, 1993), p. 242.

24 Franks, *All or Nothing*, p. 294.

This transformation is of course incomplete as it only concerns the limited sphere of moral practice. It is the task of a philosophy of history to make this sphere limitless. It does so via prolepsis. Here philosophy as philosophy of history intensifies its teleological drive, because it anticipates the future of the fully attained goal of human nature. By then humanity has fully shed its immoral and amoral aspects. Natural limits have been overcome so that human nature is completely at one with the purpose of the categorical imperative at the endpoint of history.

It is this sense of the limitless that contrasts Kant's approach toward history and nature from that of both Spinoza's and Herder's. Spinoza's critique of anthropomorphism focuses on the limits of human cognition and Herder submerges philosophy into anthropology to put humanity in its place. It is a Spinozan place: one where the human does not have the holistic or all-encompassing overview enjoyed by God or nature.

Kant is of course aware that humanity in its present state is limited. Indeed his transcendental philosophy delineates human limitations. Crucially, however, it does so with a view toward establishing an a priori system that is not limited by epistemological constraints (on which Spinoza's critique of anthropomorphism focuses): "Transcendental philosophy is the science of pure synthetic *a priori* knowledge from concepts"[25] and it therefore paves the ground for "the self-creation (autocracy) of ideas, into a complete system of the objects of pure reason."[26]

In the *Opus Postumum* Kant significantly re-anthropomorphizes Spinoza's thought claiming that the "Spirit of man is Spinoza's God."[27] Kant can, however, only reveal God as "the spirit of man" through the anticipation of a fully rational state of human existence. This is precisely what is performed by and through his philosophy of history: it leaves behind "brute nature" and focuses instead on "the great stage of supreme wisdom which contains the purposes of all the others—the history of mankind."[28] The history of mankind realizes freedom from natural instinct as the purpose or spirit of man, which the late Kant of the *Opus Postumum* equates with Spinoza's God. In order to attain an unlimited state of reason, Kant develops a philosophy of history which does away with present epistemological and moral insufficiencies. The telos of history fulfills our true moral nature. This might well be what Kant means by his peculiar conception of Spinoza's God as the spirit of man: the "history of mankind" realizes "Nature's secret plan"[29] which is the perfection of humanity into God.

Kant's philosophy of history has turned the theological conception of perfection and salvation into an immanent force. Here history breaches the gulf separating the rational realm of freedom from that of nature. This gap can,

---

25 Kant, *Opus postumum*, p. 243.
26 Ibid., 249–250.
27 Ibid., p. 255.
28 Kant, *On History*, p. 25.
29 Ibid., p. 21.

however, only be overcome by eliminating those elements in our nature that are supposedly the opposites of freedom and reason. As I have shown in *German Idealism and the Jew*, Kant and some of the idealists following him identified these elements with Judaism and the Jews.

There is, however, a much larger context for Kant's apprehension of ethnic and religious groups that runs counter to his understanding of the free, autonomous or rational. Robert Bernasconi has recently argued that Kant introduced "both the scientific conception of hereditary races with permanent limitations and the cosmopolitan conception of universal history."[30] Kant's universalism is indeed admirable and inspiring. What is, however, highly disturbing is the fact that his universalism is not an inclusive but exclusive one. As Bernasconi has put it,

> the fact that Kant was against whites killing Native Americans should not distract us from the fact that he needed the latter to kill each other—or for them to suffer some other disaster—if cosmopolitanism was to embrace all of humanity, that is to say, all that remained of humanity after the constitutionally less talented had been purged in one way or another.[31]

Historical forces have to purge those who are perceived to be less talented in order for humanity to reach the universal goal of freedom or reason. What hampers the attainment of history's telos is precisely the continued existence of what is irrational (or in Bernasconi's words "less talented"). Kant identified this lack of reason with specific ethnic and religious groups (Blacks, Jews and Native Americans, amongst others).

The philosophy of history that Kant brings to prominence is directed against the pluralistic existence of different and perhaps contradictory narratives: it anticipates the purging of Jewish, Native American and Black cultural narratives over the course of history's progression towards the attainment of Kant's idealist conception of reason or freedom. Kant's approach towards history is both antinarrative and anti-pluralistic. It is universal but at the same time exclusive, because it posits the extinction of what it perceives as imperfect or "less talented people" via history's long progression.

By contrast, in focusing on both time and drama, a philosophy such as Herder's or Lang's (or Franz Rosenzweig's as will be discussed in the following chapter) implicitly discusses the historical within the broader context of the literary. Here the actions of particular agents are thus immersed in the realm of the unpredictable, the diverse and the potentially new.[32] Philosophical systems, in contrast, reside in a realm beyond time and drama, claiming to be universal and rational. Even though he emphasizes the limits of human reason

---

30 Bernasconi, "Why do the happy Inhabitants of Tahiti Exist," p. 143.

31 Ibid.

32 In this context Edith Wyschogrod has defined life as the unpredictable: Wyschogrod, *Spirit in Ashes: Hegel, Heidegger, and Man-Made Mass Death* (New Haven, CT: Yale University Press, 1985), p. 11.

Kant accentuates these philosophical trends. He does so when he upholds a permanent and uniform conception of humanity and at the same time dismisses human diversity. In *German Idealism and the Jew*, I have shown how this radicalization of philosophy as the atemporal and the undramatic prepared the way for the exclusion of groups of people from the universality of the human.

Strikingly, Kant discusses diversity within the context of a literary approach to both science and philosophy. He faults Herder's naturalistic and pluralistic understanding of humanity. He does so by assessing Herder's way of inquiry as that worthy of a poet but not of a scientist and philosopher. "What can the philosopher now invoke here," Kant asks in his review of Herder's first part of the *Ideas*, "to justify his allegations except simple despair of finding clarification in some kind of knowledge of nature and the attendant necessity to seek it in the fertile field of the poetic imagination?"[33] "Knowledge of nature" refers to what is, for Kant, Herder's scandalous way of grounding reason in the field of nature.

In the first part of the *Ideas* Herder argues that humanity's reason is the product of human physiology: namely its upright posture. Herder makes clear that this discussion of human rationality is a clear departure from metaphysics, because it focuses on the phenomenological world rather than on categories or concepts. This grounding of reason in physiology precludes a developmental scheme of history, since humanity has already fully attained its upright posture (it does not need to fully attain it in some goal of history).

As his review makes clear, Kant is disturbed by both (a) the lack of an opposition between nature and freedom or reason and (b) the concomitant absence of a teleology which would transform the merely natural into a second state of rational nature. In this way Kant contrasts reason as a destiny—here rationality only reaches its fruition once undesirable parts of humanity have passed away—with reason as a product of nature:

> Upright posture and the rational use of his limbs were not allotted to man because he was destined to be a rational creature; on the contrary, he acquired reason by virtue of his erect stature, as the natural effect of that stature which was necessary merely to make him walk upright.[34]

History as destiny realizes Kant's idea of reason as freedom from natural or pathological deficiencies that hinder the complete implementation of the categorical imperative universally. By grounding reason into physiology—as upright posture—Herder, in contrast, has already completed its instantiation "as natural effect." There is thus no need for history understood in purposive terms, namely, as Kant calls it, as "destiny." There is also no need for the historical destruction of parts of humanity that cannot keep pace with reason's destiny.

---

33 Kant, *On History*, pp. 37–38.
34 Kant, *On History*, p. 31.

Kant insists on the importance of race, because race is the purposive force within nature. As nature's purpose it assists history's goal. There is a strong link between Kant's teleological conception of reason, in nature as well as history, and his writings on race. Race is crucial for Kant's moral philosophy and for his philosophy of history, because it "called for a purposive account."[35] Race guarantees teleology in nature which runs parallel to and supports Kant's teleology of reason. As Kant makes clear in his essay "The Use of Teleological Principles in Philosophy" (1788), race is an internal purposive force independent of outside forces such as climate: "This cause does not lie in the climate, but comes from within these people themselves."[36] Most importantly Kant argues that race is an isolating factor within a purported universal history: "Each of these races is virtually isolated."[37] So some races could become extinguished without having a detrimental affect on humanity as whole.

In isolating different races within the context of a progressive universal history of reason, Kant laid the foundation for a conception of humanity that was prone to harbor hostility toward human diversity. Following Rousseau, Kant differentiated between natural and rational societies. The distinguishing feature of the latter is the sacrifice of individual preferences for the greater good of the community. As Wolfgang Pross has recently shown, this dualistic image of the human goes hand in hand with Kant's reception of Christoph Meiner's polygenetic division of humanity into two races: "The dichotomy between *the state of nature* and *the state of culture*," Pross cogently observes, "resolves into the dichotomy between two types of humans, which are in their physical disposition completely different."[38] The rational type embarks upon the process of civilization and thus establishes culture, while, in contrast, the opposed type remains passively, and thus immutably, imprisoned in the realm of nature. Arguing against this view, Herder maintained that every human type—"savage" or "civilized"—has been born with reason: "The human race is one and the same species throughout the earth."[39] As Pross has convincingly demonstrated in his extensive commentary, Herder's monogenetic and non-dualistic anthropology radically contradicts Rousseau's and Kant's conception of humanity.[40]

So it is not particularly startling that in his review of the second part of Herder's *Ideen*, Kant harshly criticized the abolition of the universal division

---

35 Bernasconi, "Who invented the concept of race?" p. 29.

36 Kant, "The Use of Teleological Principles in Philosophy," in Bernasconi and Lott (eds), *The Idea of Race* (Indianapolis: Hackett, 2000), p. 49.

37 Ibid.

38 Wolfgang Pross, "Anmerkungen zu Seite 389" in Wolfgang Pross, ed., *Johann Gottfried Herder: Band III/2.Ideen zur Philosophie der Geschichte der Menschheit. Kommentar* (Darmstadt: Wissenschaftliche Buchgesellschaft, 2002), p. 594.

39 Herder, *Ideen zur Philosophie der Geschichte der Menschheit Text/ Herder Werke Vol III/1* (ed.), Wolfgang Pross (Darmstadt: Wissenschaftliche Buchgesellschaft, 2002), p. 229.

40 Pross, *Kommentar* in Pross (ed.), *Johann Gottfried Herder Werke Vol III/2*, p. 227.

of humanity into the merely natural and the rational. One result was that Kant, in effect, denied human rights to the inhabitants of Tahiti, asking of Herder:

> Does the author mean that if it were the case that the happy inhabitants of Otaheite, having never been visited by civilized nations, would be destined to live in their quiet indolence for another thousand of centuries, one could then give a satisfactory answer to the question why they exist and whether it would not be as well that these islands were occupied with happy sheep and cattle rather than with humans who are happy with sheer consumption/pleasure (*Genuss*)?[41]

On this view, *Genuss*, that is to say the sheer pleasure of consumption, makes the human mutate to the bodily level of the animal. As a consequence, Kant argues that Tahiti might as well be "cleansed," its inhabitants replaced by sheep and cattle. The latter would be as happy as the former but more useful for the subsistence of human society.

This demotion of one part of humanity to the level of the animalistic forms a substantial part of Kant's philosophy of history. In his "Idea for Universal History from a Cosmopolitan Point of View" Kant makes clear that the "men, good-natured as the sheep they herd, would hardly reach a higher worth than their beasts; they would not fill the empty place in creation by achieving their end, which is rational nature."[42] For this reason rational nature turns historical. It introduces competition and strife so that over time those communities which have established the greatest distance from "the beast" overtake those that still remain mired to the lowly sphere of the beastly:

> Thanks be to Nature, then, for the incompatibility, for heartless competitive vanity, for the insatiable desire to posses and to rule! Without them, all the excellent natural capacities of humanity would forever sleep, undeveloped. Man wishes concord; but Nature knows better what is good for the race; she wills discord.[43]

Over the discordant path of history human nature turns divisive, separating those who have won in the competition from those who lost out. According to Kant racial differences offer proof positive of such division. This is why Kant reacted vehemently against Herder's dismissal of racial divisions: "Whereas Kant was among those who advocated a division into only four or five kinds, Herder advocated recognition of the diversity of human peoples; whereas Kant focused on color divisions, Herder saw continuity: 'colors run

---

41　Kant, "Rezension zu Johann Gottfried Herders Ideen," in Wilhelm Weischedel, ed., *Schriften zur Anthropologie, Geschichtsphilosophie, Politik und Pädagogik* (Frankfurt a. M.: Suhrkamp, 1964), pp. 781–806, p. 805.

42　Kant, *On History*, pp. 15–16.

43　Ibid., p. 16.

into one another.'"[44] Bernasconi here cites the crucial quote from the second part of the *Ideas* on which Kant vents his angry response in his second review of 1785. Herder argues for the unity underlying human diversity:

> In brief neither four or five races nor exclusive varieties exist on this earth. The colors run into each other; the formation serve the genetic character; and on the whole in the end everything mutates into shades of one and the same picture which is spread throughout all spaces and times of the earth.[45]

The scattering of qualities does not imply division, because there is no hierarchical divide between what is spread out. Kant takes issue with precisely such dismissal of hierarchy and competition. In his review of the second part of the *Ideas* Kant first duly notes Herder's abandonment of the notion of race: "The division of the human species into races does not find favor with our author; he is especially hostile to the classification based on hereditary coloration, probably because he does not yet clearly conceive the notion of race."[46] According to Kant, such dismissal of racial division does not only disqualify Herder as a scientist but also calls into doubt his philosophical credentials. This is so because racial divisions are the empirical proof for the necessity of moral and political hierarchies. Kant takes issue with Herder's pluralistic understanding of humanity: "But what if the true purpose of providence would not be this shadow of happiness that each man forms of himself, but rather the endlessly growing and progressing activity,"[47] he questions Herder's notion of reason (Vernunft) as a diverse form of listening (Vernehmen). Countering Kant's conception of reason as pure, Herder defines reason as autonomy's heteronomy— as the self's cognizance of itself and the other:

> From this we see what reason (*Vernunft*) is: a name which in recent publications is often used like an inborn automat and which as such leads to nothing but misinterpretation. Theoretically and practically reason is nothing but something that is heard (*Vernehmen*); an acquired proportion and direction of ideas and forces to which humanity has been formed according to its organization and way of life.[48]

This notion of reason as type of listening is not only hermeneutic—focused on understanding the other—but it also runs parallel to the natural running together of human differences—an argument with which Herder dismisses immutable difference proclaimed by Kant's science of race. In a similar way in

---

44 Bernasconi, "Who invented the concept of Race?" p. 28.
45 Pross, ed., *Johann Gottfried Herder Werke Vol III/1*, p. 231.
46 Kant, *On History*, p. 47.
47 Ibid., p. 50.
48 Pross, ed., *Johann Gottfried Herder Werke Vol III/1*, pp. 133–34.

which the different colors of the skin run into each other, cultural differences are part of a common human denominator. Reason recognizes difference but does not make it absolute. It bridges over what is different while not equating what differs from each other. Herder's peculiar combination of difference and universalism inspired Goethe's critique of theological and philosophical ideologies of exclusion. Goethe's classicism clearly has taken on board Herder's critique of an appraisal of ancient Greece to the detriment of Egypt and Israel.

CHAPTER 7

TALKING HUMANLY WITH THE DEVIL: FROM ROSENZWEIG VIA SPINOZA TO GOETHE'S HOSPITALITY IN *FAUST* AND *IPHIGENIA ON TAURIS*

To express my ideas briefly: Goethe was the Spinoza of poetry. The whole of Goethe's poetry is animated by the same spirit that is wafted towards us from the writings of Spinoza. That Goethe paid undivided allegiance to the doctrine of Spinoza is beyond doubt. At any rate, he occupied himself with it throughout his life; in the introductory passages of his Memoirs, as in the concluding volume recently published, he has frankly acknowledged this to be the case. I cannot now recollect where I have read that Herder, losing his temper at finding Goethe permanently engaged with Spinoza's works, once exclaimed, "If Goethe would just for once take up some other Latin book than one of Spinoza's!" Heine, *Religion and Philosophy in Germany*.

This chapter focuses on the way in which Goethe developed and deepened Herder's Spinozist approach toward sacred texts. As we have seen in the preceding chapters, Herder appropriated and transformed Spinoza's naturalism by making it compatible with a non-dogmatic understanding of religion. Goethe follows Herder when he propounds a highly unorthodox theology in both his rereading of the Faust tradition and in his idiosyncratic interpretation of the Iphigenia myth. In this chapter I will introduce Goethe via the highly original, and thus far, neglected link which Franz Rosenzweig establishes between, what he calls, the "unrevealed truth" of Spinoza's paganism and the fluidity which Goethe introduces into literary and theological discussions through his peculiar characterization of evil (in his tragedy *Faust*) and the non-civilized (in his drama *Iphigenia on Tauris*).

Like Herder, albeit to a far lesser extent, Goethe engaged in biblical criticism. I will introduce Goethe's representation of how Faust translates the first sentence of the Gospel according to John via a brief analysis of his aphoristic essay *Israel in the Desert*. This essay sheds light on Goethe's relationship with sacred texts: one that is equally removed from the derisory tone of Enlightenment thought as it is remote from the dogmatic ethos of religious orthodoxy.[1] Goethe depicts Moses as staggering through the desert. This dizziness of the

---

1   For a discussion of this point see Peter Hofmann's *Goethes Theologie* (Paderborn: Schöningh Verlag, 2001); Willy Schottroff's "Goethe als Bibelwissenschaftler" in D. Kimpel/J. Pompetzki (eds), *Allerhand Goethe. Seine Wissenschaftliche Sendung aus Anlaß des 150. Geburtstages und des 50. Namenstages der Johann-Wolfgang-Goethe-Universität in Frankfurt am Main* (Frankfurt a. M.: Peter Lang, 1985), pp. 111–137; Gerhard Sauder's "Der junge Goethe und das religiöse Denken des 18. Jahrhunderts" *Goethe-Jahrbuch* Vol. 112 (1995), pp. 97–110 and H. B. Nisbet's "Religion and Philosophy" in *The Cambridge Companion to Goethe* (Cambridge: Cambridge University Press, 2002), pp. 219–231.

purported founder of Jewish monotheism links him backwards, as it were, to the religious uncertainty and plurality of polytheistic or "pagan" religions (strikingly Freud relies on Goethe's characterization of a staggering, dizzy Moses, when he propounds his peculiar theory of Judaism's Egyptian origins in *Moses and Monotheism*).

The brief description of Goethe's Moses establishes a spring board for a larger discussion of Goethe's Spinozist or, in Rosenzweig's unprejudiced usage of the term, "pagan" reading of the Christian Faust and the Greek Iphigenia myth. As translator of these myths Goethe relies on what he describes as the "ghostly" quality of Spinoza's thought. Spinoza's thought seems to induce a desert like dizziness by doing the work commonly associated with that of a ghost: it haunts seemingly autonomous entities with their opposite so that the mind becomes dependent on the body. Even the "high Lord" God does not approach the devil as his antagonist but undertakes what seems to be impossible for humans: he speaks humanly with Mephistopheles.

1. Rosenzweig's New Thinking and Goethe's Spinozist Paganism

In his essay on "The New Thinking" Franz Rosenzweig propounds a philosophical, literary and theological defense of paganism. Indeed he depicts the first part of his magnum opus *The Star of Redemption* as a radical departure from the old philosophy in so far as it is pagan rather than narrowly metaphysical. Such a statement needs to be unpacked. In a sense Rosenzweig contrasts the pagan with the metaphysical. What does he understand by the term metaphysics? Rosenzweig's old thinkers are metaphysicians, because they try to reach down to the essence behind and beneath the things of the phenomenal world. The "meta" of metaphysics denotes this search for an essence. Once this search has reached its goal, the old philosophy would (so it hopes) be capable of capturing the static and thus unchangeable truth of the physical world we encounter day after day. Rosenzweig begs to differ. Rather than apprehending the truth of our world, the old thinking proffers a distorted image of it. According to Rosenzweig, metaphysics reduces any given entity to what it is not. No wonder then that he detects behind metaphysics a kind of thinking which he demotes as old and from which he sets out to depart.

Rosenzweig's qualms about metaphysics, however, do not have primarily to do with knowledge concerns (i.e. epistemology). They have a much larger reach, because Rosenzweig addresses not merely an academic discipline (i.e. that of philosophy) but the complexity of human life in its entirety. This complexity expands over three broad realms: world, humanity and divinity. Reducing one of these entities to another metaphysical thought is not only theoretically or epistemologically questionable (i.e. it distorts our ways of knowing) but it is also problematic in terms of social practice, because it does violence to life not merely in the conceptual but in the performative sense: life as experienced in the three dimensionality of the worldly, the human and the divine. Rosenzweig's approach to what he calls "The New Thinking" opens with a plea for the radical separateness of these three entities.

Why does he do so? Rosenzweig argues that it is only by virtue of being distinct that each part of the three dimensional assembly comprising world, humanity and divinity can have a life of its own in the first place. In order to interact with each other, each must—for the time being at least—be detached from the others. Whereas philosophy's metaphysical quest for essences reduces the one to the other and, equally and, perhaps most importantly, the other to the one:

> The world is by no means permitted to be the world, God by no means permitted to be God, man by no means permitted to be man, rather all must "really" be something totally different. If they were nothing else but actually only what they are, then philosophy—heaven forbid and forfend—would ultimately be superfluous! At least a philosophy which absolutely would ferret out something "entirely different." Indeed, as far as my university knowledge suffices, this is what all previous philosophy wanted.[2]

Rosenzweig qualifies this bleak assessment of "all previous philosophy" later on, while singling out the work of Spinoza. He in fact turns Spinoza into a Godfather of sorts: namely, into the intellectual patron of the arguments developed in the first part of the *Star of Redemption*. There Rosenzweig establishes the radical distinctness of world, humanity and divinity. None of these entities can be reduced to another. In Spinozist fashion Rosenzweig insists on each entity as a substance and Spinoza famously defined substance as "what is in itself and is conceived through itself, that is, that whose concept does not require the concept of another thing, from which it must be formed."[3] Spinoza, however, also insists on the interdependence of independent entities.

Following Spinoza's thought about the interdependence of what is independent, Rosenzweig discusses in the second part of *The Star of Redemption* how the worldly, the human and the divine relate to each other precisely because each is separate and can only be "conceived through itself." Spinoza paves the ground for Rosenzweig's new thinking not only on account of his conception of substance but also because of his all-encompassing approach to life. Spinoza avoids hierarchical rankings as much as possible: he does not privilege the human over and above the divine or natural and neither does he extol the divine or natural over and above the human. Rosenzweig admires Spinoza's

---

2 Rosenzweig, *Philosophical and Theological Writings*, trans. end ed. with Notes and Commentary, by Paul W. Franks and Michael L. Morgan (Indianapolis, IN/ Cambridge: Hackett), p. 115.

3 Spinoza, *Ethics*, ed. and trans. by Edwin Curley with an introduction by Stuart Hampshire (New York: Penguin, 1996), p. 1.

holistic approach. It is this mishmash of self-enclosed substance thinking and a non-hierarchical interlinking view of the human, divine or natural which seems to lay the intellectual foundations for what Rosenzweig calls "The New Thinking."

What precisely is new about it? Whereas the scholasticism preceding Spinoza was theological, the idealism subsequent to Spinoza was anthropological. According to Rosenzweig, Spinoza occupies a unique and utterly new position, because he is neither strictly theological nor strictly anthropological:

> If Spinoza, at the beginning of his work [i.e. his *Ethics*], passes on the scholastic concept of substance to the great Idealists of 1800—being in this respect the significant mediator between two epochs of European thought, precisely because he understood substance neither theologically like the epoch that just passed by nor anthropologically like the coming epoch, but rather cosmologically-naturalistically, thereby rendering substance formal and also mutable—then he defines substance, famously (that impertinent word of the literati may stand here without the reader having to blush, for he usually knows the first sentences of philosophical books), as that which is in itself and is conceived through itself. I could perhaps explain the intention of the difficult constructive parts of the three books of the first volume [of the *Star of Redemption*] no better than if I say that there it is shown, for each of the three possible bearers of the essence concept [i.e. world, humanity, divinity], how it fulfills this definition in its special way.[4]

Through his understanding of substance as that which "is in itself and is conceived through itself" Spinoza criticizes anthropomorphic conceptions of God. This critique of theology and philosophy does not make Spinoza into a theologian. Neither does it turn him into a thinker who is exclusively concerned with human, or, in other words, anthropological issues. Rather Spinoza addresses nature, life and the cosmos in their entirety without privileging one part over another. Rosenzweig argues that this Spinozist element constitutes the paganism of the *Star of Redemption*. He does not condemn but rather appreciates paganism as the foundation for a new kind of thinking: "insofar as the first volume of the *Star* seeks to set out elemental contents of experience, purified from the admixture with which thinking might occupy in them, it has to become exactly this, a philosophy of paganism."[5] A philosophy of paganism is one which uncovers experience freed from the reductions and distortions of thinking. Rosenzweig defines paganism as nothing less than the truth in its "unrevealed form."[6]

While the pagan lacks revelation, it is nevertheless less violent than a metaphysical philosophy or a revelatory theology. Pagan truth is non-violent and mild, whereas the reduction to essence which metaphysical thought practices

---

4   Rosenzweig, *Philosophical and Theological Writings*, p. 117.
5   Ibid., p. 120.
6   Ibid.

do work in a voracious manner. Philosophical insight arrests life and thus deprives it of its lifelines in order to be better able to consume it.[7] According to Rosenzweig, this philosophical approach is sickening and he contrasts the consuming interest of philosophy and theology with the mellow and peaceful light that illuminates our understanding of life when we read the work of, perhaps the greatest German writer, Goethe:

> Wherein, then, lies the difference between healthy human understanding and sick human understanding which, exactly like the old philosophy, the philosophy of "philosophical astonishment"—astonishment means standstill—sinks its teeth into something that it will not let go before it "has" it in its entirety? Healthy human understanding can wait, can keep on living, has no "*idée fixe*"; advice comes when the time comes. This secret is the whole wisdom of the new philosophy. It teaches, to speak with Goethe, the "understanding at the right time"—
>
>> "Why is the truth so woefully
>> Removed? To the deepest ground banned?
>> None understands at the right time, how near and broad
>> The truth would be, how lovely and mild."[8]

What Rosenzweig describes here is the absence of dogma, creed, of an *idée fixe* in works of literature. A nondogmatic approach towards theology and philosophy is premised on a narrative or literary sensibility. Rosenzweig's narrative philosophy abandons the stasis of dogma, because it instantiates a thinking in and with time.

There is a fascinating correlation between Rosenzweig's New Thinking and Spinoza's conception of the mind as the idea of the body. As Genevieve Lloyd has convincingly shown, the "mind, as idea of the human body, has a past."[9] The body's immersion in time requires a narrative or timely approach toward understanding the mind.[10] Rosenzweig's New Thinking performs this task: it traces ideas through a narrative, time-bound itinerary. Rosenzweig describes Spinoza's and Goethe's work as revival of a pagan or nondogmatic conception of humanity. Rosenzweig appreciates the intellectual and social advantageous paganism (thus understood) but he also acknowledges its shortcomings.

2. Goethe's Moses and the Spinozist Literature of the Desert

According to Rosenzweig, Spinoza's philosophy is a narrative one. It is pagan, because it accurately focuses on the ever-changing nature of life and because

---

7   For a discussion of Rosenzweig's critique of Hegel's voracious philosophy see chapter 8 of *German Idealism and the Jew*.

8   Rosenzweig, *Philosophical and Theological Writings*, p. 123.

9   Lloyd, *Spinoza and the Ethics*, p. 97.

10 See Ibid., pp. 96–97.

it is not concerned with revelation. There seems to be similarities between Rosenzweig's understanding of the pagan and his conception of Goethe's literature. Literature uncovers the truth in its "unrevealed form." Rosenzweig differentiates himself from Spinoza and Goethe in his attempt at introducing a modern version of revelation. At the end of the *Star*, Rosenzweig arrives at a new conception of revelation. This is, however, the end of a journey that has passed through and has been informed by Spinoza's and Goethe's narrative or pagan thought. Spinoza's and Goethe's narrative thinking offers a blueprint of an all-inclusively broad and non-violent world: in Goethe's words (as cited by Rosenzweig in the quote above), it is the broad and mild truth of literature.

Literature is a space that allows for time and it is a time that asks for patience. Here there are no conclusions, no outcomes, and no final truths. What we encounter is the lovely and mild appearance of the truth of literature that lives in, through, and with time and thus never reaches a clearly defined end or goal. The space and time of literature is that described by the title of a recent book by David Jasper: *The Sacred Desert*. Jasper argues that "art and literature can offer an authentic response to the desert, since they too are universal, beyond all confessional limitations."[11] Goethe in fact locates his access to religion and the sacred texts of the Bible in the highly disorienting and dislocating space of the desert and so he calls his main essay on Moses and the Bible *Israel in the Desert (Israel in der Wüste)*.[12]

In this essay Goethe focuses on the dizziness infused by the desert, a dizziness that causes loneliness and at the same time its opposite: a relation to universal human experiences "beyond all confessional limitations." Goethe's Moses is similar to his Faust: both are men of action. Goethe strikingly characterizes Moses as a "*man of the deed*" (*Mann der That* italics in the German original).[13] The deed in question here is not that of clearly delineated actions. It cannot be so, precisely because Moses does his work in the desert, which is a place that calls our sense of being placed into question: it thus exudes and infuses dizziness. Rather than being pragmatic Goethe's Moses—here again like Faust—is "by his nature driven to the most daunting/greatest undertaking imaginable" (*durch seine Natur zum Größten getrieben*).[14] Similar to Faust, Moses' daunting ambitions cause him to err, to commit crimes even: Goethe here mentions Moses' cold blooded act of killing an Egyptian in his youth ("*von dem ersten Meuchelmord an*") and the following acts of cruelty ("*durch alle Grausamkeiten durch*").[15] Yet Goethe does not condemn the personality of Moses. He abstains from a judgmental approach.

---

11 Jasper, *The Sacred Desert: Religion, Literature, Art, and Culture* (Oxford: Blackwell, 2004), p. 6.

12 Goethe, *West-Östlicher Divan. Vol 1*, ed. by Hendrik Birus (Frankfurt a. M.: Deutscher Klassiker Verlag, 1994), pp. 229–248.

13 Goethe, *West-Östlicher Divan. Vol. 1*, p. 247.

14 Ibid.

15 Ibid.

Goethe interprets Moses' crimes in the context of the dizzy, ambiguous and non-confessional space of the desert which is also that of literature. Moses as "the man of the deed" creates Israel, he forms a "tremendous mass of people" (*"ungeheuren Volksmasse"*).[16] Moses' way of proceeding is the opposite of a clearly defined set of objectives and creeds. Goethe's Moses errs, because he does not walk through the desert; rather he dizzily staggers (*taumeln*) through it.[17] This staggering, dizzying approach is part of a literary access into philosophy and theology. As we have seen, Rosenzweig uncovers the philosophical foundations of this literary philosophy in the pagan (or nondogmatic), non-revelatory thought of Spinoza. Strikingly, Rosenzweig establishes a convincing link between Spinoza and Goethe: both are highly heterodox and according to Rosenzweig they share a religious sensibility that goes under the name of paganism. He sees the repercussions of paganism enacted or performed in the work of Goethe who characterized himself as a pagan and who was quite frank about his indebtedness to the work of Spinoza.[18]

3. Goethe's Sense of Selfhood and Spinoza's Notion of Self-Preservation (conatus)

Goethe's relationship with Spinoza is a long lasting and personal one. He emphasizes the intellectual and at same time intimate acquaintance with Spinoza's writing and thought in his autobiography *Poetry and Truth* and his *Italian Journey* (his account of his travels through Italy). In *Poetry and Truth* Goethe speaks of a "necessary elective affinity" (*notwendiger Wahlverwandtschaft*)[19] between his own character and that manifested in the writing of Spinoza's *Ethics*: "This intellect/spirit/ghost (*Geist*) who so decisively influenced me and who had such an impact on my whole way of thinking was Spinoza."[20] The term *Geist* resonates with what Goethe discusses a few paragraphs previously as the "ghostly" copresence of the past within contemporary everyday life. Here he articulates his "sense of the oneness of past and present: a view which has brought something ghostly (*etwas Gespenstermäßiges*) into the present."[21] This ghostliness characterizes Goethe's rapport with Spinoza's

---

16 Ibid.
17 Ibid.
18 See John Armstrong's *Love, Life, Goethe. How to be Happy in an Imperfect World* (New York: Penguin, 2006), p. 38. For a fascinating discussion of Goethe as "the Spinoza of science" see Robert J. Richard's *The Romantic Conception of Life: Science and Philosophy in the Age of Goethe* (Chicago: University of Chicago Press, 2002), pp. 376–390.
19 Goethe, *Werke. 'Hamburger Ausgabe': Autobiographische Schrifften II. Vol. 10*, ed. By Erich Trunz (Nördlingen: Beck, 1989), p. 35.
20 Ibid.
21 Ibid., p. 32.

writing and thought. We could say that Goethe felt visited by the ghost (*Geist*) of Spinoza. In this sense, Spinoza is dead and yet alive as a spirit/intellect/ghost: he haunts the past as well as the present.

What does Goethe admire most in Spinoza's writing and thought? A direct and yet somewhat confusing answer would be "ghostliness." What Goethe means by the "ghostly" is not only the haunting of the present by the past but also the general fusion and confusion of opposites (i.e. mind and body; nature and culture; monotheism and paganism etc.). In his *Specters of Marx* Derrida employs the word ghost with a similar concern for outdoing dualisms which is precisely what attracted Goethe to Spinoza: "If we have been insisting so much since the beginning on the logic of the ghost," writes Derrida, "it is because it points toward a thinking of the event that necessarily exceeds a binary or dialectical logic, the logic that distinguishes or opposes *effectivity or actuality* (either present, empirical, living—or not) and *ideality* (regulating or absolute non-presence)."[22] Goethe locates in Spinoza's philosophy this ghostly work of thought which confounds various dualisms between the mind and the body.

Against this background it is not surprising that Goethe focuses on the *Ethics,* because it is in his magnum opus that Spinoza most clearly deviates from his philosophical mentor Descartes. This becomes abundantly clear when Spinoza maintains that the mind is the idea of the body.[23] Goethe enthuses about Spinoza's *Ethics* as follows:

> I cannot give an account of what I have read out (*herausgelesen*) of this work and what I have read into (*hineingelesen*) it. Suffice it to say that here I found a calming of my passions (*Leidenschaften*); here seems to open up a broad and free view over the sensuous and the moral world.[24]

Strikingly Goethe goes on to connect this Spinozist approach towards both the passions and morality's dependence on sensuality with Spinoza's idiosyncratic view on self-preservation as unselfishness: "What, however, most of all captivated me in him was the limitless unselfishness (*grenzenlose Uneigennützigkeit*) which shone through each sentence [i.e. of the *Ethics*]."[25] It is this absence of selfishness that, at least according to Goethe, constitutes Spinoza's understanding of eternity. Spinoza's eternity reconciles liberalism (that may tend towards selfishness) with a communitarian approach which emphasizes unselfishness.

In Moira Gatens and Genevieve Lloyds words, "a Spinozisitic perspective may dissolve the false opposition between liberal and communitarian approaches

---

22 Derrida, *Specters of Marx. The State of Debt, the Work of Mourning & the New International,* trans. by Peggy Kamuf (New York: Routledge, 1994), p. 63.

23 See Gatens and Lloyd, *Collective Imaginings,* p. 37.

24 Goethe, *Werke. 'Hamburger Ausgabe' Vol. 10,* p. 35.

25 Goethe, *Werke. 'Hamburger Ausgabe' Vol. 10,* p. 35.

by conceiving the distinction between individual and community in reciprocal rather than oppositional terms."[26] Those who see the preservation of themselves linked to the preservation of that which is different—which is not directly related to them—are partaking of eternity. They share eternity, because their separate lives are interlinked with the universal flow of life as it unfolds over the past, present and future. From the perspective of eternity, the self preserves itself by being unselfish. Admittedly these unselfish selfhoods are not spared mortality: they perish as isolated and disconnected individuals but they survive after their corporeal death in precisely what connects them to the larger ongoing life of humanity here and now. Here the freedom from selfishness paradoxically presupposes a concern for the well-being of the self: only by ensuring the success of my life can I hope to contribute to the life of others, be that in the short-term context of the present or from the eternal perspective of the future or combining both.

Goethe's life exemplifies the ethical validity of this concern for the well-being of the self. John Armstrong has recently written a fascinating philosophical essay about what Goethe's writing and life has to say to us in our contemporary society of consumerism. He too focuses on the question of the self. According to Armstrong Goethe has resolved the seemingly "inescapable conflict between mental culture and material success."[27] Whereas material success is commonly associated with selfishness, mental culture often represents the opposite: unselfish dedication to the apparently selfless life of the mind. As Armstrong has brilliantly shown, Goethe is important, because he outdoes this binary opposition between self and unselfishness. Goethe's life seems to contain a message in a bottle which Armstrong admirably deciphers as follows:

> It would be a pity if Goethe were to remain a mere name associated only with an intriguing novel and a famous but not-much-read play. Not because we need to be better informed about the past. Rather, Goethe is worth listening to now. Although he was an outstanding intellectual and artistic figure, Goethe was very much a "Weltkind"—to use one of his favorite words: "a creature of this world". He had an appetite for engaging with the world as it is—for facing the realities of authority, for "getting on", for finding out how things work, for concrete success. He was not intimidated by the material world, or by the largely philistine powers that hold sway in it.[28]

Goethe connected his sense of the self, or, in other words, his subjectivity, to universalism: to the concern for the well-being of others. This does not mean that the self abandons its selfishness. What it does mean, however, is that selfish behavior which is rational (according to Spinoza's understanding of the intellectual love of God) assists rather than obstructs the flourishing of the community at large.

---

26 Gatens and Lloyds, *Collective Imaginings*, p. 132.
27 Armstrong, *Love, Life, Goethe*, pp. 4–5.
28 Ibid., p. 4.

Deepening and developing Spinoza's notion of the intellectual love of God, Goethe proclaims that we are only universal by remaining subjective. This questioning approach towards the binary opposition between the self and the universal leaves either side of the opposition intact. Both remain where they are but while remaining where they are, they perform each other's concerns: by being subjective, the self contributes to the preservation of the universal and by being universal, universalism assists in the perseveration of the self.

And yet universalism and the concern for the self are diametrically opposed positions. They are antagonistic. In a sense Spinoza's notion of the *conatus* (self-preservation) describes this antagonism between the self and the universal. In Spinoza's usage the term *conatus* itself becomes another word for antagonism. Herein consists the true originality of Spinoza's take on self-preservation: the self that preserves itself is more than merely itself, because it incorporates that element that is antagonistic to it, which is precisely the attention devoted to that which is other than the self, that is the universal. Spinoza employs the irrational, in the sense of nonuniversal, term of subjectivity (i.e. the self that preserves itself) in order to describe the work of reason as the preservation of life in its entirety.

What governs the logic of Spinoza's *conatus* is the seemingly paradoxical formula according to which x can only be x by not merely being x: by partaking of a larger alphabetical context where it relates to letters that are not x but a, b, c etc. In this way, the self that preserves itself only preserves itself by preserving that which is not itself. This back and forth between independence and interdependence is what Rosenzweig has in mind when he describes the outline of his "New Thinking." More recently, Žižek has described the logic of the paradoxical state of an x that can only be true to itself by not coinciding with itself as follows: "the only way for universality to come into existence, to 'posit itself' 'as such', is in the guise of its very opposite, of what cannot but appear as excessive 'irrational' whim."[29] Spinoza's *conatus* seems to be such an excessive irrational whim, because it appears to tout the position of an exorbitant self: one that keeps preserving itself. It is precisely this seemingly irrational excess of subjectivity (i.e. selfhood) that helps fulfill the eternity of the universal. Spinoza's *conatus* and Goethe's seemingly selfish concern with getting on in the world both occupy not a self-contained but an intrinsically antagonist position: their subjectivity is also universal so that subjectivity and universalism emerges as "not only not exclusive," but as "two sides of the same coin."[30] There cannot be a subject without the plurality of antagonistic subjects which are nevertheless interrelated and thus *are* the universal.

Goethe's wish to "get on" is therefore not merely selfish or materialistic or irrational; it has an intellectual truth to it which is precisely that of universalism. What Armstrong describes as Goethe's realism—an approach to the world

---

29 Žižek, "Carl Schmitt in the Age of Post-Politics," in Chantal Mouffe (ed.), *The Challenge of Carl Schmitt* (London: Verso, 1999), pp. 18–37, p. 35.

30 Ibid., p. 36.

that does not gloss over unsavory or mundane/materialistic aspects but nevertheless sees intellectual/spiritual validity in these same demoted aspects—is what fascinates Rosenzweig as the pagan, non-revelatory rationality of both Spinoza's and Goethe's work. Rosenzweig appreciates Goethe's and Spinoza's worldly outlook. According to Rosenzweig it represents the truth, albeit the truth that goes without the other-worldly sphere of revelation. From Rosenzweig's perspective, however, Spinoza's and Goethe's understanding of eternity is certainly pagan: it is a worldly view of immortality.

Goethe's encounter with Italy deepened his self-perception as a pagan. In his *Italian Journey* Goethe interprets Spinoza's ethical teachings as a quasi-pagan pathway to eternity. Residing in the center of Catholicism, in Rome, Goethe sees eternity emerge in a strikingly Spinozist way. On 18 August 1787 while coming to terms with life in "the eternal city," Goethe evokes Spinoza's writing and thought in order to focus on the infinity of the finite world: "The form (*Gestalt*) of this world perishes, and I want to follow exclusively Spinoza's teaching and concern myself with what is everlasting (*bleibende Verhältnisse*) and procure the eternity (*Ewigkeit verschaffen*) of my soul/spirit/ghost/intellect (*Geist*)."[31] Goethe here invokes Spinoza's intellectual love of God. This type of love is intellectual, because it presupposes that we realize what keeps nature or God from destruction and self-destruction. As such it keeps the selfish passions in check. Self-mastery here is not necessarily an ascetic exercise. The reigning in of the passions has nothing to do with hostility towards pleasure. Instead the self masters its affects in order to insure the sustainability of its joy in sheer existence.[32] Keeping the passions in check is not an end itself. Rather it is a means for performing a new kind of self-preservation: a Spinozist one where the boundaries of the self turn porous so that selfhood overlaps with the life of the other and of others.

The constellation Goethe establishes between Spinoza's idiosyncratic notion of self-preservation and the eternity of Rome is not a marginal aspect of his writing and thought. His *Faust* closes with an appraisal of a peculiar eternity. To be more precise, at the end of his *Faust II* Goethe interprets the infinity of Spinoza's intellectual love of God as the "eternal feminine": "the eternal feminine elevates us" (*Das Ewig-Weibliche/Zieht uns hinan*) are the final two lines of his dramatic magnum opus.[33] While it is impossible to reduce to one term what Goethe means by the expression "the eternal feminine," it is worthwhile correlating this expression with his Spinozist understanding of eternity. Goethe's Spinoza inspired interpretation of the eternal does not connote the other-worldly realm of heaven. Instead it refers to Spinoza's ethical teaching on which Goethe focuses in Rome when he resolves to concern himself only with everlasting things.

---

31 Goethe, *Werke. 'Hamburger Ausgabe.' Autobiographische Schriften III*. Vol. 11, Erich Trunz (ed.), Nördlingen: Beck, 1989, pp. 386–387.
32 See Armstrong's *Love, Life, Goethe*, p. 44.
33 Goethe, *Werke. 'Hamburger Ausgabe.' Dramen I*, p. 364.

Spinoza discovers eternity in a life that is shaped by the intellectual love of God. In his "Letter from the Pastor of *** to the New Pastor of ***," Goethe radicalizes Spinoza by arguing that God is nothing less than loving oneself and others. Here Spinoza's intellectual love of God plainly and explicitly transmutes into a subjective and inter-subjective sphere. In Goethe's *Letter* a Protestant Pastor asks a colleague to abstain from the urge to impose his faith upon others. This may well be an implicit critique of Lavater's missionary zeal. Lavater repeatedly attempted to convert the Jewish Enlightenment philosopher Moses Mendelssohn to Christianity. Responding to these repeated attempts to bring about his conversion to Christianity Mendelssohn questioned absolute truth claims in religious discourse. His magnum opus *Jerusalem. Or on Religious Power and Judaism* closes with a plea for diversity. According to both Goethe and Mendelssohn, "diversity is evidently the plan and purpose of Providence."[34] Instead of enforcing his faith Goethe's Protestant Pastor attempts to prompt his colleague to realize how his religious convictions might result in ethical actions that preserve not only his life but also those who belong to a religion that differs from his own. Significantly, Goethe's mentor Herder discusses Spinoza's thought as philosophy of love that has overcome the divisiveness of religious convictions:

> Love is the highest reason, as it is the purest, divinest volition. If we are unwilling to believe Saint John on this point, then we may believe the doubtless still more divine *Spinoza*, whose philosophy and morality entirely revolves around this axle.[35]

Whereas Saint John clearly belongs to the Christian tradition, Spinoza offers a non-confessional ethics of love.

Goethe speaks of "the central point of our faith, Eternal Love."[36] In what ways does the "eternal love" in question here relate to Spinoza's intellectual love of God and what are the implications of this possible relation? This section closes by attending to the first part of this question. Spinoza' intellectual love of God constitutes a clear realization of what it means to be part of nature/God. Being part of nature or God stipulates that one conceptualizes self-hood as a partaking of otherness. Spinoza's intellectual love of God eventuates in a non-hierarchical approach towards the relationship between distinct entities such as the distinction between mind and body or the differentiation between the puportly human and the allegedly nonhuman. As will be discussed

---

34   Mendelssohn, *Jerusalem. Or on Religious Power and Judaism*, trans. by Allan Arkush; introduction and commentary by Alexander Altmann (Hanover, NH: Brandeis University Press, 1983), p. 138.

35   Herder, *Philosophical Writings*, p. 216.

36   Goethe, "Letter from the Pastor of *** to the New Pastor of *** from the French. 1773", trans. by Paul E. Kerry with the assistance of Peter Clayson and John Fowles, in *Literature and Belief. Special Issue: Goethe and Religion* (Vol 20: 2000): 1–11, p. 11.

in the following section, Goethe creatively assimilated this non-dualistic approach from his first Spinoza studies of May 1773 onwards.[37]

4. From Spinoza' Intellectual Love of God to Goethe's Religion of Love

In his *Letter* Goethe has his Pastor celebrate a new understanding of religion as the absence of hierarchical divisions. How does he question religious hierarchies? Taking into account the discussion in the previous paragraphs, it is not surprising that he does so by referring to the concept of love. Radicalizing Spinoza's intellectual love of God, Goethe conceptualizes religion as consubstantial with acts of love and so Goethe's Pastor exclaims:

> Religion! Let everyone feel as he could and then go with brotherly love among all sects and parties—then how it would please us, to see the godly seeds bear fruit in so many different ways. Then we could cry out: praise God, that the kingdom of God is found here where I did not seek it.[38]

Religion comes to fruition where one least expects it. Here we encounter the opposite of teleological i.e. goal oriented ways of thinking and behaving: the religious person finds what he seeks precisely by the absence of planning and calculation. In a religious universe one finds what one is seeking by paradoxically the absence of seeking.

Religion introduces a new space for the allocation of time and attention, one that transcends goal oriented forms, be they the search for treasures or the calculation that goes with financial transaction, or military planning or other forms of teleology. By introducing a space and time beyond teleological constructions, religion confounds established forms of relating to the world. How does it do so? Religion unties what has been firmly bound together by academic, financial, and social conventions. This act of untying loosens rather than ossifies dualistic and hierarchical approaches to the world. It reveals finding not as the opposite of seeking, instead it includes not seeking into a sphere from which it has previously been excluded: that of finding. Antagonistic principles (not seeking—finding) do not collide with each other but rather fulfill each other (not seeking becomes revealed as fulfilling its seemingly opposed principle: finding). Philip Goodchild's interpretation of what it means "to do theology" is pertinent in the context of Goethe's Spinozist and thus heterodox understanding of religion. Goodchild has recently argued that the "investigation of the powers and principles by which time, attention and devotion are

---

37 See David Bell's *Spinoza in Germany from 1670 to the Age of Goethe* (London: The Institute of Germanic Studies, 1984), p. 149.

38 Goethe, "Letter from the Pastor of * * * to the New Pastor of * * * from the French. 1773," p. 11.

distributed belong [. . .] to the discipline of theology."[39] Theology in this all-encompassing sense of allocating contemplative time describes Goethe's reading of what it means to be truly religious. To be more precise, Goethe's understanding of religion as love describes the ability to allocate time and devotion to a spiritual and intellectual appreciation of worldly goods.

Religion turns attention away from the competitive and hasty principle of the mantra "divide and conquer" to what Goethe would call a peculiar form of love that does not seek to conquer and thus does not divide but instead slowly and lovingly confounds ossified divisions. Goethe's Spinozist approach towards religion establishes via acts of untying relations between so far mutually opposed and hierarchically graded elements. This means that the untying in question itself enacts its antagonistic other. Goethe reverses the common meaning attached to words so that the act of untying connects, rather than what is the conventional denotation of the term, separates.

Strikingly, Goethe reads the concept religion against the grain. The act of untying contradicts the very semantic field of the Latin root of the term, because the verb *religo* denotes the act of binding. Yet the poetic usage of *religo* embraces Goethe's connotation of unbinding (Catullus uses the verb to mean unbinding rather than binding when he writes: *Cybele religat juga manu*).[40] The Latin word that forms the semantic foundation for the notion religion thus incorporates the very antagonist principle which fascinates Goethe.

The tying and at the same time untying work of religion also confounds the binary opposition that governs the dualism between the profane and the secular. The religious does not exclude the profane nor does it banish the secular. What is seemingly opposed (the secular) or inferior to it (the profane) actualizes its inner and outer manifestations. Goethe here subscribes to Herder's highly unorthodox and Spinoza inspired theology. It is a theology that is inclusive rather than exclusive. It is a theology that questions rather than affirms hierarchies, be they religious, political, social or economic. As a result of this non-hierarchical approach, diversity rather than a clearly defined homogenous ideal or goal emerges as the inscrutable plan of God's providence.

God as the creator of nature cannot be clearly confined to one set of creeds, identities or even one set of practices. He is to be discovered in the infinite diversity of nature (human society included): his seeds thus "bear fruit in so many different ways." This conception of religion as not merely love but the actual love of everything, however strange it may seem, eventuates in the abandonment of religious hierarchies and, even more radical, the dissolution of organized religion: "And once and for all, the idea of a hierarchy is completely against the concept of a real community of believers."[41] This questioning approach to the hierarchical eventuates in Goethe's radical critique of a visible Church: "Regard, my dear brother, even the time of the apostles just

39 Goodchild, *Theology of Money* (London: SCM-Canterbury Press, 2007), p. 6.

40 Lewis and Short, *Latin Oxford Dictionary* (Oxford: Clarendon Press, 1991), p. 1557.

41 Goethe, "Letter from the Pastor of***to the New Pastor of***," p. 11.

after Jesus' death and you will have to confess there was never a visible Church on earth."[42] Here Goethe's reading of the Bible is remarkably similar to that of Spinoza. This is so because both Spinoza and Goethe describe Jesus as an unorthodox thinker: without a Church and without a set of doctrines. Both dismiss creeds and the fideistic element of Christian theology. Instead they focus on Jesus actions: on his *justitia* and his *caritas*. Goethe's understanding of religion is quite close to Moses Mendelssohn's in his *Jerusalem* where Mendelssohn distinguishes between revealed religion and revealed legislation. The former is dogmatic and fideistic while the latter emphasizes the importance of both the performance of certain actions and the avoidance of certain actions. Mendelssohn sees Judaism as more amenable to a deistic modern understanding of religion, because it does without creeds and dogmas. As Karin Schutjer has shown, Goethe is so close to Mendelssohn's Spinozist/ nondogmatic interpretation of Judaism that he paradoxically perceives it as being in competition with his own unorthodox interpretation of Christianity. Goethe sides with Mendelssohn against the attempts at conversion by the evangelist Lavater. Yet, Goethe articulates an anti-Semitic exclusion of Jews from a utopian American society in his novel *Wilhelm Meister's Years of Wandering*, because he sees Judaism as being almost identical with his own action-based view of religion.[43]

What Rosenzweig sees in both Spinoza's and Goethe's work as the truth of paganism, is precisely this emphasis on deeds and the precision of things as they are outside the metaphysical nomenclature established by theology. It is the truth of deeds and things untouched by the revelation of the word (*logos*). The *logos* (word) of theology recedes. Instead we are confronted with deeds of love. These deeds of love stipulate a world where all things are worth loving. As will be discussed in the following sections, this heterodox approach to religion characterizes Goethe's *Faust* and his *Iphigenia on Tauris*. At the hands of Goethe's *Faust* the term "love" acquires a whole range of highly ambiguous meanings ranging from desire to worldly ambitions and of course to curiosity as the craving for knowing the secrets of nature and the universe. This quasi-erotic quest for knowledge is what arouses Faust's passion for theology.

5. Faust's Anthropomorphism or the Deed Which is Scriptural

A case in point is Faust's famous translation of John 1.1. Strikingly Goethe's Faust willfully misreads theology's logos as deed. He does so while trying to translate John 1.1 in the second scene of *Faust I*:

> Tis writ, "In the beginning was the Word."
> I pause, to wonder what is here inferred.

---

42   Ibid., p. 7.

43   Schutjer, "Beyond the Wandering Jew: Anti-Semitism and Narrative Supersession in Goethe's *Wilhelm Meisters Wanderjahre*," *German Quarterly* 77 (Fall 2004): 389–407 (403).

The word I cannot set supremely high:
A new translation will I try.
I read, if by the spirit I am taught,
This sense: "In the beginning was the Thought."
This opening I need to weigh again,
Or sense may suffer from a hasty pen.
Does thought create, and work, and rule the hour?
Twere best: "In the beginning was the Power."
Yet, while the pen is urged with willing fingers,
A sense of doubt and hesitancy lingers.
The spirit comes to guide me in my need,
I write, "In the beginning was the Deed."[44]

Faust moves further and further away from the literal sense of scripture. This aversion to a faithful translation may give the impression as if Faust were here engaged in a quest for allegorical meaning. He actually refers to a quasi-metaphysical, quasi-theological authority: to the *Geist* (spirit/ghost/intellect) whom he asks for assistance in his work of reading. The *Geist* in question here is, however, quite removed from orthodox theology. It is a rather subversive spirit: one that reads sacred scripture against the grain. As part of this sub-version of theology Faust establishes a trinity of terms that increasingly dis-tance themselves from the *logos* of sacred scripture until the third element in this "unholy" trinity produces the opposite of "the word": what surfaces instead is "the deed." The first attempt at translating *logos* as thought or mean-ing (*Sinn*) could be interpreted as metaphysical/allegorical reading of John 1.1. This is indeed the case but Faust does not like it. Far from being a principle of creation, thought distorts the workings of nature ("Does thought create, and work, and rule the hour?").

So Faust refers to Herder's notion of vital force (*Kraft*) but this too does not capture nature's or God's powers of creation. The manifestation of this cre-ative principle represents the deed. This is on what Faust's interpretative quest settles. As the first scene of the play amply illustrates, the deed is, however, unsettling too. Why is this so? The deed as translation of the scriptural *logos* is itself only a word. It denotes "deed" but remains itself nothing else but a denotation. When we first meet Faust, he confronts us, in his opening mono-logue, with the gulf that separates the "vital force" (*Wirkenskraft*) and the seed (*Samen*) of deeds from mere "words" (*Worten*).[45] Faust's translation of theo-logy's *logos* as deed offers a rather short-lived and deluded satisfaction. The focus on deeds as good works would move Faust into close proximity of tra-ditional Catholicism where salvation does indeed depend on the performance

---

44 Goethe, "*Faust, Part 1* (1808), tr. Philip Wayne, Penguin, 1949, Scene ii, 'Faust's Study'" in D. Jasper and S. Prickett (eds), *The Bible and Literature. A Reader* (Oxford: Blackwell, 1999), p. 87. Goethe, *Werke. 'Hamburger Ausgabe'. Dramen 1*, Vol 3, p. 44.

45 Goethe, *Werke. 'Hamburger Ausgabe'. Dramen 1*, Vol 3, p. 20.

of good earthly acts. As Žižek has pointed out, it is Protestantism that has introduced the "shift from act to sign" so that "from the perspective of predestination, a deed becomes a *sign* of the predestined Divine decision."[46] Faust attempts to close the gap between sign and act, which Protestant theology has introduced to the conception of world, humanity and nature. The subject matter of Goethe's play is Faust's failure to do so.

One could read Goethe's tragedy in terms of how literature triumphs over life and this would indeed be one way to interpret the Gretchen subplot of the play: Faust is so ruthless to his lover Gretchen and her family because he values his itinerary as literary/scriptural character over and above what he seems to be desiring, but in the end abstains from obtaining, fulfillment in a settled state of embodied life.[47] Faust's is a failed attempt at closing the Protestant gulf that introduces a split between sign and deed into God himself, which makes the play, as the title page, proclaims a modern tragedy. Žižek has given a precise explanation as to why Faust's concern with the deed lies at the heart of the difference between classical and modern tragedy:

> In political terms, the difference between classical tragedy and modern tragedy is the difference between (traditional) *tyranny* and (modern) *terror*. The traditional *hero* sacrifices himself for the Cause, he resists the pressure of the Tyrant and accomplishes his Duty, cost what it may; as such he is appreciated, his sacrifice confers on him a sublime aura, his act is inscribed in the register of Tradition as an example to be followed. We enter the domain of modern tragedy when the logic of the sacrifice for the Thing compels us to sacrifice this Thing itself.[48]

Faust is the modern hero of tragedy insofar as he does violence to what he loves most: the most striking example of Faust's lethal love is of course the ruin he brings upon Gretchen, the girl he loves most.

How can we account for Faust's destructive effects on what he deems closest to himself? Goethe's tragedy proposes a novel reading of an established folk tale when he interprets Faust's traditional pact with the devil in terms of the destruction wreaked by the self as precisely the destruction of the self. In Goethe's *Faust* "we enter the domain of the *monstrosity of heroism*, when our fidelity to the Cause compels us to transgress the threshold of our 'humanity.'"[49] What, however, compels Faust to transgress the threshold of his humanity; or, in other, more traditional words, to form a pact with the devil? It is what Spinoza has critiqued as the anthropomorphic conception of God or nature. Faust's quest for the inner secret that holds nature together (*was die Natur im Innersten zusammenhält*) is nothing else but to acquire the sort of

---

46 Žižek, "Carl Schmitt in the Age of Post-Politics," p. 20.
47 For a discussion of how Gretchen is sacrificed to literature see Kenneth D. Weisinger, *The Classical Façade: A Nonclassical Reading of Goethe's Classicism* (London: The Pennsylvania State University Press, 1988), pp. 61–100.
48 Žižek, "Carl Schmitt in the Age of Post-Politics," p. 20.
49 Ibid.

knowledge that would enable him to be the creature of knowledge. Faust has truly internalized Bacon's dictum according to which knowledge is power. Knowledge of the deed would turn him into a performer of the deed. Faust's settling on the deed as the modern replacement of the word is, however, itself unsettling, because the act in question here remains firmly bound to the world of signs: it is after all only a translation.

Straight from the opening of the play, Faust searches for ways of closing the gap between act and sign. This is certainly not a humble undertaking, because through it he attempts to metamorphose into the power of God or nature. The quest for this power causes acts, not of creation, but of destruction. In his opening monologue Faust himself realizes this gap between the denotative and the performative when he realizes that his talk about the revelation of nature's powers (*Die Kräfte der Natur rings um mich her enthüllen?*) is nothing else but a work of fiction: a play (*Welch Schauspiel! Aber ach! Ein Schauspiel nur!*).[50] Later on during this same scene there appears a ghost who mocks Faust's venture of casting himself as God or nature. The ghost in question here is Goethe's ghost of nature. What he says resembles Spinoza's critique of anthropomorphic conceptions of the divine in his *Ethics*.

The ghost flatly rebukes Faust's talk about nature as nothing else but an anthropomorphic mirror of himself rather than that of nature (*Geist. Du gleichst dem Geist, den du begreifst, Nicht mir! Verschwindet*).[51] Like Spinoza, Goethe's ghost argues that human attempts at reaching down to the knowledge of God evidence nothing but a limited human wisdom and not that of the deity. Deeply shocked (*Zusammenstürzend*) by such harsh critique Faust attempts to establish the traditional theological separation between God and nature. He props up his self-esteem by referring to his creation as a human rather than merely natural being: as a human being he *is* the image of God, the biblical creator of nature. If he is not like nature what is his likeness like? (Faust here ironically refers to the biblical account of humanity's creation in the image of God). He asks Goethe's ghost of nature:

FAUST (deeply shaken): I do not resemble you?
Who then?
I am the image of God after all!
And I do not even resemble you?[52]

In true Spinozist fashion Goethe's ghost of nature reveals Faust's conception of nature as nothing else but a self-conception and self-deception (i.e. anthropomorphism). Ironically the modern hero Faust desperately clings to the theological separation between God and nature in order to ward off the ghost's stringent Spinozist critique of anthropomorphism. In his ensuing conversion

---

50　Goethe, *Werke*. '*Hamburger Ausgabe*' *Dramen 1* Vol. 3, p. 22.
51　Ibid., p. 24.
52　Ibid. My translation.

with his student Wagner,[53] Faust insists on being an image of God rather than of nature:

> I, the image of God, deem to be already
> Quite close to the mirror of eternal truths.[54]

The mirror of eternal truth merely represents the observant self which is caught not in deeds but in words, as Faust's translation of John 1.1 illustrates. In rejecting the biblical *logos* for the Faustian deed, Faust ironically becomes deeper and more irresolvable entangled into the turmoil of signifying processes which have been cut loose from lived embodiment. One of the lessons to be gathered from Spinoza's *Ethics* is that it is indeed illusory to oppose written thought (or *logos*) to the embodied deed. Contrary to Descartes, Spinoza combines rather than separates thinking things and extended things. His understanding of life as self-preservation (*conatus*) embraces both the mind and the body: "The *conatus*, the drive to self-maintenance and coherence, is a universal feature both of any person's mind and of his body."[55] According to Spinoza the mind (thought) is the idea of the body (deed) and we oppose these two entities with each other at our peril. Gretchen's and Faust's tragedy illustrates this peril. Faust who sets out to solve the riddle of the universe only propounds it. In the same way Faust who attempts to capture the essence of God, evokes God's traditional adversary: Mephistopheles.[56]

6. *Talking Humanly with the Devil: From* Faust *to* Iphigenia

Strikingly Rosenzweig ends his essay on "The New Thinking" with Mephistopheles' words in the first part of Goethe's *Faust*: here Rosenzweig refers to "the greatest poet of the Germans, whose Mephistopheles, to Faust's impatient call, 'many a riddle must be solved there,' replies: 'yet many a riddle is also propounded.'"[57] Mephistopheles here subscribes to a timely and thus patient approach to life and literature. Understanding is an infinite task. It only appears to be at an end when we equate our limited human view with the

---

53 As Benjamin Bennett has clearly shown there is another irony as regards Faust dismissive attitude towards his pedantic pupil Wagner. Faust resembles what he abhors rather what he is searching for (i.e. the creative powers of nature). He resembles Wagner: Bennett, *Goethe's Theory of Poetry. Faust and the Regeneration of Language* (Ithaca: Cornell University Press, 1986), p. 21.

54 Goethe, *Werke. 'Hamburger Ausgabe' Dramen 1* Vol. 3, p. 27.

55 Stuart Hampshire, *Spinoza and Spinozism*, p. xxviii.

56 And Mephistopheles, as Benjamin Bennett has pointed out represents the opposite of Faust's quest for knowledge of God's creative powers: Bennett, *Goethe's Theory of Poetry*, p. 71.

57 Rosenzweig, *Philosophical and Theological Writings*, p. 139.

omniscience and omnipotence of a deity and this is the anthropomorphism of theology and philosophy which Spinoza criticizes in his *Ethics*; a critique on which Goethe elaborates, as we have seen, in his *Faust*.

Goethe's *Faust* opens with a Rosenzweigean focus on reading, thinking and time. In the first Prologue the theatre director confronts the poet with the question of how we are able rejuvenate old texts. This is of course an undertaking with which Goethe is engaged in both *Iphigenia on Tauris* and *Faust*. Both are old texts which have to do with issues of the sacred and, closely associated with it, the question of the self and the other. The theatre director complains that the audience has read far too much: "they have read horrible amounts of literary staff" (*Allein sie haben schrecklich viel gelesen*).[58] The director is of course concerned with practical issues: how to entertain the audience who already knows the old texts.

Goethe radically rereads the old story of the frustrated scholar Faust who strikes a deal with the devil and after a highly exciting but sinful life winds up in the flames of Hell. That Goethe breaks with the established theological Faust tradition becomes amply clear in the second prologue which takes place not in the theatre but in the more elevated and certainly more sacred place of heaven. Here we are privy to an amicable conversion between God and the devil. Faust is traditionally a play about sin and its consequences, but at the beginning of the Prologue the three angels Raphael, Gabriel and Michael unanimously depict creation and the world as having never undergone anything like the fall. Sin is in fact conspicuous by its absence. The three angels unanimously praise God's "deeds which are glorious now as on the first day," the day of creation. This world is certainly not troubled by original sin. Could this lack of concern for original sin have anything to do with the redemption brought about by the new Adam, Jesus Christ? We hear nothing about Jesus; neither do we hear anything about the trinity.

Instead of the trinity we encounter something close to friendship that seems to bind God to the devil and the devil to God. Indeed, God himself denies any ill feelings towards Mephistopheles. He explicitly says to him that he "has never hated people like him" (*Ich habe deinesgleichen nie gehaßt*).[59] In a way the devil even agrees with the worldview of the uncorrupted angels in so far as he also denies any corruption and confirms the pristine non-lapsarian nature of the world: "the small God of the world remains always the same and is as astounding as on the first day" (*Der kleine Gott der Welt bleibt stets von gleichen Schlag,/Und ist so wunderlich als wie am ersten Tag*).[60] Mephistopheles does of course not like this state of affairs and his perception of God's creation is "as always cordially bad" (*wie immer, herzlich schlecht*).[61] What the devil particularly dislikes is what Rosenzweig criticizes as the old thinking. Mephistopheles is piqued by "the semblance of heavenly light" which God has

---

58 Goethe, *Werke. 'Hamburger Ausgabe' Dramen 1*, Vol.3. p. 10.
59 Ibid., p. 18.
60 Ibid., p. 17.
61 Ibid.

bestowed upon humanity. He reproaches God for having endowed humanity with the *logos* (reason):

> I wish you had not given him [i.e. humanity] the semblance of heavenly light; he calls it reason (*Vernunft*) and employs it merely to be more animalistic than any animal.[62]

The devil here engages in a critique of theological and philosophical thought which is akin to Spinoza's analysis of the way in which humanity's assumed rationality is bound up with the animalistic realm of the appetites and the passions. Mephistopheles here delineates a naturalism that is as radical as that propounded by Spinoza and Spinoza's naturalism, "the insistence that human being's are completely immersed in the natural order and are not to be understood outside it, is the most uncompromising naturalism that can be imagined."[63]

God's interaction with Mephistopheles is mild and accommodating; especially if compared with the conflicts in the human world which are often justified by appeals to an higher realm, be it God, be it reason, or the secular vistas of a better world (i.e. nationalism, Stalinism, fascism, etc). It is therefore not surprising that the prologue in heaven closes with an expression of warmth and gratitude: Mephistopheles is quite pleased that a "high Lord" such as God "speaks so humanly with the devil himself" (*Es ist gar hübsch von einem großen Herrn,/So menschlich mit dem Teufel selbst zu sprechen*).[64] This is quite an important quote and the import of its semantic field is often lost in translation.

David Luke translates "So menschlich mit dem Teufel selbst zu sprechen" in a metaphorical sense, namely as "man to man talk."[65] However, the "humanly," the "menschlich" of the German original, is important. To begin with it sheds an ironic light on what Mephistopheles criticized as the animalistic use of reason within humanity itself a few lines previously. This ironic twist is quite illuminating, because it brings to the fore that God is more human than humanity, precisely because he is able to talk humanly with the devil. Humans fall prey to voraciousness, and are, in Mephistopheles' words, animalistic due to their quasi-heavenly, logos based, and apparently rationalistic hostility towards what they perceive as the devil. The devil in question here is of course not Mephistopheles, who gets along quite cordially with the "high Lord" in heaven, but another human individual; or another religious and/or ethnic group who promulgate and/or lives out what is perceived to be a wrong, irrational or satanic point of view or way of life.

We can detect a further ironic reference here: one that concerns the public reputation of Spinoza as a devil of sorts within the seventeenth- and

---

62 Ibid.
63 Hampshire, *Spinoza and Spinozism*, p. xxiv.
64 Goethe, *Werke. 'Hamburger Ausgabe' Dramen 1* Vol. 3, p. 19.
65 Goethe. *Faust. Part One*, trans. by David Luke (Oxford: Oxford University Press, 1998), p. 12.

eighteenth-century philosophical discourse.[66] From the seventeenth- until well into the middle of the eighteenth-century, Spinoza did not only serve as a convenient target which academics and clergymen could attack in order to prove their orthodoxy, but worse still during this era, Spinoza was commonly associated if not identified with the devil himself.[67] Fred Beiser has vividly depicted the satanic horror which the sheer mentioning of Spinoza's name could evoke between around 1670 and around 1750:

> Such was Spinoza's reputation that he was often identified with Satan himself. Spinozism was seen as not only one form of atheism, but as the worst form. Thus Spinoza was dubbed the "Euclides atheisticus", the "princeps atheorum."[68]

Goethe composed the Prologue in Heaven around 1800. So at this time the association of Spinoza with Mephistopheles would have been a historical rather than an actual event. Nevertheless, the sheer fact that a philosopher whose motto was to be non-scandalous and cautious (*caute*) could yet still be equated with the devil around the time Goethe was born illustrates the highly ideologically charged nature of attributing a devilish character to any given individual or group.

Rather than warranting condemnation, the true nature of condemnation is self-referential: it condemns itself. As René Girard has pointed out, "Satan or the devil, which are interchangeable titles in the New Testament, is the 'accuser,' the power of accusation and the power of the process resulting in blaming and eliminating a substitute for the real cause of the community's troubles."[69] Even though it targets particular people and groups, evil seems to be an impersonal force that does its work via what Girard calls mimetic contagion: "There is no real subject within this mimetic contagion, and that is finally the meaning of the title 'prince of this world,' if it is recognized that Satan *is* the absence of being."[70] Goethe's God is so relaxed while talking to Mephistopheles, because he knows that evil is not a force that necessarily threatens anyone.

The high Lord of the Prologue in Heaven seems to have taken on board Spinoza's discussion of good and evil as modes of thinking rather than as constituting existing things: "As far as good and evil are concerned, they also indicate nothing positive in things, considered in themselves, nor are they anything other than modes of thinking, or notions we form because we compare

---

66 For a discussion of the early Spinoza reception see Michael Czelinski-Uesbeck's *Der Tugendhafte Atheist: Studien zur Vorgeschichte der Spinoza-Renaissance in Deutschland* (Würzburg: Könighausen & Neumann, 2007).

67 Czelinski-Uesbeck points out that at the beginning of the eighteenth century anyone was labeled an atheist who deviated from orthodox theology. See Ibid., p. 24.

68 Beiser's *The Fate of Reason*, p. 48.

69 Girard, *I see Satan Fall like Lightening*, translated with a foreword by James G. Williams (New York: Orbis Books, 2001), p. xii.

70 Ibid., p. 69.

things to one another."[71] Goethe's God can afford to be relaxed in his dealings with the devil because his understanding of evil is Spinozist. He knows that evil is an imaginary or, in other words, abstract category which humanity adapts in order to express its various aversions. Clearly Goethe's God has pondered Spinoza's argument according to which

> the true knowledge of good and evil is only abstract, *or* universal, and the judgment we make concerning the order of things and the connection of causes, so that we may be able to determine what in the present is good or evil for us, is imaginary, rather than real.[72]

Good and evil are abstract and universal categories which we impose upon particular experiences. The imaginary nature of good and evil arises in the gulf that separates the abstract nomenclature from the complexity of particular experience.

Goethe radicalizes Spinoza's critique of abstractions as products of the imagination, when he opts for a remarkable form of indecision (or what Derrida would later call ghostliness) in political and moral debates. In an important essay John K. Noyes explained why, unlike Herder, Goethe does not launch into a clear condemnation of harmful political practices such as colonialism and other forms of exploitation. The decisive issue is paradoxically indecision:

> I would argue that it is this indecision that prevents Goethe from taking the same stance that Herder had taken on the detrimental effects commerce and colonialism have on other cultures, or from consequentially developing his views on colonial violence. To Herder it was quite clear that human activity involves a moral choice between improving the lot of others and exploiting them for one's own material gain. Because Goethe problematizes the concept of choice (again most notably in *Elective Affinities*), both improvement and exploitation begin to blur into the same natural principle of circulation. It is through the movements of capital that nature-as-commerce can enter into association with pantheistic nature and nature as social harmony. In this sense it can be said that economic nature acquires a certain fluidity that makes its essence increasingly indeterminate—or to Goethe's eye, nature becomes a field that can and must be described in multiple registers.[73]

Goethe reads Spinoza's discussion of good and evil as part of a description of nature as being fluid rather being fixed into a specific essence (i.e. either good or evil). The fluidity that marks nature in its entirety calls for indecision as the

---

71 Spinoza, *Ethics*, p. 115.
72 Ibid., p. 149.
73 Noyes, "Goethe on Cosmopolitanism and Colonialism: *Bildung* and the Dialectic of Critical Mobility," *Eighteenth-Century Studies* 39 (Winter 2006), pp. 443–462 (457).

most realistic and adequate response to the ceaseless shifting which is nothing else but nature's peculiar way of existing. The words we adapt to depict one particular aspect of nature are thus constantly subject to revision, because things are not as they seem to our limited perception. In this way a threat only becomes a threat once we make it into one. This is precisely what Goethe's God has truly grasped. In contrast to humanity, the high Lord engages in a friendly manner with Mephistopheles and does not condemn him. This open-mindedness offers a striking contrast to the judgmental and often violent tone which characterizes human interaction with what has been perceived as the devil or as devilish: Spinoza and Spinozism.

In Goethe's Prologue in Heaven, the devil appraises his amicable dealings with God as the hidden meaning behind the theological concept according to which humanity has been created in the Divine image: humans are only able to imitate the 'high Lord' of creation once they will have learned to become well-disposed to what they perceive as a threat. In a sense Mephistopheles criticizes the reductions which Rosenzweig has in mind when he questions the old thinking and to which Spinoza's interpretation of substance as that "which is in itself and is conceived through itself" offers an alternative. This Spinozist alternative avoids reducing an entity to something that it is not. A human being or human ethnic and/or religious group is not the devil. Likewise no part of humanity can claim to be God or to be closer to God than any other part of humanity. Again this would be a reduction brought about by reason. It is a reason and logos based reduction that, as Mephistopheles points out, has serious social, religious and political repercussions: this abuse of reason makes humanity more violent or more voracious than any violence encountered in the animal world.

Mephistopheles' gratitude to God for engaging with him on a human rather than a voracious level has another important point of reference. Scholars have so far ignored the way in which Mephistopheles' description of his interaction with the "high Lord" alludes to Goethe's characterization of his classicist play *Iphigenia on Tauris*. They have interpreted Goethe's expression "absolutely devilishly human" as description of his Iphigenia drama to denote the radically nontheological, non-transcendent character of the play.[74] They have ignored its ironic and philosophical/theological reference to the amicable relationship between the devil and the Almighty in *Faust*. In a letter of 19 January 1802 to Schiller Goethe characterizes his "Hellenizing play" (*gräzierendes Schauspiel*) as "absolutely devilishly human" (*es ist ganz verteufelt human*).[75] What does Goethe mean by "devilishly human?"

In order to unpack this term we have to return to Mephistopheles' sentence about God speaking humanly with the devil. As we have seen in this context

---

74 Weisinger, *The Classical Façade*, p. 108.
75 *Der Briefwechsel zwischen Schiller und Goethe*, Vol. 2 (Frankfurt a. M.: Insel, 1977), p. 929.

there is an implicit and ironic contrast with human communities who cannot speak humanly with the devil. By being unable to do so they become more animalistic, in the sense of violent (i.e. voracious) than animals. Their use or rather abuse of reason in forms of thought that reduces the other to a satanic entity serves to justify this violence on moral, theological or political grounds. According to Goethe the litmus test for being human is precisely this capacity to speak humanly with what strikes us as dangerous, threatening or immoral— in short, devilish. Hence his characterization of *Iphegenia on Tauris* as "absolutely devilishly human" play. It is humanistic precisely because it engages rather than excludes the devil. Is this not what God does in the Prologue in Heaven? This seems to be Goethe's understanding of humanity being formed in the image of divinity. To imitate the "high Lord" we must be able to speak humanly, not only with those whom we consider to be respectable and a part of our society, but also with those who are excluded, who are marginalized, and with those who are seen as a threat and provocation to our ethnic and religious identity.

This capability to engage with rather than to cheat and conquer the barbarian is of course what distinguishes the main protagonist of Goethe's play *Iphigenia* and what sets her apart from the Greek sources. Goethe emphasizes this distance to the classical sources when he calls the play "absolutely devilishly human." In doing so he both counteracts to and accepts Schiller's critique of the play as violating classical conceptions of tragedy. According to Schiller (letter of April 4, 1797) Goethe composes individual characters á la Shakespeare, whereas the ancient Greeks put on stage "idealistic masks and not true individuals" (*idealistische Masken und keine eigentliche Individuen*).[76] Harking back to Spinoza's analysis of good and evil as abstractions, Goethe agrees with Schiller while at the same time disagreeing with him. How does he do so? He argues that his play is indeed nonidealistic. However, he also maintains that this absence of idealism frees *Iphegenia on Tauris* from abstractions and thus makes it more truthful in the sense of realistic (in the following chapter we will see how George Eliot sees a close affinity between her realism and that of Goethe and Spinoza). In his reply to Schiller's critique Goethe describes the abstract stylization of characters in both ancient poetry and ancient sculpture.[77] Goethe links this abstract characterization to what Spinoza has described as the imaginary nature of terms like good and evil which equate a particular experience with a universal value judgment. Goethe understands his art as a way of making fluid the abstract nature of moral value judgments; be they the distinction between good and evil or the divide that presumably separates the barbarian (non-Greek Thoas) from the civilized (Iphigenia's Greek family).

---

76 *Der Briefwechsel zwischen Schiller und Goethe*, Vol. 1, p. 364.
77 Ibid., p. 365.

7. Goethe's Iphigenia *and the Equality of Athens and Jerusalem*

In *Iphigenie auf Tauris* Goethe puts on stage the deleterious divide between the civilized and the barbarian. His play is a revision of Euripedes' Iphigenia drama. Goethe shifts the emphasis away from the relation between gods and men to a concern with intercultural conflict. Whereas in Euripides the deity Artemis asks for human sacrifices, Goethe turns this sacrificial aspect into the main social trait that distinguishes the barbarism of the Taureans from the civilization of the Greeks.[78] Yet the play questions the social and cultural validity of a binary opposition between the civilized and the primitive. How does it do so? The second scene of the play presents a conversation between Agamemnon's daughter and Arkas, a messenger of the king of Tauris. In this dialogue Iphigenia conceives of the foreign as the homely. Here she implicitly alludes to the violence inherent in her own Greek family history (i.e. the curse of Atreus). In this way she learns to understand the barbarism that forms part of her "civilized" home.

Thoas, the King of Tauris, confronts Iphigenia with the history of violence that pertains to her own Greek background (see Act 5/Scene 3, lines 1937–1943). Goethe's and, by implication Herder's, notion of *Humanität* eludes the binary opposition between civilization and barbarism. Hierarchical rankings of culture result in the perpetration of violence. They are attempts at the elimination of humanity's indebtedness to nature. The other appears in the light of the nonhuman, be it the natural (revealingly primitive people are called *Naturvölker* in German) or the animalistic. As Adorno has astutely put it in his famous essay "On the Classicism of Goethe's Iphigenia" ("*Zum Klassizismus von Goethes Iphigenie*"), "Iphigenia negotiates the notion of humanity out of the experience of its antinomy."[79] In Tauris the homely thus appears to be strange.

When her brother Orestes arrives on the island (just after having killed his mother Clytemnestra) he tries to persuade his sister to elope with him without saying goodbye to Thoas, the King of Tauris. The play here questions the enlightenment's self-understanding as civilization. As Adorno has put it, "*by dint of his antithesis to myth Orestes threatens to fall prey to it.*"[80] The play centers on Iphigenia's refusal to treat "the barbarian" in a humiliating manner. She informs him of her intention to leave Tauris together with her brother. This news enrages Thoas. Iphigenia's sense of grace, however, soothes him and

---

78 Goethe's revision of both the Iphigenia myth and the Faust folktale could be best described in terms of Walter Benjamin's notion of interruption. See John T. Hamilton's *Soliciting Darkness. Pindar, Obscurity, and the Classical Tradition* (Cambridge, MA: Harvard University Press, 2003), p. 245.

79 Adorno, *Noten zur Literatur. Gesammelte Schriften Band 11*, ed. by Rolf Tiedemann (Darmstadt: Wissenschaftliche Buchgesellschaft, 1998), 500.

80 Adorno, *Noten zur Literatur*, 512.

he allows her to set sail with Orestes for her Greek homeland (see Act V/ Scene 3, lines 1983–1991).

In the closing dialogue of the play, Iphigenia does not celebrate the enlightenment notion of tolerance. Instead she argues that it is the practice of hospitality that bridges over ethnic divisions and conflicts. What role does this closing dialogue play within the overall structure of a drama that attempts to renegotiate the meaning of the terms civilized and barbarous? Why does Goethe avoid the Enlightenment term "tolerance?" As Derrida has recently pointed out, the "word 'tolerance' is first of all marked by a religious war between Christians, or between Christians and non-Christians."[81] Most importantly, this concept introduces a hierarchical divide between those who are tolerant and those who are tolerated. It thus presupposes a ranking between different religious and ethnic groups.

This is why Derrida prefers the notion of hospitality to that of tolerance. The former engages with the foreign within a non-hierarchical context, while the latter only refrains from the physical extinction of what appears to be strange or alien:

> But tolerance remains scrutinized hospitality, always under surveillance, parsimonious and protective of its sovereignty. [. . .] We offer hospitality only on the condition that the other follows our rules, our way of life, even our language, our culture, our political system, and so on. That is hospitality as it is commonly understood and practiced, a hospitality that gives rise, with certain conditions, to regulated practices, laws, and conventions on a national and international— indeed, as Kant says in a famous text, a "cosmopolitan"—scale. But pure or unconditional hospitality does not consist in such an *invitation*. [. . .] Pure and unconditional hospitality, hospitality *itself*, opens or is in advance open to someone who is neither expected nor invited, to whomever arrives as an absolutely foreign *visitor*, as a new *arrival*, nonidentifiable and unforeseeable, in short, wholly other. I would call this a hospitality of *visitation* rather than *invitation*.[82]

Derrida thus takes issue with the implicit hierarchical gradation which "tolerance" as "scrutinized" hospitality establishes between those who invite and those who are invited. An invitation unfolds according to "regulated practices, laws and conventions." Iphigenia, by contrast, undergoes a visitation while enjoying Thoas' hospitality. She realizes that her Greek standard of civilization fails to establish her superiority if confronted with the assumed barbarism of Tauris. Iphigenia thus recognizes how civilization is sustained by the copresence of its fantasized other: how barbarism always already exists on equal terms with the civilized aspirations of Greek culture. This collapse of binary

---

81 Giovanna Borradori, *Philosophy in a Time of Terror. Dialogues with Jürgen Habermas and Jacques Derrida* (Chicago: University of Chicago Press, 2003), p. 126.

82 Borradori, *Philosophy in a Time of Terror*, 128–129.

oppositions does not exclusively exist in the supposedly self-referential realm of language. It has social consequences, because it confounds the hierarchical construction of what it means to be Greek (civilized) or non-Greek (barbarian).

In her closing dialogue with Thoas, Iphigenia thus does not establish a legal or political treatise. Rather she depicts the prospect of a future interaction between the homely and the strange that unfolds via visitation rather than invitation. A "friendly hospitality" (*freundlich Gastrecht*) will bridge the gulf between different cultural communities. The different thus remains different but is no longer separated from what seemingly opposes it. Now disconnected difference becomes familiar. Significantly Iphigenia includes Thoas into her family. At the end of the play she emphasizes that his difference has in fact entered her family home. She no longer considers his strangeness in a detached legal or political manner as separated sphere of existence. Even though he is not related to her family, Iphigenia includes him into her kinship group. This becomes abundantly clear when she calls him "father":

> Let hospitality be the link between us.
> Then we shall not forever be cut off
> And driven apart. Dear to me
> And valued as my father was, so are
> You now; my soul will always bear this mark
> Upon it.[83]

Hospitality thus de-eternalizes geographic and cultural separation. Significantly, Iphigenia does not depict the Greeks as initiator of this cordial relationship. Rather, the "friendly hospitality" of which she speaks traces the itinerary of a visitation: it moves from Tauris to Greece (*Von dir zu uns*). It literally arrives on Greek shores as a visitor. Unfortunately this aspect of visitation is lost in English translation: the German original clearly states that it is due to the "barbarian" rather than the "civilized" that separations are breached, which could result in violence if they remain cut off from each other. The link between you (the "barbarian") and us (the Greeks, the "civilized") moves "from you to us" (*Von dir zu uns*). According to Iphigenia, Thoas the barbarian, rather than her own people, prevents a potential clash of civilizations by initiating a visitation that turns porous a rigid nomenclature, dividing the "barbarian" from the "civilized," or, a propos Faust, "good" from "evil." Previously, Iphigenia has rejected her brother Orestes' demand to deceive "the barbarian Thoas" by revealing the destruction of the other as coinciding with self-destruction:

> I have never learned the practice of deceiving,
> Of tricking someone out of something. Lies!

83　Goethe, *Plays. Egmont. Iphigenia in Tauris. Torquato Tasso*, trans. and ed. by Frank G. Ryder (New York: Continuum, 2002), p. 143. Goethe, *Werke. 'Hamburger Ausgabe' Dramatische Dichtungen III* Vol. 5, p. 67.

Oh, wretched lies! They do not free the heart
As any word spoken in truth can do.
They bring no solace to us, only fear
To those who forge them secretly, come back
Like arrows sped from bows, turned by a god,
Striking the marksman.[84]

The image of the arrow that a god turns back upon the one who first set it off, describes the opposite of Spinoza's notion of self-preservation: the self that sets out to destroy the other only destroys itself. This seems to be God's or nature's inevitable course and humanity ignores to take cognizance of this itinerary at its peril. If it does so it risks self-destruction. The study of god or nature is thus a practical and political task: it ensures the well-being of a given individual or given group.[85] It eventuates in Goethe's daring interpretation of the biblical account of the creation of humanity in the image of God: humanity only lives up to its divine origin if it is open to a specter-like visitation by what it considers to be threatening and inferior. Only then does it truly imitate God, He who seems to have an open door policy as regards the devil in both the biblical book of *Job* and in Goethe's *Faust*. The following chapter will analyze the way in which George Eliot's realism performs a similar kind of visitation. As we shall see, Eliot conceptualizes realist literature as critique of ideological exclusion.

---

84 Goethe, *Plays*, p. 121. Goethe, *Werke. 'Hamburger Ausgabe' Dramatische Dichtungen III* Vol. 5, p. 45.

85 According to Walter Burkert this abstention from a wild form of self-preservation is a universal economic phenomenon: Burkert, *Creation of the Sacred.* (Cambridge, MA: Harvard University Press, 1996), p. 140.

CHAPTER 8

THE SIGNIFICANCE OF THE INSIGNIFICANT: GEORGE ELIOT'S *DANIEL DERONDA* AND THE LITERATURE OF WEIMAR CLASSICISM

1. Introduction: Spinoza, the Literature of Weimar Classicism, and how Eliot Distinguishes Morality from Ideology

In the previous chapter we have seen how Goethe characterized Spinoza's thought as ghostly. We have also analyzed the ways in which he reinterpreted pagan (*Iphigenia*) and folk myths (*Faust*) in terms of a certain haunting that confounds the exclusionary devices of ideological agitation. In this way Goethe's God does not exclude or banish his supposed adversary, the devil. Spinoza's ghost (or, in other words, Spinoza's legacy) seems to trigger visitations that outdo various kinds of dualism as well as to upend the cultural and political validity of forms of exclusion.

This chapter focuses on how Eliot distinguishes morality from the practices of exclusion that characterize the workings of ideology. Eliot's critique of ideology emerges from her reading of Spinoza and the literature of Weimar Classicism. Spinoza's analysis of theology as anthropomorphism and Goethe and Herder's attempt to develop a new kind of literature that comes close to the impartiality of scientific observation constitute the intellectual background of Eliot's definition of morality. What causes Eliot's discomfort with a possible confusion of the moral with the ideological? There is a striking clash between ideology and what Lawrence Rothfield has called "the 'critical' realism of Balzac, Flaubert, and Eliot."[1] Rothfield links the discourse of critical realism to the meticulousness that characterizes the sciences.[2] He pinpoints the emergence of critical realism sometime "near the end of the eighteenth century."[3] This is precisely the time when Goethe and Herder redefined the literary along scientific lines, influenced by Spinoza's scientific approach toward the study of nature.

The first part of this chapter discusses Eliot's appreciation of an impartial mode of writing, which steers free of ideological distortions and which she associates with the literary project of Weimar Classicism. A second issue involved in Eliot's critique of ideology will be discussed in the main part of this article. Ideology in whatever form is based on practices of inclusion and exclusion: ideology refers to morality in order to justify the exclusion of certain groups of people from mainstream society. By distinguishing morality from

---

1 Lawrence Rothfield, *Vital Signs: Medical Realism in Nineteenth-Century Fiction* (Princeton, NJ: Princeton University Press, 1992), p. 8.
2 Ibid., p. 18.
3 Ibid., p. 8.

ideology Eliot therefore distances morality from practices of exclusion in general and of the exclusion of the Jews in particular. But she does not confine her analysis of ideology to the ethical sphere alone. Instead she relates ethics to aesthetics and vice versa. Ideology is not only a moral failure; it also produces art that distorts reality. Formally, it is realism that critiques such fictions of the real. Eliot finds in both Spinoza's *Ethics* and in the literature of Weimar Classicism intellectual support for this understanding of critical realism.

Finally, I consider Eliot's artistic working through of both Spinoza and the literature of Weimar Classicism. Section 2 analyzes the character Daniel Deronda as embodiment of the Herderean capability to see the world from another person's point of view. It is this capability that makes him seem morally eccentric and insignificant to society at large. Sections 3 and 4 analyze intertextual references to two Goethe works. It will be shown that here too Eliot further develops Goethe's distinction between morality and ideology: her allusions are to two plays by Goethe that recognize those who have been excluded by various ideological practices.

2. The Legacy of Spinoza and the "Immoral Literature" of Goethe

In the Mid-1850s Eliot set out to translate Spinoza's *Ethics*. This translation "was finished (though it was not published) in the spring of 1856."[4] As part of his critique of Descartes' mind-body dualism, Spinoza questions the presumed harmony between the mind's conception of things and the actual constitution of these things.[5] Spinoza argues that human cognition does not present an accurate account of nature. Instead it forms "universal ideals of natural things as much as" it does "of artificial ones."[6]

For an accurate understanding of Eliot's critique of the alleged immorality of Goethe's work it is crucial to take into account Spinoza's argument that mental constructs are distortions of the real. Spinoza discusses the difficulty of separating the fictional from the mentally constructed as part and parcel of his critical inquiry into the fallacious foundations of certain moral propositions. He argues that the idea of sin comes into being at the point at which the mind realizes how nature diverges from cognitive models: "So when they [human minds] see something happen in Nature which does not agree with the model they [human minds] have conceived of this kind of thing, they believe that Nature itself has failed or sinned, and left the thing imperfect."[7] Here then

---

4 Tim Dolin, *George Eliot* (Oxford: Oxford University Press, 2005), p. 27.
5 Spinoza's questioning of Descartes mind-body divide has a realist agenda: the mind cannot exist without its empirical, corporeal foundation, and so Spinoza calls the mind the idea of the body. According to Rothfield this interdependence between consciousness and corporeality also marks the literature of critical realism: Rothfield, *Vital Signs*, p. 166.
6 Spinoza, *Ethics*, 114.
7 Ibid.

morality itself can fall prey to fictitiousness. If it does so, it becomes immoral, because it labels as sin or failure anything that does not coincide with its cognitive model of the world. In this way morality turns discriminatory and exclusive.

Spinoza thus criticizes a morality that has turned into ideology. At this point the moral can justify the exclusions practiced by the ideological. It is this possible confusion of morality with the exclusionary practices of ideology that is a major concern within the literature of Weimar Classicism. Eliot sees in the literature of Weimar Classicism a force that avoids the subjugation of morality to ideology. Whereas an ideological morality excludes and discriminates against certain groups of people, critical realism attempts to be inclusive. In her essays, Eliot praises the literature of Weimar Classicism for such a large and all-inclusive perspective. The method of German classical literature is that of non-specialization. As she makes clear in "The Future of German Philosophy," "Lessing, Herder, Goethe, and Schiller [. . .] were productive in several departments."[8] She goes on to highlight the creative potential of such a non-exclusive approach: "Those who decry versatility—and there are many who do so in other countries besides Germany—seem to forget the immense service rendered by the *suggestiveness* of versatile men, who come to the subject with fresh, unstrained minds."[9] It is, however, not only the non-versatile, specialized scholar (whom Eliot calls "exclusive inquirer"[10]) who has much to learn from the literature of Germany's classical age. Related to the issue of versatility as discussed in the quote above, is the literary attempt to provide an impartial representation of reality: Herder's and Goethe's works exemplify a striving for impartiality while always being cognizant that they cannot fully attain a completely unbiased approach. In her characterization of Daniel Deronda, George Eliot illustrates Herder's theoretical work on versatility as empathy with the oblique, the neglected and the almost forgotten past. Rather than concur with the judgmental conclusions a given society has established as moral truths, Deronda attempts to understand the life and opinions of those who are moral outcasts.

This attitude bears a striking resemblance to Goethe's refusal to spell out moral judgments, which distinguishes his literary work from much of the moralistic literature of the eighteenth and nineteenth centuries. Significantly, in her essays, Eliot defends Goethe's novel *Wilhelm Meister* against the charge of constituting immoral literature. In the English society of the eighteenth and nineteenth centuries, Goethe, as Rosemary Ashton has pointed out, "had been chosen to stand for the general tendency of German literature to corrupt."[11]

---

8   George Eliot, "The Future of German Philosophy," in *The Essays of George Eliot*, ed. Thomas Pinney (London: Routledge, 1963), p. 149.

9   Ibid.

10 Ibid.

11 Rosemary Ashton, *The German Idea: Four English Writers and the Reception of German Thought, 1800–1860* (Cambridge University Press, 1980), p. 148.

Eliot asks: "But is *Wilhelm Meister* an immoral book?"[12] She explains that Goethe's lack of moral bias does not make him an immoral writer. An impartial approach accounts for this lack of direct moral judgment, and itself produces a text capable of gripping the reader's attention:

> As long as you keep to an apparently impartial narrative of facts you will have earnest eyes fixed on you in rapt attention, but no sooner do you begin to betray symptoms of an intention to moralise, or to turn the current of facts towards a personal application, then the interest of your hearer will slacken, his eyes will wander, and the moral dose will be doubly distasteful from the very sweet-meat in which you have attempted to insinuate it.[13]

And yet, Eliot acknowledges that a state of impartiality can never be fully reached. The writer who aims at a non-biased representation of characters thus composes "an apparently impartial narrative." Impartiality has therefore an impact on literary style.

What, however, are the implications of an impartial literary style for an accurate understanding of the immorality inherent in harsh moral judgments? Literature that sets out to present its narratives in an impartial and realistic mode enables its readers to learn from particulars rather than abstractions. Eliot clearly attributes greater pedagogical potential to an attention to anthropological particularity than to the generality of moral rules:

> But a few are taught by their own falls and their own struggles, by their experience of sympathy, and help and goodness in the "publicans and sinners" of these modern days, that the line between the virtuous and the vicious, so far from being a necessary safeguard to morality, is itself an immoral fiction.[14]

Here she contrasts the existential ("their own falls and their own struggles") with the cognitively constructed ("the line between the virtuous and the vicious"). She differentiates between actions and the moralistic meaning which is imposed upon them. The gulf that separates the existential (the realm of actions and nature's causality) from the cognitive construction of meaning gives rise to anthropomorphic fiction, a phenomenon Spinoza analyzed in his *Ethics*. These anthropomorphic fictions are ideological, because they serve to justify discriminations against certain groups of people. For example, according to Spinoza anthropomorphism depicts God as someone who wages war against certain communities in the same way in which human societies do.

In her essay on *Wilhelm Meister* Eliot takes forward Spinoza's critique of anthropomorphism when she focuses on the exclusionary force of moral judgments. She appreciates the Spinozistic heritage by way of Goethe's work.

---

12   George Eliot, "The Morality of Wilhelm Meister," in *Essays of George Eliot*, p. 144.
13   Ibid., p. 145.
14   Ibid., p. 147.

In the eighteenth and nineteenth centuries Spinoza was commonly identified as the prime cause responsible for the presumed immorality of Goethe's writings. In fact, the famous Spinoza controversy was triggered by Lessing's enthusiasm for Goethe's poem "Prometheus."[15] An espousal of Goethe's work thus testified to one's Spinozist affiliations. In what ways did Goethe's *Wilhelm Meister* in particular and the literature of Weimar Classicism in general inform the conception of *Daniel Deronda*? As Marc E. Wohlfarth has pointed out, Eliot composed her last novel in the form of the *Bildungsroman*.[16] It thus of course defines itself in relation to *Wilhelm Meister*, the *locus classicus* of this generic type. Most importantly, the theme of nationalism as discussed in *Daniel Deronda* has its historical and intellectual point of reference in the writer, poet, theologian and cultural critic Herder. Herder was the first to make the case for the national independence of ethnic groups that were oppressed by imperial rule. His work was thus the driving force behind Eastern European and Jewish strivings to recuperate a national identity. Saleel Nurbhai and K. M. Newton have recently shown that:

> The form of nationalism favored by Eliot was of an anti-imperialist nature. It was associated with the desire to replace domination with self-determination— a similar motivation to that which provoked the struggles of the working classes and which could be interpreted in cabbalistic terms as the golems' search for self-awareness.[17]

The reference to the cabbala and to the golem might well be pertinent in the present context. It is, however, equally true that Eliot derived her specific understanding of an anti-imperialist nationalism from Herder's cultural theory. In an important study Bernard Semmel has thus traced Eliot's support of "cultural pluralism" to the "eighteenth-century German historian whom she referred to as 'the great Herder' [Eliot to Mr. and Mrs. Charles Bray and Sara Hennell, 5 August 1849]."[18]

A significant upshot of Herder's and Goethe's study of Spinoza is their respective appreciation of diversity in human and natural history. The textual and thematic references in *Daniel Deronda* to writers and works of Weimar

---

15 See Gérard Vallée, *The Spinoza Conversations between Lessing and Jacobi: Text with Excerpts from the Ensuing Controversy* (Lanham, MD: University Press of America, 1988).

16 See Marc E. Wohlfarth, "Daniel Deronda and the Politics of Nationalism," *Nineteenth-Century Literature* 53 (1998) p. 192.

17 Saleel Nurbhai and K. M. Newton, *George Eliot, Judaism, and the Novels: Jewish Myth and Mysticism* (New York: Palgrave, 2002), p. 153.

18 Bernard Semmel, *George Eliot and the Politics of National Inheritance* (Oxford: Oxford University Press, 1994), p. 13. The general relevance of Herder's anti-imperialist approach to diverse national communities has also been noted by Hao Li in his discussion of *Daniel Deronda*: Li, *Memory and History in George Eliot: Transfiguring the Past* (Basingstoke: Macmillan, 2000), 156–57.

Classicism have thus as their focal point the legacy of Spinoza's writing and thought. The novel's narrative voice associates the figure of Mordecai with that of Spinoza. Both live on the margins of society: the "consumptive-looking Jew, apparently a fervid student of some kind, getting his crust by quiet handicraft"[19] resembles in his lifestyle the seventeenth-century philosopher Spinoza (he is "like Spinoza"[472]). The two intellectuals share a voluntary affiliation with the poor and other social outcasts.

Mordecai's historical consciousness, however, opens up a gulf that distinguishes his thought from that of the seventeenth-century philosopher. In his slightly dismissive approach toward history and language Spinoza clearly clings to Descartes's ideal of scientific inquiry. His *Theological-Political Treatise* sharply differentiates between philosophical truth and the unreliability of historical knowledge: "Again," he emphasizes, "philosophy rests on the basis of universally valid axioms, and must be constructed by studying Nature alone, whereas faith is based on history and language."[20] As George Levine has pointed out, with Mordecai, in contrast, Eliot acknowledges "the connection between science and what appears to be mysticism."[21] The Spinozist thought of Goethe's and Herder's work fills this gap that separates the end of the seventeenth from the middle of the nineteenth century.

The relationship between Charles Darwin's scientific inquiry and Eliot's literary work is pertinent to this discussion. As Gillian Beer has shown, Darwin set the tone for Victorian scientific inquiry precisely by unfolding his explorations through a deliberately unstable, mythic and poetic linguistic register. He presents his thought in the multivalency of metaphor and in what Gillian Beer has called "an imaginative reordering of experience."[22] What precisely characterizes the poetic and speculative element of Darwin's writing and thought? Here too Spinoza's philosophy of nature was influential. Darwin received Spinoza's idea through the mediation of the literature of Weimar Classicism (that of Goethe in particular whose work incorporates both fiction and scientific inquiry).[23]

As a consequence of his literary education, Darwin deepens and develops Spinoza's anti-teleological and anti-hierarchical critique of anthropocentrism. Gillian Beer refers to Darwin's "copious imagination" which draws upon "the richness of the perceptual world."[24] This literary and imaginative approach

---

19 George Eliot, *Daniel Deronda*, ed. Terence Cave (London: Penguin, 1995), pp. 471–72. This edition hereafter cited in text.

20 Spinoza, *Theological-Political Treatise*, trans. Samuel Shirley, with introduction and notes by Seymour Feldman (Indianapolis: Hackett, 1998), p. 169.

21 George Levine, "George Eliot's Hypothesis of Reality," *Nineteenth Century Literature* 35 (1980): 19.

22 Beer, *Darwin's Plot: Evolutionary Narrative in Darwin, George Eliot, and Nineteenth-Century Fiction* (Cambridge: Cambridge University Press, 2000), p. 95.

23 For a detailed discussion of this point, see Richards, *The Romantic Conception of Life*.

24 Beer, *Darwin's Plot*, p. 73.

furthers Darwin's Spinozist aversion to both hierarchical constructions and teleological explanations of natural phenomena: "Because it refused the notion of precedent Idea with its concomitant assumption of preordained Design, Darwin's method of description placed great emphasis upon congruities within the multiple materiality of the world."[25] Darwin's Spinozist refutation of a teleological order has serious consequences for the plot of the Victorian novel:

> The question of congruity between language and physical order is evidently related to teleological issues, just as narrative order brings sharply into focus the question of precedent design. Victorian novelists increasingly seek a role for themselves within the language of the text as observer and experimenter, rather than as designer or god. Omniscience goes, omnipotence is concealed.[26]

The eclipse of teleology gives rise to the elevation of that which has commonly been demoted to insignificance in a vertical order of things. Spinoza attempted to make the insignificant philosophically significant. The exclusionary mechanisms implicit in ideology make room for a nonideological and thus non-hierarchical understanding of morality. In the seventeenth and eighteenth centuries Spinoza was infamous for having pulled down the hierarchical divide between the realms of the transcendent (God and the mind) and the immanent (Nature and the body). Goethe and his former mentor Herder set out to adapt this Spinozist undertaking to the changed context of the end of the eighteenth and the beginning of the nineteenth century. They took issue with some tendencies in Enlightenment thought which condemned both the poetic-mythic and the historical past to insignificance.

This brief account of Spinozism and its influence on eighteenth- and nineteenth-century literature sets the stage for the following discussion of Eliot's characterization of Deronda as personifying the significance of the insignificant. By so doing, Eliot distinguishes between morality and practices of exclusion which characterize the workings of ideology. Ultimately I will consider the so far neglected role of two Goethe works alluded to in *Daniel Deronda*: *Tasso* and *Iphegenia auf Tauris*. Eliot refers to these two plays in passages which question the exclusion of Jews from Victorian society. She thus refers to Goethe's work in order to distinguish between morality and discriminatory practices of ideology.

3. Herder's Historical Reason and Deronda's Poetics of the Everyday

As I have discussed in my 2003 book *German Idealism and the Jew*, important strands within Enlightenment thought tended to characterize Jews and Judaism as insipid. Within the latter part of the eighteenth century modernity was

---

25 Ibid.
26 Ibid, p. 40.

seen to demote the historical past to insignificance and the future of humanity seemed to promise its immanent perfectibility. Voltaire was the first to coin the expression "philosophy of history," when he published his introduction to his vast historical work *Essai sur les moeurs* separately under the title *La Philosophie de l'Histoire* (1765). In his *Essai* Voltaire poked fun at Jewish history and dismissed its moral, cultural and historical validity.[27]

In response to Voltaire's ridicule of both Judaism and Jewishness, Herder declared that he becomes a Jew when he reads the Old Testament. In his *Letters Concerning the Study of Theology* he thus contrasts his understanding of historical reason with Voltaire's philosophical approach: "You see," he addresses the reader,

> how sacred and valuable I find these [Jewish] books and how much—as a response to Voltaire's mockery—I am a Jew, when I read them, for do we not have to be a Greek or a Roman when we read Greeks and Romans. Each book has to be read in its contextual spirit.[28]

Turning to *Daniel Deronda*, this mode of historical empathy distinguishes Deronda's attitude toward the oblique and the foreign from that of other representatives of English culture such as Mr Grandcourt. As a young man Deronda implicitly subscribes to a Herderean notion of historical reason. His patron

> Sir Hugo let him quit Cambridge and pursue a more independent line of study abroad. The germs of this inclination had been already stirring in his boyish love of universal history, which made him want to be at home in foreign countries, and follow in imagination the travelling students of the middle ages. He longed to have the apprenticeship to life which would not shape him too definitely, and rob him of the choices that might come from free growth. (p. 180)

This passage foregrounds Deronda's Herderian empathy with the spatially and temporally distant: he "wants to be at home in foreign countries" and he sets out to imitate the boundary-crossing travel arrangements that formed a substantial part of the educational curriculum of the middle ages. His ideal of an interdisciplinary apprenticeship also evokes the notion of *Bildung* that informs Goethe's *Wilhelm Meister*. Eliot, as we have seen, recommends such nonspecialist approach in her essays (as will be discussed below).

Ironically Deronda discovers his identity through such apparent loss of self-hood. He empathizes with the despised and the oblique and yet this empathy

---

27 See Adam Suttcliffe, *Judaism and Enlightenment* (Cambridge: Cambridge University Press, 2003), pp. 231–46.

28 Herder, *Briefe das Studium der Literatur betreffend, in Herders Sämmtliche Werke*, vol. 10, ed. Bernhard Suphan [Berlin: Weidmannsche Buchhandlung, 1879], p. 143). Goethe followed Herder's approach as emphasized in Goethe's autobiography *Dichtung und Wahrheit*. See *Goethes Werke. Hamburger Ausgabe*, vol. 9, ed. Erich Trunz (Munich: Beck, 1982), p. 140.

makes him literally find himself in the other. Eliot dwells on his "strong tendency to side with objects of prejudice" (p. 206). This is not say that she unrealistically removes him from exposure to anti-Jewish sentiments. She makes clear that

> Deronda could not escape (who can?) knowing ugly stories of Jewish character-istics and occupations; and though one of his favorite protests was against the severance of past and present history, he was like others who shared his protest, in never having cared to reach any more special conclusions about Jews than that they retained the virtues and vices of a long oppressed race. (206)

The narrative voice of Eliot's last novel characterizes the status of Judaism within Victorian society as nothing else but "as a sort of eccentric fossilised form which an accomplished man might dispense with studying and leave to specialists" (p. 363). Significantly the higher echelons of English society clas-sify Deronda as someone who is socially irrelevant, that is to say, as someone who is only of specialist interest: He appears an insignificant eccentric.

It is precisely his sympathetic approach to those who do not conform to a code of propriety that makes him seem eccentric. As the narrator points out, "Daniel had the stamp of rarity in a subdued fervor of sympathy, an activity of imagination on behalf of others, which did not show itself effusively, but was continually seen in acts of considerateness that struck his companions as moral eccentricity" (p. 178). In a truly versatile manner Deronda thus combines moral qualities (sympathy) with the gift of the artist (imagination). For Mr. Grandcourt such eccentricity reduces a person's social significance. Deronda's lack of status makes Gwendolen compare his position with that of Mrs. Glasher and her children (chapter 29). What connects Deronda to Mrs. Glasher is that they share the context of social exclusion. Gwendolen makes the connection:

> Gwendolen, whose unquestioning habit it had been to take the best that came to her for less than her own claim, had now to see the position which tempted her in a new light, as a hard, unfair exclusion of others. What she had heard about Deronda seemed to her imagination to throw him into one group with Mrs Glasher and her children; before whom she felt herself in an attitude of apology—she who had hitherto been surrounded by a group that in her opinion had need to be apologetic to her. Perhaps Deronda was himself thinking these things. Could he know of Mrs Glasher? (p. 335)

Through an acquaintance with the fate of Mrs Glasher and her children, Gwendolen becomes all of a sudden confronted with the dark side of success. The passage quoted above enters into her internal dialogue about the ambigu-ity of gain. Does gain have a relation to loss? Deronda seems to figure as the conscience within her internal dispute about the sustainability of her path towards social and financial success. She seems to know the risk associated with her marriage and yet she marries nevertheless.

Deronda plays such a marginal role in the "English part" of the novel, precisely because his presence is repressed: Gwendolen's repression of her affection for him is symptomatic of the way in which Deronda's personality does not seem to be socially acceptable. Only through this suppression of the knowledge of her affection for Deronda is Gwendolen able to conform to the ideology that prescribes marriage to women as a path to social advancement. As Slavoj Žižek has pointed out, ideology does not primarily have the function of an illusion. On the contrary the ideological denotes reality:

> ideology is not simply "false consciousness", an illusory representation of reality, it is rather this reality itself which is already to be conceived as "ideological— *'ideological' is a social reality whose very existence implies the non-knowledge of its participants as to its essence*—that is, the social effectivity, the very repro-duction of which implies that the individuals 'do not know what they are doing.'"[29]

Gwendolen's sense of reality would collapse if she were not to marry Grandcourt. She is not interested in Grandcourt as an individual—in stark contrast to her real but repressed interest in Deronda. The novel offers an extraordinarily subtle presentation, over some three hundred pages, of Gwendolen's reasons for marrying Grandcourt. This presentation focuses on both her incompletely acknowledged attraction to Deronda and the social pressures that make her choose marriage as an illusory attainment of freedom. The marriage to Grandcourt is certainly not a "romantic" affair. Instead it offers the prospect of social respectability and financial independence.

In her external dealings Gwendolen has to focus on Grandcourt and avoid Deronda. This has to be reality if she wants to be consistent with the demands of the ideology that governs her society. Conversely, in the internal dialogue (as quoted above) she focuses on Deronda. Significantly she asks whether he might know of Mrs Glasher. She seems to fear knowledge. She wants to repress the relation between gain and loss, which Deronda seems to bring to light. This knowledge of the coincidence between failure and success preconditions Deronda's imaginative sympathy: for him this division within humanity does not exist. At the end of the novel he is not an ethnocentric nationalist, and as Kwame Anthony Appiah has recently pointed out, "in claiming a Jewish loyalty—an 'added soul'—Deronda is not rejecting a human one."[30]

What thematic and structural role does Deronda's imaginative sympathy play within the larger ambit of the novel? *Daniel Deronda* has often been criti-cized for a lack of compositional coherence. Deirdre David has described the novel as "fatally, if seductively, split, for Eliot is unable to reconcile her fine

---

29   Slavoj Žižek, *The Sublime Object of Ideology* (London: Verso, 1989), p. 21.
30   Appiah, *Cosmopolitanism: Ethics in a World of Strangers* (New York: Norton, 2006), p. xvii.

study in psychological and social realism with the strange, difficult and sometimes virtually unreadable Deronda narrative of Jewish identity."[31] Why does
this issue of disconnection figure so prominently in critical discussions of a
work of fiction whose narrative strands set out to interconnect what seems to
be disjointed? Gillian Beer has rightly taken issue with the posited dualism of
English and Jewish society:

> Indeed, to conceive of Jews and English entirely in dualistic terms misses
> the point that what Eliot is exploring in the novel is not polarity but
> common sources: the common culture, story, and genetic inheritance of
> which the Jews and the English are two particularly strongly intercon-
> nected expressions, which raises questions of transmission.[32]

Yet critics tend to allocate a binding force only to the miraculous, quasi-
fairy tale nature of the novel: so far they have exclusively allocated this con-
necting force to its Jewish strand. In an important article George Levine has
thus discussed *Daniel Deronda* in terms of Eliot's break with the previous
realism of *Adam Bede, Felix Holt* and *Middlemarch*.[33] He attributes this break
to Deronda's and Mordecai's non-commonsensical idealism.

How, though, did Eliot define realism in her preceding work? In the famous
chapter of *Adam Bede* entitled "In which the story pauses a little," she explains
how inclusion of the oblique and the socially insignificant distinguishes a realistic mode of writing from a style geared to aesthetic rules and lofty theories:

> Therefore let Art always remind us of them ["old women scraping carrots with
> their work-worn hands, those heavy clowns taking holiday in a dingy pot-house,
> those rounded back and stupid weather-beaten faces that have bent over the
> spade and done the rough work of the world"]; therefore let us always have men
> ready to give the loving pains of a life to the faithful representing of common-
> place things—men who see beauty in these commonplace things, and delight in
> showing how kindly the light of heaven falls on them.[34]

Her realist mode of writing thus defamiliarizes what has become familiar.
It endows the everyday with an aura of the miraculous. In this approach Eliot
subscribes to a nonutilitarian understanding of the factual, an element common to Victorian writing and thought.[35]

---

31 Deirdre David, *Fictions of Resolution in Three Victorian Novels: "North and South,"*
    "Our Mutual Friend," "Daniel Deronda" (London: Macmillan, 1981), p. 135.
32 Beer, *Darwin's Plot*, p. 182.
33 Levine discusses this break with realism in relation to *Middlemarch*: Levine,
    "George Eliot's Hypothesis," p. 18.
34 George Eliot, *Adam Bede*, with an introduction by Leonee Ormond (London:
    Everyman, 1996), p. 201.
35 Beer has pointed out how this romantic type of materialism characterizes both
    Darwin's science and late nineteenth-century literature: Beer, *Darwin's Plot*, p. 74.

According to Eliot, realism discovers the significance of the seemingly insignificant. It brings to the fore the aesthetic ("who see beauty in these commonplace things") and the spiritual ("delight in showing how kindly the light of heaven falls on them") quality of commonplace things. This is, however, precisely Daniel Deronda's approach.[36] The narrative voice of Eliot's last novel evokes the famous chapter on realism in *Adam Bede* when it describes Daniel as neither romantic nor empiricist: "To say that Deronda was romantic would be to misrepresent him; but under his calm and somewhat self-repressed exterior there was a fervor which made him easily find poetry and romance among the events of everyday life" (p. 205). I believe that Deronda's poetics of everyday life establishes a connective thread between the Jewish and the English strands of the novel.

In order to address this issue it is necessary to look at the opening chapter where Daniel seems to cast an ironic gaze on Gwendolen who is enthralled by her pursuit of gain while gambling. To him, who sees poetry in everyday life, the exorbitant commercial glamour of the Leubronn casino appears to be "dull" (9). Alluding to this opening scene of the novel, Gwendolen will later justify her passion for gambling by saying that it "is a refuge from dulness [*sic*]," to which Daniel responds that "what we call the dulness of things is a disease in ourselves" (p. 411). What causes this disease that makes the commonplace appear to be dull and insignificant? Gwendolen's passion for gambling has a striking relation to the presence of market economic transactions. Gambling and the market economy are driven by a desire for gain. The notion of "gain" relies on the existence of its opposite, namely, "loss."

This binary opposition between gain and loss shapes a hierarchical division that separates the valuable from the valueless, the significant from the insignificant. Deronda's openness to the poetry within the realism of the everyday confounds various economic, ethnic and social hierarchies. Those who differentiate between loss and gain subscribe to a judgmental way of thinking. Deronda's "keenly perceptive sympathetic emotiveness," which does not go without a "speculative tendency" (p. 496), refrains from judging human life according to a gain-loss equation. On the contrary: "what he felt was a profound sensibility to a cry from the depth of another soul; and accompanying that, the summons to be receptive instead of superciliously prejudging" (p. 496). Deronda's receptiveness may have roots in Herder's understanding of reason

---

36 The appreciation of insignificance has of course a point of reference in both various Jewish and Christian sources. In this respect E. S. Shaffer has analyzed Daniel Deronda as Jesus figure. She makes it clear that Eliot stands in stark contrast to the institutional interpretation of Jesus. As Shaffer emphasizes, Eliot takes into account the historical critical perspective of Friedrich Strauss and others: Shaffer, *"Kubla Khan" and the Fall of Jerusalem: The Mythological School in Biblical Criticism and Secular Literature, 1770–1880* (Cambridge: Cambridge University Press, 1975), p. 181.

as a historical as well as an anthropological sensitivity. Eliot's depiction of Deronda's "profound sensibility to a cry from the depth of another soul" is influenced by Herder's conception of empathy as the capacity to feel oneself into (*fühle dich hinein*) the psychic position of some one else.[37] Rational inquiry presupposes the capacity to put oneself into the place of another, across the divides that separate the present from the past and the culturally distant from the familiar. Herder defines reason as the ability to listen: *Vernunft* (reason) is *Vernehmen* (to receive, to listen). Deronda's receptivity to the oblique, the despised and to the historical past in fact offers an intriguing illustration of Herder's understanding of reason as active listening.[38] Deronda does not confine history to the realm of the dead. Instead, he engages in a conversation with the almost forgotten past and thereby discovers his identity. He thinks "himself imaginatively into the experience of others" (p. 511). This receptive quality bridges temporal as well as geographical and cultural divisions. It presupposes the collapse of hierarchical rankings and ideological exclusions.

4. The Intertextuality of the Tasso Motive

Critics have so far paid little attention to various intertextual references to the literature of Weimar classicism in Eliot's last novel.[39] This book offers the first detailed analysis of allusions in *Daniel Deronda* to two plays that Goethe composed during his Weimar period. And a critique of hierarchical rankings and ideological exclusions lies at the heart of various allusions to two of Goethe's works in *Daniel Deronda*.

This section analyzes how the scandal surrounding Klesmer's marriage to Catherine, the daughter of Mrs. Arrowpoint, draws on Goethe's play on *Tasso*'s breach of social proprieties. The drama (*Ein Schauspiel*, in Goethe's words) *Torquato Tasso* focuses on two conceptions of art: one sees the arts as

---

37 He does so in his *This too a Philosophy of History*. See Herder, *Werke: Band 1 Herder und der Sturm und Drang 1764–1774*, ed. Wolfgang Pross (Munich: Hanser, 1984), p. 612.

38 See Herder, *Werke: Band III/1 Ideen zur Philosophie der Geschichte der Menschheit* (ed.), W. Pross, Darmstadt: Wissenschaftliche Buchgesellschaft, 2002), p. 133.

39 The specific allusions to Goethe's *Tasso* and his *Iphigenie auf Tauris* are not, however, the only textual references to the literature of Weimar Classicism. For example, Mrs. Meyrick's daughter Mab discusses the biblical book of Revelations in the light of Schiller's *Ode to Joy*: "Call it a chapter in Revelations," Mab explains to her mother, "it makes me sorry for everybody. It makes me like Schiller—I want to take the world in my arms and kiss it" (*Deronda*, p. 198). Mab is paraphrasing Schiller's *Ode to Joy*. A hymn to an inclusive universalism: "Be embraced, you millions/I give this kiss to the whole world." On this view Schiller's poetry thus outlines an inclusive universalism.

a means of reinforcing class status, whereas the other questions this conception of aesthetics as conforming to various social, economic and ethnic hierarchies. Goethe's *Tasso* emphasizes the non-hierarchical nature of artistic work. On this view art establishes the interdependence of human difference, be it in terms of class, ethnicity or gender. Goethe thus endows *Tasso* with a Spinozist poetics: poetry (and, by implication, other forms of creativity) exemplifies human interconnectedness. The aesthetic realm thus illustrates Spinoza's dictum that "man is a God to man" (*hominem homini deum esse*).[40]

In her translation of Ludwig Feuerbach's *The Essence of Christianity* (1854), Eliot employs a phrase similar to Spinoza's *hominem homini deum esse*. Here, however, the focus is on suffering rather than on the Spinozist joy in the preservation of life: "Nothing else than this: to suffer for others is divine; he who suffers for others, who lays down his life for them, acts divinely, is a God to men."[41] Goethe's play *Tasso* depicts this kind of suffering: the poet *Tasso* suffers on account of social hierarchies but he also alleviates suffering through the composition of poetry. *Tasso* primarily remedies his suffering through his creative work and yet his creative work has a social aspect because one of its aims consists in assisting its audience in the difficulties they may encounter in their lives. Poetry represents a divinely human gift to remedy injustice and inequality.

The *Tasso* motive of the novel therefore connects Deronda's nonjudgmental approach to the all-pervasive theme that centers on issues of loss and gain. But Eliot reworks central elements of Goethe's drama *Tasso*. In what follows I analyze how a subplot in *Daniel Deronda* inverts the tragic outcome of Goethe's play about the Italian Renaissance poet. In Goethe's drama, *Tasso* commits a faux pas by giving the impression of proposing to marry Leonora, the sister of the Duke of Ferrara. Why does this accusation pave the way to his social death? In proposing to Leonora, *Tasso* violates the feudal hierarchy that governs his society. He thus defiles the court that has employed him as a literary servant. In Goethe's play, *Tasso* often articulates his discontent with his position. In this way he compares his life to that of a prisoner. By contrast, poetry represents to him a signifying space free of the social hierarchy.

In an important subplot within *Daniel Deronda* Eliot deftly rearranges the story line of Goethe's play: she focuses attention on the theme of gain and loss. It is this promise of gain that infuses the social order with a quasi-libidinal aura. In Eliot's account, however, gain loses its appeal. In the main plot of the novel the prospect of success sets free libidinal energy. This energy dissipates itself in the construction of a fantasy. The fantasy in question here confers meaning on a life that triumphs over those who have failed socially and financially. A case in point is of course Gwendolen. Her story illustrates the quasi-erotic appeal of gain: she marries in order to advance socially and financially.

---

40 Spinoza, *Ethics*, p. 133, and his *Opera*, vol. 2, p. 234.
41 Feuerbach, *The Essence of Christianity*, trans. Marian Evans, 2nd ed. (London: Trübner, 1881), p. 60.

Crucially the subplot that inverts *Tasso*'s tragic violation of the social order depicts libidinal attachment as rupture with the social hierarchy, dividing those who gain from those who lose. The *Tasso* motive is crucial because it offers a striking contrast to Klesmer's and his beloved break with the social order. The daughter of the wealthy and would-be aristocratic Mrs Arrowpoint marries the musician Klesmer (employed by her mother in a way similar to *Tasso*'s position as literary servant at court) and thus loses her social and financial position—she literally abandons her heritage. The Klesmer couple thus reinterprets loss as gain. In doing so it enacts *Tasso*'s critique of the social order that gives consistency and quasi-libidinal appeal to various constructions of social hierarchy.

The Klesmer couple offers a striking contrast to Gwendolen's marriage. For Gwendolen, hierarchy imbues everyday life with an air of excitement. This is so because a hierarchical structure holds out the promise of gain. Here she can prove her superiority. Life as such is dull. It only becomes stimulating in the moment of triumph. True, both the market and the gambling hall seem to disregard class, ethnic and gender differences. This state of equality is, however, deceptive. Gambling establishes an equal playing field in order to test the strong pleasures of its participants:

> Those who were taking their pleasure at a higher strength, and were absorbed in play, showed very distant varieties of European type: Livonian and Spanish, Graeco-Italian and miscellaneous German, English aristocratic and English plebeian. Here certainly was a striking admission of human equality. (p. 8)

This concession to egalitarianism gives way to the agonistic principle of gain and loss.

Ironically, gambling does not establish Gwendolen's superiority; rather, it causes the loss of her necklace. Daniel Deronda sees the irony but he does not judge her. On the contrary he assists her by redeeming her necklace (p. 330). His non-hierarchical perception of reality is such that he does not condemn those who participate in the hierarchy of the gain-loss formula. The novel narrates how those who lose are in fact those who desire gain. Gwendolen's gambling disaster, on a microcosmic level, foreshadows the loss of her family fortune due to market speculation. Mrs. Davilow explains this state of affairs to Gwendolen. Mr. Lassmann who dissipated the wealth of the family on the market actually meant to increase it. Gwendolen, however, accuses Lassmann of theft; to which Mrs Davilow replies as follows: "No, dear, you don't understand. There were great speculations: he meant to gain. It was all about mines and things of this sort. He risked too much" (p. 233). Wish for gain thus leads to loss.

Gwendolen does not learn the true nature of the relation between gain and loss. She remains ignorant and her ignorance ultimately causes her tragedy. She succumbs to a tragic blindness. As the epigraph to chapter 21 makes clear, her will to power is the offspring of ignorance ("who having a practiced vision may not see that ignorance of the true bond between events, and false conceit of means whereby sequences may be compelled—like that falsity of eyesight which overlooks the gradations of distance, seeing that which is afar off as if it were within a step or a grasp—precipitates the mistaken soul on destruction?", p. 227). Yet her marriage to Mr. Grandcourt seems to enable her to scale the hierarchical ladder that promises a firm grasp of social prestige and significance. Her attainment of power is thus the outcome not of knowledge but ignorance. In this way the epigraph to chapter 21 poses the question as to the entanglement of power with powerlessness: "It is a common sentence that Knowledge is power; but who hath duly considered or set forth the power of ignorance?" (p. 227). The power of ignorance is precisely the enticement of ideology. Gwendolen attempts to establish a position of influence not knowing that this quest for supremacy will make her powerless. The ruin of her family fortunes makes her "taste the bitterness of insignificance" (p. 292). Her marriage to the wealthy and influential Mr. Grandcourt seems to offer a way out of social and economic obscurity. Grandcourt's name encapsulates the hierarchical nature of his life. Yet this court will imprison Gwendolen. She pays scant attention to the fact that the loss-gain relation determines not only the economic and ethnic spheres of social hierarchy. It also shapes gender relations. This is why, as woman, she cannot gain through marriage. Her economic and social gain is thus bound to turn out a loss.

Here the gain-loss theme connects Gwendolen to the Jewish strand of the novel. Both Jews and women are defined by a loss of action. The epigraph to chapter 51 describes the Greek poetess Erinna as emblematic of the gender hierarchies within society:

> Erinna is condemned
> To Spin the byssus drearily
> In insect-labour, while the throng of
> Of Gods and men wrought deeds that poets wrought in song.
>
> (p. 624)

In chapter 42 Mordecai differentiates the Greek from the Jewish people along lines that separate activity from passivity. Gentile children "admire the bravery of those who fought foremost at Marathon. . . . But the Jew has no memory that binds him to action" (p. 529). Gwendolen attempts to gain room for action through her marriage to Grandcourt. She marries in order to obtain "rank and luxuries" (p. 669) and yet the court of her married life turns out to be like a gilded prison.

She has "no choice but to endure insignificance and servitude" (p. 315). The reference to insignificance and servitude has a parallel in Goethe's *Tasso*. This parallel has a rather ironic bearing on Gwendolen's ignorant gain-loss calculation. In Goethe's play *Tasso* frequently characterizes himself as being confined to a state of servitude as subject of Alfons II, Duke of Ferrara. In a subplot that connects the novel's Jewish with its English strand, a reversal of

Tasso's tragedy takes place that starkly contrasts with the misery of Gwendolen's marriage.

Here the heroine and the hero perceive the unity of binary opposites. They forsake the gain of family fortune and thus avoid the tragedy of loss.[42] In this subplot the German Jewish musician figures as a modern reincarnation of Goethe's *Tasso*. He marries the daughter of Mrs. Arrowpoint. Mrs. Arrowpoint tells Gwendolen of her intention to write a book about *Tasso*. "So many," she declares, "have written about *Tasso*, but they are all wrong." She goes on to comment on the theme of madness, imprisonment and marriage:

> As to the particular nature of his [i.e. *Tasso*'s] madness, his feelings for Leonora, and the real cause of his imprisonment, and the character of Leonora, who, in my opinion is a cold-hearted woman, else she would have married him in spite of her brother, they are all wrong. I differ from everybody. (p. 46)

Ironically the subplot of her daughter's love affair—rather than Mrs. Arrowpoint's book project—differs from the main plot of Goethe's *Tasso*. In the novel Mrs. Arrowpoint in fact plays the role of Leonora's brother: she interdicts her daughter's marriage to Klesmer. In the play the Italian poet stands condemned for his breach of social propriety. He breaks social hierarchies when he seems to propose to Leonora, the sister of the Duke of Ferrara. Mrs. Arrowpoint's daughter, in contrast, marries the German-Jewish artist. In so doing she severely disappoints her mother, who wants her to marry Mr. Grandcourt.

This marriage designates gain whereas the union with Klesmer amounts to a loss of social and economic power. Mrs Arrowpoint castigates her daughter Catherine for her intention to become the fiancée of the German-Jewish musician:

> You will be a public fable. Every one will say that you must have made the offer to a man who has been paid to come to the house—who is nobody knows what—a gypsy, a Jew, a mere bubble of the earth. (p. 246)

In response to this onslaught Catherine evokes the genius of *Tasso*: "Never mind, mamma. . . .We know he [i.e. Klesmer] is a genius—as *Tasso* was" (p. 246). Mrs. Arrowpoint then reminds her daughter that it is "a woman's duty not to lower herself" (p. 247). Catherine abandons her position within the hierarchical gradation that shapes Victorian society. She marries Klesmer

---

42 Esther in *Felix Holt* offers an intriguing comparison to this embrace of loss. After having rejected Harold Transome's marriage proposal and after having married the destitute Felix Holt, Esther gains prominence as someone who "had renounced wealth, and chosen to be the wife of a man who said he would always be poor" (George Eliot, *Felix Holt, The Radical*, ed. William Baker and Kenneth Womack [Peterborough, ON: Broadview Press, 2000], p. 505).

and her parents disinherit her. Is her loss really a loss? Unlike Goethe's play, her and Klesmer's story does not end in dramatic upheaval. How does it accomplish this feat of an ordinary ending?

The Klesmer couple configures gain as a loss. They willingly abandon the family fortune of the Arrowpoints as if it were a poisonous appendage. In doing so they give themselves the "pure gift," which in Derrida's words,

> should have the generosity to give nothing that surprises and appears *as* gift, *nothing that presents itself as present, nothing that is*; it should therefore be surprising enough and so thoroughly made up of a surprise that is not even a question of getting over it, thus of a surprise surprising enough to let itself be forgotten without delay. And at stake in this forgetting that carries beyond any present is the gift as remaining [*restance*] without memory, without permanence and consistency, without substance or subsistence; at stake is this rest that is, without being (it), beyond Being, *epekeina tes ousias*.[43]

By foregoing the gift of inheritance, the Klesmer couple has reached the state that Derrida has thus characterized as the "pure gift." When Mrs. Arrowpoint draws a line in the sand by making it clear that the marriage would disinherit her daughter, Klesmer responds by conflating fortune with misfortune: "Madam, her fortune has been the only thing I have had to regret about her" (p. 248). The couple thus abdicates any relation to the loss-gain formula that holds Gwendolen in its grip.

The reversal of *Tasso*'s tragic violation of social proprieties in the Klesmer subplot starkly contrasts with the main narrative account of Gwendolen's marriage to Grandcourt: Here too the inheritance of a gift plays a significant role. Whereas the Klesmer couple freely rejects the passing on of the Arrowpoint family fortune, the already married Gwendolen is in no position to return the gift of Grandcourt's former mistress Mrs. Glasher. On the day of her marriage to Mr. Grandcourt, Mrs. Glasher has a couple of valuable diamonds delivered to Gwendolen. These diamonds were Grandcourt's gift of love to his former mistress. They represent gain. Here however, the gift is poisonous. The inheritance of the diamonds is deeply fraught: "It was as if an adder had lain on them" (p. 358). They embody what Derrida has described as the constitutive feature of a *pharmakon*: they exemplify a gift that is a curse.[44]

The narrator dwells on the lethal residue of inheritance: "Truly here were poisonous germs and the poison had entered into this poor young creature" (p. 359). In a "spell-bound" state Gwendolen reads Lydia Glasher's letter and "suddenly" gives in to "a new spasm of terror." When Grandcourt sees her in this disposition he wonders whether this is "a fit of madness" (p. 359). Such dementia does not take hold of Klesmer. Klesmer and Catherine walk in the

---

43 Jacques Derrida, *Given Time. I, Counterfeit Money*, trans. Peggy Kamuf (Chicago: University of Chicago Press, 1994), p. 147.

44 See Jacques Derrida's *Dissemination*, trans. Barbara Johnson (Chicago: University of Chicago Press, 1981), pp. 63–171.

footsteps of the Italian poet when they denounce the hierarchical code which rules the proper marriage arrangement for high-ranking women. Why does their plot nevertheless contrast with that of *Tasso* (and by implication that of Gwendolen)? They not only threaten but enact a break with societal stratifications, whereas *Tasso*, as Goethe's play repeatedly emphasizes, lacks room for action. *Tasso* lives in a state of servitude where action is prohibited (*Das Handeln bleibt mir untersagt*).[45] Conversely, Gwendolen marries in order to gain socially as well as economically. As a result of a marriage arrangement she falls prey to something resembling madness (if only temporarily).

Most importantly, the fit of dementia takes place at precisely the point where the opposition between gain and loss disintegrates into a state of coincidence: the one who gains loses. When Gwendolen dimly perceives the emptiness of gain the meanings of the social order that has sustained her sense of reality collapse. A void opens up. This emptiness results from the momentary sight of the now apparent gulf that divides the signifier (gain) from the signified (which turns out to be loss).

As Jacques Lacan has extensively discussed, "normal" psychological functions depend on the quilting point where signifier and signified are knotted together.[46] The ends of this point have been tenuously sewed together at the moment when the copiousness of meaning, which the signifier potentially signifies, has been reduced to and firmly identified with one specific signified. When, however, experience contradicts this identification (as is the case when gain turns out to be loss), the quilting point breaks asunder. This is precisely the case at the moment and place (Mr. Grandcourt's luxurious mansion) where Gwendolen realizes that Mrs. Glasher's gift is poisonous. She dimly recognizes then that the sign "gain" has such a superabundance of meaning that it can in fact announce the opposite of the only significance the subject has so far invested in it.

Gwendolen manages to come to terms with reality by suppressing this recognition. She thus does not completely identify with the unscrupulousness implicit in the pursuit of personal gain, as represented by her financier husband Grandcourt. Instead she appeases her scruples by focusing her attention on Deronda as someone who, she imagines, calls into question that which she nevertheless does (namely marrying Grandcourt in order to advance socially and financially).[47] This then is her unknown known: the desire for supremacy

---

45 *Torquato Tasso* act 4, scene 3, line 2549.

46 See Lacan, *The Psychoses. The Seminar of Jacques Lacan. Edited by Jacques-Alain Miller. Book III 1955–1956*, trans. Russell Grigg (London: Routledge, 1993), pp. 268–323.

47 As Slavoj Žižek has pointed out, this refusal to identify with a given ideological position paradoxically helps the enactment of ideology: "an ideological identification exerts a true hold on us precisely when we maintain an awareness that we are not fully identical to it, that there is a rich person beneath it: 'not all is ideology, beneath the ideological mask, I am also human person' is the *very form of ideology*, of its 'practical efficiency'" Žižek, *The Plague of Fantasies* (London: Verso, 1997), p. 21.

causes the experience of failure. It is precisely this overlap between gain and loss that Klesmer, as a truly fortunate modern-day *Tasso*, announces when he depicts his fiancée's inheritance as a poisonous burden.

5. Goethe's Iphigenia *and the Equality of Athens and Jerusalem*

In her revision of the *Tasso* motive Eliot introduces the element of ethnic tension. As we have seen Mrs. Arrowpoint takes exception to Klesmer's ethnic background.

Goethe's play by contrast exclusively focuses on the Italian poet's presumed violation of the hierarchical social code that governs marriage arrangements. But Gillian Beer has pointed out that these two spheres were closely inter-linked with each other in Victorian writing and thought: "The fascination with race is for many Victorian writers essentially a fascination with class. Race and class raise the same questions of descent, genealogy, nobility, the possibility of development and transformation."[48]

The novel alludes to another of Goethe's Weimar plays, one which revolves around the contrast between different ethnic communities. This section focuses on allusions to Goethe's *Iphigenia* in the context of Mirah's relation to her brother. The intertextual references to both Goethe's *Tasso* and his *Iphigenia* connect the novel's English with its Jewish strand. Both foreground the theme of loss and gain. It is this theme that unites the seemingly piecemeal aspects of the novel. Intertextual references are not ends in themselves in *Daniel Deronda*. Rather, they bring to the fore Eliot's criticism of a narrow conception of national identity.[49] They instantiate the novel's intrinsic connection with world literature, because they delineate "the way in which cultures recognize them-selves through their projections of 'otherness.'"[50] The allusions to both Jewish history and the literature of Weimar classicism connect the novel to transna-tional literature. Homi K. Bhabha has described transnational writing as fol-lows: "Where, once, the transmission of national traditions was the major theme of a world literature, perhaps we can now suggest that transnational histories of migrants, the colonized, or political refugees—these border and

---

48 Beer, *Darwin's Plot*, p. 189.

49 The foregrounding of these intertextual references contributes to the sense of artis-tic construction. As Saleel Nurbhai and K. M. Newton have recently pointed out, it is this sense of the imaginary that distinguishes Eliot's last novel from fiction composed in a realist mode: "What distinguishes Eliot from such writers [as John Buchan and Kipling] is the awareness in her Jewish novel that any literary repre-sentation of Jews will be a construction. The novel itself is preoccupied with con-struction. Deronda constructs his own identity as a Jew and Eliot foregrounds her own literary construction by, for example, creating a polarized relationship between Deronda as Noble Jew and Lapidoth as Evil Jew that functions allegori-cally" (Nurbhai and Newton, *George Eliot, Judaism and the Novels*, p. 20).

50 Homi K. Bhabha, *The Location of Culture* (London: Routledge, 1994), p. 12.

frontier conditions—may be the terrain of world literature."[51] Strikingly, in his reformulation of the meaning of world literature, Bhabha recuperates Goethe's conception of the term.[52] Eliot's allusion to two plays by Goethe seems to have a programmatic character, evoking a sense of cultural interconnectedness. Eliot's literary allusions question the validity of national boundaries, foregrounding the isomorphism of self and other.

So I read Eliot's allusions to another Goethe work. In a more pronounced manner than in *Tasso*, in *Iphigenie auf Tauris* Goethe puts on stage the deleterious divide between the civilized and the barbarian (see previous chapter). By alluding to Goethe's reworking of Euripides's play, Eliot thus moves the supposed contrast between Gentile and Jew into a wider historical and cultural context. This has an important bearing on Mordecai's Spinozist quest for the formation of particular identity that does not contradict universalism. He is particularly concerned with redressing the prioritization of the Hellenistic heritage over Jewish history. His endeavor to establish an equilibrium between different cultural formations mirrors Klesmer's disregard of hierarchical constructions within the social and the economic spheres. By comparing Mordecai's relation with Mirah to that of Iphigenia and Orestes, Deronda implicitly puts the Greek and the Jewish worlds on a par with each other.

The intertextual reference to Goethe's drama about *Iphigenia* is significant for a new understanding of Eliot's *Daniel Deronda*. In this context, it is worth inspecting the points where allusions to the Iphigenia motif occur in the novel. Long before Deronda discovers that he is a Jew, he compares the Jewish plot of the novel to Greek myth. The specific myth is that of Orestes and Iphigenia: he associates Mirah's search for her brother with that of Orestes for his lost sister. "To Deronda this event of finding Mirah was as heart-stirring as anything that befell Orestes or Rinaldo" (p. 205). Against the conventions of his time, Deronda puts the Jewish and the classical/Christian worlds (Rinaldo's Crusade context as depicted in *Tasso*'s *Gerusalemme liberata*) on a par with each other. Significantly, nineteenth-century anti-Semitism equated the Jews with the barbarians and contrasted them with the civilized Greeks. Deronda, by contrast, shows as much empathy for the life of contemporary Jewry as he does for the texts and artifacts of ancient Greece: "Deronda had as reverential an interest in Mordecai and Mirah as he could have had in the offspring of Agamemnon" (p. 544). In an intriguing parallel to Goethe's play *Iphigenie auf Tauris*, Deronda is not Mirah's kin, just as the "barbarian" Thoas is not Iphigenia's father, but Deronda nevertheless becomes accepted as a proper father figure. (Agamemnon, Iphigenia's physical father, famously set out to sacrifice his daughter; Artemis saves the latter and transports her to Tauris where, in Goethe's account, Thoas acts like a true father.) In this way the allusions to Goethe's play relate Jews (perceived as "barbarians") to the Greeks. Through a creative reworking of Goethe's play, Jews are associated with the

---

51   Ibid.

52   See John Pizer's "Goethe's 'World Literature' Paradigm and Contemporary Cultural Globalization," *Comparative Literature* 52 (2000): 213–27.

Greeks while almost celebrating the difference. The Jewish past becomes as relevant as the Greek past in Eliot's oeuvre.

The redemption of the Jewish past was a burning question for various Jewish writers and thinkers in the nineteenth century. Leopold Zunz, who, together with the poet Heinrich Heine, was one of the active members of the *Wissenschaft des Judentums*/Society for the Culture and Science of the Jews, strongly believed that anti-Semitism and assimilation would ring in the end of Jewish history.[53] Zunz embarked on historiographical research in order to give Judaism "a dignified burial."[54] With his thorough scholarly work he set out to rescue the future remembrance of Jewish history. Eliot highlights this state of affairs when she cites a key passage from Zunz's *Die Synagogale Poesie des Mittelalters* as the epigraph for chapter 42:

> Wenn es eine Stufenleiter von Leiden gibt, so hat Israel die höchste Staffel erstiegen; wenn die Dauer der Schmerzen und die Geduld, mit welcher sie ertragen werden, adeln, no nehmen es die Juden mit den Hochgeborenen aller Länder auf; wenn eine Literatur reich genannt wird, die wenige klassische Trauerspiele besitzt, welcher Platz gebührt dann einer Tragödie die anderthalb Jahrtausende währt, gedichtet und dargestellt von den Helden selber?
>
> If there are ranks in suffering, Israel takes precedence of all the nations—if the duration of sorrows and the patience with which they are borne ennoble, the Jews are among the aristocracy of every land—if a literature is called rich in the possession of few classic tragedies, what shall we say to a National Tragedy lasting for fifteen hundred years, in which the poets and the actors were also the heroes? (p. 517)

This quote is more than a *cri de coeur*: it goes to the heart of the contrast between Jew and Greek that structures the novel's Iphigenia theme. Zunz depicts Jewish history in aristocratic terms, precisely by relating it to the world of suffering that constitutes Greek tragedy. Those who have been despised, and have been condemned to endure with patience centuries filled with pain, are exactly for this state of abjection on equal terms with those who epitomize nobility: the ancient Greeks. Here loss clearly becomes gain.

According to Zunz, the derided Jews outdo the revered Greeks in Greekness: whereas the Greeks only composed a few tragedies, Jewish history constitutes tragedy that reaches from the contemporary age back to the mythic time of the Hebrew Bible. The whole history of the Jews therefore represents the work of art, which can only fragmentarily be found in Greek tragedies. The demoted life of the Jews, in actual fact, presents ("gedichtet und dargestellt von den Helden selber") that of which the writings and artifacts of ancient Greece are only fantasized representations.

---

53 For a detailed discussion of Leopold Zunz and the *Wissenschaft des Judentums*, see Mendes-Flohr and Reinharz, *The Jew in the Modern World* , pp. 207–40.

54 I am indebted to long-standing discussion with Paul Mendes-Flohr (University of Chicago and Hebrew University, Jerusalem) about all this. See Mendes-Flohr's *German Jews: A Dual Identity* (New Haven, CT: Yale University Press, 1999).

This quotation from Zunz's *Die Synagogale Poesie des Mittelalters* introduces a chapter, where the relation between Greek and Jew (Iphigenia and
Mirah) moves into a Spinozist context. Mordecai, whom Deronda has previously compared to Iphigenia's brother Orestes, here engages in a discussion
about the Jewish past at the pub The Hand and Banner, which is the regular
meeting place of the club "The Philosophers." In this philosophical society,
Mordecai discusses Spinoza's work within the context of affiliations and
disaffiliations with the Jewish past:

> Baruch Spinoza had not a faithful Jewish heart, though he had sucked the life of
> his intellect at the breasts of Jewish tradition. He laid bare his father's nakedness
> and said, "They who scorn him have the higher wisdom." Yet Baruch Spinoza
> confessed, he saw not why Israel should not again be a chosen nation. Who says
> that the history of and literature of our race are dead? Are they not as living as
> the history and literature of Grèece and Rome, which have inspired revolutions,
> enkindled the thought of Europe, and made the unrighteous powers tremble?
> These were an inheritance dug from the tomb. Ours is an inheritance that has
> never ceased to quiver in millions of human frames. (p. 536)

In the first part of his statement Mordecai refers to Spinoza's heresy: he compares the seventeenth-century philosopher to the Biblical Ham who uncovered
his father Noah. Yet the *herem* (ban), which the Sephardic Jewish community
of Amsterdam imposed upon Spinoza, did not result in a complete disaffilia-
tion with Jewish history. In the *Theological-Political Treatise* Spinoza nurtures
the possibility that the Jews will "establish once more their independent state,
and that God will again choose them."[55] Mordecai, who characterizes Spinoza
as rationalist philosopher, argues that Enlightenment thought does not necessarily demote the past to insignificance. At this point it becomes apparent why
Eliot translates the term "Tragödie," which Zunz employs to describe Jewish
history, as a "National Tragedy." As has been intimated above, Zunz did not
believe in the futurity of Jewish history. He feared that enlightenment thought
and modern culture would do away with Jewish difference. Mordecai, in contrast, argues for the compatibility between cultural/religious difference and
the rationality of an enlightened philosopher such as Baruch Spinoza.

Here the term nation denotes not the homogenous but the diverse. Modernity cannot do without particularity (that is, national identities) if it wants to
avoid the homogeneity of a monolithic state, which would of course in itself be
an unacknowledged particular entity (as Žižek has argued "one should fully
accept the paradoxical fact that the dimension of universality is always sustained by the fixation on some particular point"[56]). Mordecai therefore questions an understanding of universality that obfuscates its particularity:

> Can a fresh-made garment of citizenship weave itself straightway into the flesh
> and change the slow deposit of eighteen centuries? What is the citizenship of him

---

55 Spinoza, *Theological-Political Treatise*, 47.
56 Žižek, *The Plague of Fantasies*, p. 104.

who walks among a people he has no hearty kindred and fellowship with, and has lost the sense of brotherhood with his own race? It is a charter of selfish ambition and rivalry in low greed. (528)

The garment represents the imposition of a monolithic abstraction upon the embodied forms of human diversity. Like Spinoza, Mordecai opts for the heretical act of uncovering. Both thinkers repeat Ham's sacrilege against the father figure: Spinoza became a heretic by offending the religious orthodoxy of his time, and in a different but related way Mordecai, walking in the footsteps of the maverick enlightenment thinker Herder, introduces the open acknowledgement of particularity into the universality of rationalist thought.

How does particularity manifest itself? According to Mordecai, it denotes the vitality of the past within the changed context of the present. This survival of the past within the here and now defines Jewish history. Gentile society reveres the ancient Greeks, precisely because they are dead ("were an inheritance dug from the tomb"), and it despises the Jews on account of their persistence. Anti-Semitism gives rise to the fantasy of life that cannot be put to death, that is so filled with enjoyment that its vitality constantly renews itself. This then is the supposed threat of the Jews: life that does not need to fear death.[57] Mordecai emphasizes this phantasmagoria of unquenchable life that spurs anti-Semitism: "Ours is an inheritance that has never ceased to quiver in millions of human frames." This contrast between ancient Greeks as inhabitants of the tomb and Jews as bearers of eternal life has a point of reference in the historiography of Heinrich Graetz.

Between 1853 and 1870 Graetz set out to counter anti-Semitism as well as to revive a sense of Jewish identity by writing a multivolume *History of the Jews* from biblical times to contemporary Europe. In the concluding volume of this truly monumental work, Graetz gives an etiology of anti-Semitism. Here he formulates the contrast between death (ancient Greece as adored in present-day German culture) and eternal life (the survival of the Jews), which Eliot's Mordecai implicitly picks up in his speech about Spinoza and the redemption of the past within the present (Eliot was of course familiar with Graetz's *magnum opus*). Graetz asks his readers how we can account for the fact that modern German culture discriminates against Jewish civilization and lavishes praise on Greek and Roman antiquity. Like Eliot's Mordecai, he explains this discrepancy with reference to the presence of an ongoing and vital Jewish culture within the contemporary world. Rather than being praised for their cultural achievements, the Jews are discriminated against precisely because they, unlike the ancient Hellenes, continue to exist.[58]

---

57 For a brilliant discussion of a similar return of the dead in Honoré de Balzac's *Le Colonel Chabert*, see Cathy Caruth, "The Claims of the Dead: History, Haunted Property, and the Law," *Critical Inquiry* 28 (2002): 419–41.

58 For a detailed discussion of Heinreich Graetz's response to anti-Semitism, see Mack, *German Idealism and the Jew*, 98–107.

As a result of their continued existence, the Jews are perceived as a threat:

> Jaundiced malignity and hatred are silent at the grave of the illustrious man; his merits as enumerated there are, in fact, as a rule overrated . . . Just because of their continued existence, the merits and moral attainments of the Hebrews are not generally acknowledged.[59]

Mordecai develops and deepens Graetz's critique of both anti-Semitism and the cult of Hellenism, when he pinpoints Jewish survival as the stone of offence that gives rise to all kinds of feelings of envy and rivalry. Why does the continuation of life provoke such outbursts of hatred? The arrest of movement, that is to say, the freezing of a living process establishes the decipherment of its purported meaning: "immobility," as Žižek writes, "makes a thing visible."[60] The literature and the artifacts of ancient Greece are significant, precisely because they belong to a nonexisting civilization: their past is literally passed (in the words of Mordecai, it belongs to the tomb).

Ancient Jewish customs are "alive while dead": they bridge the gulf between the deadness of prehistory and the palpitation that runs through present day life (Mordecai's "inheritance that has never ceased to quiver in the millions of human frames"). This very paradox makes Judaism "insignificant" in the eyes of the English society in which Daniel Deronda has been brought up. The past that has not been frozen but continues to live in the present provokes anger in those who structure their lives according to a differentiation between the contingency and meaninglessness of the past (be it "primitive," "Jewish," or "superstitious") and the goal-oriented significance of history's progress, of which the current state of affairs is, of course, the culmination. As Žižek has put it, "life is the horrible palpitation of the 'lamella,' the non-subjective ('acephalous') undead drive which persists beyond ordinary death; death is the symbolic order itself, the structure which, as a parasite, colonizes the living entity."[61] By questioning the symbolic order Daniel Deronda walks in the footsteps of Goethe's *Tasso* and Iphigenia. By putting himself into the place of those who have been excluded by this order, he literally finds his life and his inheritance. The novel turns the common understanding of meaning and significance upside down. It traverses the chain of signification so that the insignificant turns into the significant and loss reemerges as gain. The following concluding discussion focuses on how Freud's psychoanalysis unfolds another chapter of the persistence of Spinoza's non-hierarchical vision.

---

59 Heinrich Graetz, *History of the Jews*, vol. 5, *From the Chmielncki Persecution of the Jews in Poland (1648 C.E.) to the Present Time (1870 C.E.)*, trans. Bella Löwy (Philadelphia: Jewish Publication Society of America, 1895), p. 707.

60 Žižek, *The Plague of Fantasies*, p. 87.

61 Ibid., 89.

Conclusion: Freud, Spinoza or how to be Mindful of the Mind

Spinoza is, in effect, the "philosopher as such," with his subjective stance of double outcast (excommunicated even from the community of the outcasts of Western civilization); this is why we should use him as a paradigm that enables us to discover the traces of a similar displacement, a communal "out-of-joint," with regard to all other great philosophers, up to Nietzsche, who was ashamed of the Germans and proudly emphasized his alleged Polish roots.

Žižek, The Parallax View

I am utterly amazed, utterly enchanted. I have a precursor, and what a precursor! I hardly knew Spinoza: that I should have turned to him just now was inspired by "instinct." Not only is his over-all tendency like mine—making knowledge the most powerful affect—but in five main points of his doctrine I recognize myself; this most unusual and loneliest of thinker is closest to me precisely in these matters: he denies the freedom of the will, teleology, the moral world order, the non-egoistic, and evil.

Nietzsche, letter of July 30, 1881 to Franz Overbeck

1. Overview of the Discussion so Far

This book has traced the ways in which Spinoza's critique of anthropomorphism, in both theology and philosophy, sparked off a series of shifts that profoundly changed our understanding of nature, history, literature (see the discussion of George Eliot's realism in the preceding chapter) and science. As we have seen, Spinoza's new conception of nature inspires in Herder a novel account of human history. Herder decenters cultural history by submerging it into the life of nature and the cosmos at large. Whereas Kant (and later, following Kant's approach, Hegel) "secularizes the historical concept of divinity, and equally sacralizes his own humanistic morality,"[1] Herder questions the privileged role which humanity presumes for itself. According to Kant the unfolding of reason would be at the same time the realization of human freedom. In this way Kant and Hegel's history is decisively human centered: over time the merely natural and only minimally developed endowment of reason accelerates—thanks to the antinaturalistic statutes of a civilized modern body politic—until we will live a fully rational life and hence will have fully realized freedom via the suspension of natural impulses.

---

1 Yirmiyahu Yovel, *Spinoza and Other Heretics: The Adventures of Immanence* (Princeton, NJ: Princeton University Press, 1989), p. 8.

Herder moves our understanding of time away from the Kantian focus on the human. Instead of privileging humankind Herder accentuates the isomorphism of humanity and nature. This becomes amply clear when he deviates from the Kantian view of humanity's original endowment as one of reason and concentrates instead on biology. By submerging humanity (anthropology) into nature (biology), Herder clearly refers back to Spinoza who, as Hampshire has put it, "gives the strong impression of thinking like a biologist, as opposed to those philosophers who in his time were trying to think like physicists, particularly Descartes and Hobbes."[2] Herder famously submerges humanity into nature when he claims that the physiology of standing upright distinguishes the human from other animals. In so locating the origins of our history, not in a divine or rational but in a physiological and animalistic realm, Herder undermines the quasi-divine status with which Kant and later Hegel endows our rationality. As Yrimiyahu Yovel has astutely pointed out, Kant's transcendental philosophy pinpoints the limits of the knowable only in order to overcome them:

> Kant's qualified philosophy of human immanence is thereby both human centered and anti-naturalistic, two features which Kant passed on to Hegel [. . .]. The critique of reason is also, for Kant, its declaration of independence. Despite its finitude—and also because of it—human reason takes over the role of God as legislator for both nature and morality. Unable to prove or disprove the existence of God (and other major theological claims), human reason assumes this finitude as a binding norm, forbidding itself to rely upon external authorities and reaffirming its power to produce of itself, as the explication of its own inherent structure, the metaphysical features of natural objects and the fundamental moral commandments.[3]

It may be impossible for us to fully know nature or God but this epistemological limit holds out the promise of the immanent creation of a quasi-divine morality and quasi-divine human nature. This creation is the work of our autonomy. Kant contrasts his novel conception of what it means to be autonomous with metaphysics' traditional quest for complete insight into nature or God. He demotes this quest to what he calls heteronomy. Heteronomy denotes the law of the external so that if we were able to fully understand nature or God we would not attain our law (which would be autonomy) but only the law of what is extraneous to us, which is precisely nature or God. By imposing limits on the quest for knowledge of the external world, Kant empowers humanity to construct its own world in a limitless manner. We may not understand what is not us but we are potentially omniscient and omnipotent when it comes to building our own world. Kant is the true architect of a modernity that subjugates nature to the autonomous will of human rationality. This is, however, a rationality that is premised on the command of such subjugation.

---

2 Hampshire, *Spinoza and Spinozism*, p. xlvii.
3 Yovel, *Spinoza and other Heretics: The Adventures of Immanence*, pp. 7–8.

2. *Freud's Spinozist New Science*

Freud defines his new science against Kant's modernity. Freud ironically characterizes Kant's Copernican revolution as "old science." What makes it old is its presumption of intra-human omniscience and omnipotence. Contra Kant, Freud argues that we are not masters in our own house. Instead our ego or our psyche is split into competing claims and commandments of which we can rarely gain control. Significantly, Freud undermines the Kantian notion of autonomy as mastering one's own house and world, when he locates the psychoanalytical revolution within the historical context of both Copernicus and Darwin: both have inflicted wounds on humanity's narcissism. Psychoanalysis deals a third and decisive blow to this kind of anthropomorphism:

> Humanity had to endure two big wounds of its naïve self-love as inflicted by science over the ages. First when it learned that our earth is not the center of the world, but a tiny part of a much bigger and unimaginable system of the world. This wound is associated with the name of Copernicus, although Alexandrinian science has pronounced something similar. The second: when biological science rendered null and void the presumed privilege of creation of man by referring to both his descent from animals and to the inerasable nature of his animalistic constitution. This reevaluation has taken place in our time under the influence of Charles Darwin, Wallace and their predecessors [i.e. Spinoza, Herder, and Goethe], which have been met not without the fiercest resistance of their contemporaries. The third and most severe wound, however, human megalomania has to endure from psychological research, which proves to the ego[4] that it is not even master in his own house, but remains dependent on pathetic information derived from something which takes place unconsciously in the life of its soul.[5]

Here Freud clearly places his new science in a historical trajectory of maverick scientists who have radically rejected humanity's anthropomorphic conception of God.

The Copernican revolution has questioned the quasi-divine place of the earth as the center of the universe and Darwin and his predecessors Spinoza, Herder and Goethe have shown how humanity forms part of natural rather than exclusively spiritual history. The most severe wound to humanity's anthropomorphic concept of God and the universe is, however, inflicted by Freud's new science. Why is this so? The preceding revolutions had to do with the strictly biological (Darwin) and astrological (Copernicus) spheres, while minimally touching upon the sphere of the mind. This is why Kant is part of the Copernican revolution: with Copernicus he acknowledges the periphery

---

4 Translating Freud's *Ich* as "ego" can be misleading: the term *ego* seems to be related to the notion of egoism. Freud's *Ich* does not encompass such semantic associations. However, I refer to the common translation of "ego" for *Ich* in order not to confuse the reader.

5 Freud, *Studienausgabe*, Vol. 1, ed. Alexander Mitcherlich, Angelika Richards and James Strachey (Frankfurt a. M.: Fischer, 1975), pp. 283–284.

of the astrological position of our habitat, the earth, but he nevertheless reclaims the autonomous mastery of humanity within its post-Copernican limits (i.e. the limits of the sublunar world).

Freud's new science is radical, because it assaults this last remaining bastion of pride: the mind. Rather than guaranteeing the proud independence of humanity from natural forces, the mind is "not master in his own house but remains dependent on pathetic information derived from something which takes place unconsciously in the life of its soul" (see larger quote above). This indefinite "something" (*von dem, was*) makes nonsense of any claim to an unambiguous self-knowledge. It therefore strongly undermines the Kantian position concerning transcending the empirical world, because of the autonomy of the rational mind.

According to Kant, reason shapes the material world in an a priori manner and, as a result, is capable of freedom from natural conditions.[6] In Freud's *Introductory Lectures* of 1933 Kant appears as the godfather of philosophers who argues that "time and place are necessary forms of psychic activities."[7] Far from being able to create stable spacial structures and temporal rhythms, the mind easily turns mindless when it removes the ego from the flow of time and also from the flow of life. This removal from time and space is consubstantial with a loss of reality which characterizes various forms of psychosis (as we have seen in Chapters 1 and 2, Spinoza tried to cure this loss of reality via his geometrical method).

In undermining Kant's conception of autonomy, Freud's new science refashions Spinoza's critique of both religion and philosophy as anthropomorphism. As Suzanne R. Kirschner has pointed out, Freudian psychoanalysis analyzes "the limitations of modernity's emphasis on rationality and autonomy."[8] Freud's new science enmeshes cultural with natural history. According to Freud we cannot overcome nature and attain Kant and Hegel's state of freedom where natural impulses are suspended. Psychoanalysis focuses on damages caused precisely by such suspension. Rather than emphasizing a future state of reason and freedom, Freud's new science tries to persuade us to commemorate a "savage" (i.e. premodern) past which, if not brought to consciousness, determines our presumably modern and civilized way of life.

3. *The Death Drive as Foundation of Life or Herder's and Goethe's Ontological Negativity*

The focus on human savagery, on aggression and self-destruction are certainly far removed from Spinoza's universe where suicide does not come naturally,

---

6 See Mack, *German Idealism and the Jew*, pp. 23–41.

7 Freud, *Studienausgabe*, Vol. 1, p. 511.

8 Kirschner, *The Religious and Romantic Origins of Psychoanalysis. Individuation and Integration in Post-Freudian Theory* (Cambridge: Cambridge University Press, 1996), p. 199.

but is instead the offspring of external societal factors. As Spinoza puts it in the third Part of the *Ethics*, "whatever can destroy our body cannot be in it."[9] Clearly Freud is cognizant of the negativity, which Herder and Goethe have introduced into Spinoza's seemingly benign naturalistic universe. It is worthwhile adding that there already is an epistemological negativity in Spinoza, which, as analyzed by Alain Badiou, focuses on the void that separates our finite human understanding from the infinity of God or Nature.[10] What Herder has introduced into Spinozist thought is a further radicalization of this void. It now turns from the merely epistemological into the ontological sphere. Spinoza, in contrast, denies that any being "has anything in itself by which it can be destroyed, *or* which takes its existence away."[11]

The issue of an ontological negativity has, to be sure, been reinforced by Charles Darwin's notion of natural selection, based not on the principle of merit but rather on that of arbitrariness, chance, or, in other words, tough luck. "We behold the face of nature bright with gladness," writes Darwin and goes on to stress nature's dark side,

> we often see superabundance of food; we do not see or we forget, that the birds which are idly singing around us mostly live on insects or seeds, and are thus constantly destroying life; or we forget how largely these songsters, or their eggs, or their nestlings, are destroyed by birds and beasts of prey; we do not always bear in mind, that, though food may be superabundant, it is not so at all seasons of each recurring year.[12]

In Darwin's work Spinoza's principle of self-preservation ceases to be cooperative while it is of course still entirely naturalistic:

> He who believes in the struggle for existence and in the principle of natural selection, will acknowledge that every organic being is constantly endeavouring to increase in numbers; and that if any one being varies ever so little, either in habits or structure, and thus gains an advantage over some other inhabitant of the same country, it will seize on the place of that inhabitant, however different that may be from its own place.[13]

Here the preservation of the self feeds on the weakness of others. Darwin's account is Spinozist in so far as it thoroughly naturalistic. His description of nature lacks, however, any ethical component and is thus removed from Spinoza's social agenda in his *Ethics*. Freud seems to intensify this naturalistic

---

9   Spinoza, *Ethics*, p. 76.

10   See Badiou, *Being and Event* (New York: Continuum, 2006), pp. 112–120.

11   Spinoza, *Ethics*, p. 75.

12   Darwin, *On the Origin of the Species By Means of Natural Selection or the Preservation of Favored Races in the Struggle for Life* (New York: Random House, 1993), p. 89.

13   Ibid., p. 227.

bleakness when he discusses the death drive which is another word for self-destruction: "A strange drive," he exclaims, "that is bent on the destruction of its own organic home!"[14] Freud is, however, far from being judgmental: following Goethe and Darwin he merely observes the life of the psyche. The intellectual working through of what has been observed does not yield a one-dimensional outcome.

Distinguishing his approach from that of Schopenhauer, Freud argues that far from being opposed to life, the death-drive is actually the very foundation of our ability to survive. It only turns deadly if it has been cut off from an organism's erotic circulation to which it originally belongs. The death-drive certainly forms part of the libido and as such it is life preserving. In this way, Freud speaks of "the way in which the two drives [i.e. of life and of death] interconnect and how the death-drive is placed at the services of Eros."[15] This intermingling of the constructive and destructive represents another shift within a Spinozist conception of an interconnected universe. Goethe—one of Freud's favorite writers—in turn transformed this holistic principle of interdependence into one of circulation where the operations of "evil" in fact support those of "goodness" and vice versa (see Chapter 7). Freud frequently refers to Goethe's and Darwin's work. What about Spinoza?

The name Spinoza seems to be conspicuous by its absence in Freud's oeuvre: most of the time he refers to him indirectly. This absence of a direct reference to Spinoza points to the indirection or, we may say, the shift that Spinoza's thought is capable of inspiring. Freud only directly addresses his debt to Spinoza when he is asked to do so. In this way the Spinozist Dr. Lothar Bickel requested of the late Freud an acknowledgement of his intellectual reliance of Spinoza. Freud's reply is affirmative:

> *I readily admit my dependence on Spinoza's doctrine.* There was no reason why I should expressly mention his name, since I conceived my hypotheses from the *atmosphere* created by him, rather than from the study of his work. Moreover, I did not seek a philosophical legitimation.[16]

The term atmosphere is of course rather vague. What Freud seems to have in mind is what he has in common with Spinoza, namely, being affiliated while at the same time being disaffiliated with the contemporaneous Jewish community and with Jewish history. Both Freud and Spinoza are double outsiders: they are not part of their own community in terms of religious affiliation

---

14 Freud, *Studienausgabe*, Vol. 1, p. 538. My trans.
15 Ibid., p. 540. My trans.
16 Quoted from Yovel, *Spinoza and Other Heretics*, p. 139. This is Freud's letter to Lothar Bickel of June 28, 1931; English translation in H. Z. Winnik, "A Long-Lost and Recently Recovered Letter of Freud," *Israel Annals of Psychiatry* 13 (1975): 1–5. German original in Leo Sonntag's and Heinz Solte's *Spinoza in neuer Sicht* (Meisenheim: Anton Hain, 1977), pp. 169–171.

though they are perceived as Jews by the non-Jewish majority of their respective societies; being seen as typically Jewish they are automatically associated with the threatening, the savage, or, in Spinoza's case, the Satanic. This perception of their ethnicity is then reinforced through the content matter of their writing and thought, which undermines in different but nonetheless related ways the anthropomorphic conception of God or, in Freud's words, humanity's megalomania.

In his letter to Bickel Freud downplays the way in which he was an actual student of Spinoza's work. As a later communication makes clear, this lack of systematic study does not mean that he was not shaped by Spinozist thought. While declining to contribute to a volume dedicated to Spinoza's three hundredth anniversary, Freud nevertheless emphasizes his intellectual debt to the Dutch Jewish philosopher: "Throughout my long life," he writes, "I [timidly] sustained an extraordinarily high respect for the person as well as for the results of the thought [*Denkleistung*] of the great philosopher Spinoza."[17] Here Freud implicitly conceives of Spinoza not as single and isolated figure; rather he sees in the name Spinoza an intellectual constellation of thinkers and writers who from Lessing, Herder, and Goethe to Darwin have introduced various shifts in the way we see humanity, not as a quasi-divine representative on earth, but as deeply enfolded within the material realm of nature.

It may well be that it is due to this non-definable and superindividual influence of Spinoza's work that Freud avoids mentioning his name in his various psychoanalytical studies. Freud sometimes alludes to Spinoza by referring to Heine as his nonreligious coreligionist (*Unglaubensgenossen*).[18] This is precisely the term Heine employs in order describe his affinity with Spinoza. Significantly Heine focuses on Spinoza's critique of anthropomorphism in both philosophy and theology. Heine is often ingenuously right by saying something that is blatantly wrong. He does this when he claims that Spinoza never denies the existence of God but always the existence of humanity. Implicitly contradicting the seventeenth and eighteenth-century charge of atheisim and the twenty-first century appraisal of Spinoza as atheist, Heine writes:

> Nothing but sheer unreason and malice could bestow on such a doctrine the qualification of "atheism." No one has ever spoken more sublimely of Deity than Spinoza. Instead of saying that he denied God, one might say that he denied

---

17 Quoted from Yovel, *Spinoza and Other Heretics*, p. 139. German original in S. Hessing (ed.), *Spinoza-Festschrift* (Heidelberg: Karl Winter, 1932), p. 221. See also S. Hessing's "Freud's Relation with Spinoza," in Hessing's *Speculum Spinozanum 1677–1977* (London: Routledge, 1977), pp. 224–239 and J. Golomb's "Freud's Spinoza: A Reconstruction," *Israel Annals of Psychiatry* 16 (1978): 275–288.

18 Freud calls Heine a *Unglaubensgenossen* in the *Future of an Illusion*, *Studienausgabe* Vp. 9, p. 183. And in his monograph on Jokes and their relation to the Unconscious he quotes the Heine excerpt where Heine uses the term *Unglaubengenosse* as a synonym for Spinoza: "'Mein Unglaubensgenosse Spinoza', sagt Heine", Freud *Studienausgabe* Vol. 4, p. 75.

man. All finite things are to him but modes of the infinite substance; all finite substances are contained in God; the human mind is but a luminous ray of infinite thought; the human body but an atom of infinite extension: God is the infinite cause of both, of mind and of body, *natura naturans*.[19]

What Heine refers to in this important quotation is precisely the topic on which I have focused in this book: namely, the shift Spinoza introduces away from thought centering on the human to one centered upon nature (on what Herder and Goethe discuss as humanity's natural history). Freud reinforces this shift when he distinguishes his new science from the presumptuous claims of both religion and philosophy.

4. Freud's Spinozist Critique of Theology and Philosophy

We can better understand Freud's conception of his "new science" by attending to his polemics against religion. In a highly ironic manner Freud argues that religion renders God anthropomorphic by endowing humanity with quasi-divine powers. This seems to be a far cry from the way in which Herder enmeshes cultural and natural history in order to emphasize the limitations of the *conditio humana*. Whereas Herder questions the rational teleologies of the Enlightenment, Freud seems to cling to a eighteenth and nineteenth-century belief in rational-scientific and technological progress. In this context it is important to point out that Freud to some extent repeated the anthropological evolutionism as advocated by James Frazer and E. B. Tylor. Jonathan Lear has recently criticized Freud's apparent belief in historical progression as follows:

> Freud's argument is persuasive *in the way he intends* only within the outlook of a particular historical epoch. Thus to vindicate Freud's argument, one would need to demonstrate the legitimacy of his historical outlook. Freud claims that "in the long run nothing can withstand reason and experience." But why should Freud of all people believe this? Has he not taught us that we are always subject to wishful and aggressive fantasies—whose origins are lost in infancy—of which we are largely unaware?[20]

Lear's question is indeed pertinent: how can we reconcile Freud's apparent belief in history's triumphal progress with his stringent and rather bleak view of human nature? As has been discussed above, Freud clearly characterizes his new science as an affront to Kant's conception of an autonomous mind that is capable of shaping his own world and history. Perhaps we can find a reason for Freud's inconsistency in his uncritical espousal of the nineteenth-century

---

19 Heine, *Religion and Philosophy in Germany*, trans. by John Snodgrass (Albany: State University of New York Press, 1986), p. 72. Heine, *Schriften über Deutschland*, ed. by Helmut Schanze (Frankfurt a. M.: Insel, 1968), p. 95.

20 Lear, *Freud* (London: Routledge, 2005), p. 212.

adoration of science with all its teleological baggage (i.e. E. B. Tylor and J. Frazer).

According to Lear, Freud's critique of religion as illusion gives way to an illusion of the future (i.e. science's triumphal progress). There is, however, another aspect to Freud's conception of his new science, which emphasizes the open and always incomplete nature of human intelligibility. There is a strong sense that this fragmentary character of science cannot be remedied through any future advancement in knowledge. Why does Freud, despite his nineteenth-century background in anthropological evolutionism (i.e. Frazer and Tylor), base his conception of psychoanalysis on the nonprogressivist footing of lack (or incompletion) and the insufficiency of civilization and its morals (or on aggression and savagery as the original foundation of morals and civilization)?

To address this question it is worth drawing attention to Eric L. Santner's brilliant discussion of a sense of "too muchness" in Freud's writing and thought. The confrontation with this topic stipulated the composition of Santner's *On the Psychotheology of Everyday Life*. Here Santner speaks of his "sense that Freud's mostly negative assessments of religion are in some way undermined or at least challenged by what I can't help but characterize as the 'spiritual' dimension of the new science he founded."[21] This "spiritual dimension" is precisely the encounter with not only a physiological but also a psychic energy of excess (or too muchness):

> Psychoanalysis differs from other approaches to human being by attending to the constitutive "too muchness" that characterizes the psyche; the human mind is, we might say, defined by the fact that it includes more reality than it can contain, is the bearer of an excess, a too much of pressure that is not merely physiological. The various ways in which this "too much," this surplus of life of the human subject seeks release or discharge in the "psychopathology of everyday life" continues to form the central focus of Freudian theory and practice. Now the very religious tradition in which Freud was raised, his protestations of lifelong secularism notwithstanding, is itself in some sense structured around an internal excess or tension—call it the tension of election—and elaborates its particular form of ethical orientation to it. For Judaism (as well as for Christianity), that is, human life always includes more reality than it can contain and this "too much" bears witness to a spiritual and moral calling, a pressure toward self-transformation, toward goodness.[22]

This excess is paradoxically humanity's limitation: it is so overwhelmed by various pressures and conflicting demands that it is incapable of mastering its own house. This sense of "too muchness" splits the ego apart into at least three incompatible force fields: one is the demand to attend to the hardship imposed by external reality (what Freud calls *Lebensnot*),[23] the second are the realms

---

21   Santner, *On the Psychotheology of Everyday Life: Reflections on Freud and Rosenzweig* (Chicago: University of Chicago Press, 2001), p. 8.

22   Ibid.

23   Freud, *Studienausgabe*, Vol. 9, p. 186.

of aggressive or sexual drives (the so called *id*) and the third, equally over-whelming and potentially destructive, are the valid, but sometimes nonsignifi-cant, moral imperatives imposed by civilization (the superego).

In his works on religious history, Freud attempts to show how the superego or civilization itself derives from the aggression and obscenity of the drives, of the id. Instead of a narrative of progression here we clearly have an account of how qualitative leaps emerge only thanks to what they apparently oppose and into what they could easily regress yet again. According to Freud, civilization begins not with the promulgation of moral doctrines but with the murder of the primeval father by his sons, who are so envious of his exclusive sexual pos-session of women that they kill him in a fit of rage. How is murder responsible for morality? It gives rise to a sense of guilt. The excessive demand of psychic and physiological drives thus gives way to the too much of self-destructive feelings of guilt. As Santner puts it in the excerpt quoted above, it is due to this excess of guilt that we attempt to be "good."

This sense of goodness, however, can easily turn into an anthropomorphic conception of God: through our moral consciousness we may feel identical with God. In this way religion does not bring about humility but megalomania. So Freud's critique of religion is in fact a Spinozist one that criticizes human self-aggrandizement. The specter of anthropomorphism looms large when Freud argues that religious folk are the most hubristic imaginable because they feel at one with the limitless power of God. According to Freud religious folk:

> give the name of "God" to some vague abstraction which they have created for themselves; having done so they can pose before all the world as deists, as believ-ers in God, and they can even boast that they have recognized a higher, purer concept of God, notwithstanding that their God is now nothing more than an insubstantial shadow and no longer the mighty personality of religious doctrine. Critics persist in describing as "deeply religious" anyone who admits to a sense of man's insignificance or impotence in the face of the universe, although what constitutes the essence of religious attitude is not this feeling but only the next step after it, the reaction to it which seeks a remedy for it. The man who goes no further, but humbly acquiesces in the small part which human beings play in the great world—such a man is, on the contrary, irreligious in the truest sense of the world.[24]

Freud argues that it is not an awareness of humanity's insignificance but a sense of its consubstantiality with the divine that characterizes religion. He makes it clear that his way of thinking here is idiosyncratic, if not ironic. This is so because we usually define religious character in the opposite manner: not in terms of anthropomorphically occupying the place of the divine but, on the

---

24 Freud, *The Future of an Illusion*, trans. By W. D. Robson-Scott (New York: Doubleday, 1964), p. 53.

contrary, in terms of accentuating human lack in the face of God or nature. According to Freud, in contrast, this sense of lack or incompletion shapes, not the world view of religion, but that of science.

Freud's notion of science is indeed new; not least because it reverses the role traditionally attributed to religion with that of his "new science." Here we encounter the opposite of a triumphal narrative of progression with which Jonathan Lear has justifiably taken issue. Rather than assuring us of our secure and secured passage to a state of complete knowledge of ourselves and our universe, Freud's "new science" focuses on our lack of self-mastery: it proves that we are not even masters of our own house. Radicalizing Spinoza's analysis of the self as being intrinsically bound up with the other, Freud denies that we are unified entities. Rather than forming a consistent whole our psyche is torn by a whirlpool of excessive demands, commands and urges. It is due to this internal strangeness or, in other words, this experience of being overwhelmed by competing drives and desires and aspirations that it is so difficult for us to take account of what is actually happening in the external world. Psychic illness results from an overflow of internal pressures so that the ego cannot see anything in its environment but an intensification or mirror image of its mental conflicts. This is of course what Spinoza criticizes as anthropomorphic distortion of nature or God according to the life of our internal appetites or passions. This distortion is nothing else but a psychotic loss of reality where we cannot accurately assess our self as being interconnected with the world external to the self. This loss of coordination between self and other brings about destruction as self-destruction.

In his *Ethics* Spinoza provides a philosophical guide for sustainable integration of the self within the world at large. According to Spinoza we achieve this coordination through the realization that we are part of what is ostensibly not us (this is the third kind of knowledge or the intellectual love God). Freud, on the other hand, chooses Herder's and Goethe's scientific approach, which is not so much metaphysical but empirical, being based not on philosophical speculation but on observation. In a quasi-empiricist manner Freud defines research "by the intellectual working through of carefully checked observations."[25] According to Freud "truth consists in the agreement with the actual external world."[26] Spinoza tackles the passions and appetites and Freud attends to the surreal reality of various drives and hyper-moral commandments in order to prepare for an accurate perception of the actual world surrounding us. Spinoza's passions and Freud's various libidinal urges and demands cause a distorted or anthropomorphic reading of nature or God. Significantly the two thinkers take these distortions seriously. They do so, because the loss of reality brought about by the passions nevertheless shapes the life of human society. According to Spinoza reason has to collaborate with the passions if it

---

25 Freud, *Studienausgabe*. Vol. 1, p. 586.
26 Ibid., p. 597.

wants to change social practices. As Moira Gatens and Genevieve Lloyd have put it:

> Spinoza's version of freedom involves a distinctive way of thinking of the relations between reason and the passions. For Spinoza, reason does not of itself have dominance over the passions, but only insofar as it involves affects—joys—which are in the rational mind more powerful than those affects which are passions. Affects can be restrained only by more powerful affects.[27]

Rather than imposing a categorical framework upon the affects, Spinoza encourages us to conduct an ethical life that is not at war with the passions but makes use of their constructive rather destructive potential. In a similar vein, Freud's new science criticizes the deleterious effects of a morality that attempts to destroy the passions. This attempt at destruction is in actuality self-destructive. Both Freud and Spinoza undermine the quasi-divine status of moral commandments. Spinoza shows how our understanding of good and evil reflects our appetites and so we call that good what we desire and evil what we loathe. These categories therefore reflect our psychic and physiological state but they distort the object that they are supposed to denote.

In Spinozist fashion Freud's "new science" questions "morality which God has presumably given to us."[28] Morality as gift from God is of course an anthropomorphic construct. Significantly Freud sees anthropomorphism operative not only in religion but also in philosophy; and that nowhere more than in Kantian moral philosophy. To illustrate his discussion of an anthropomorphic deity as foundation of morality, Freud refers to Kant's famous parallelism between the mind and the starry heavens above:

> Following the famous sentence by Kant who connects our conscience with the starry heavens, a pious person could be tempted to venerate the two as masterpieces of creation. The stars are certainly marvelous but as regards conscience, God has done an uneven and careless job [. . .]. We do not fail to appreciate the bit of psychological truth that is contained in the claim that conscience is of divine origin, but the sentence requires interpretation. If conscience is something "in us," then it is, however, not so from the beginning. It is quite a counterpart to sexual life which is really there straight from the beginning of life and is not superadded only later.[29]

Rather than following Kant and becoming a pious person, Freud here follows Spinoza when he uncovers the morals as appetites. By turning upside down the anthropomorphic narrative of conscience or reason as original divine endowment, Freud ironically makes the untidy sphere of sexual drives into the point of origin of all human values. The excess of sexual drives limits rather

---

27 Gatens and Lloyd, *Collective Imaginings*, p. 55.
28 Freud, *Studienausgabe*, Vol. 1, p. 500. My trans.
29 Freud, *Studienausgabe*, Vol. 1, p. 500.

than aggrandizes humanity's position in the universe. Instead of confirming the quasi-divine status of morality, Freud naturalizes all aspects of human society. This naturalization is so all-encompassing that it includes the realm of cultural and intellectual achievements. The work of the intellect is not the offspring of a divine gift mirroring the sublimity of the stars. Instead it emerges from the plasticity of the libido.

Freud sees in religion the main enemy of his "new science," because it does not allow for such an unsavory view of humanity's intellectual achievements. He does not take issue with art and literature, because they do not presume to be anything else but illusions. Freud's "new science" is indeed heavily indebted to works of art and literature. One could even say that he takes their purported illusion to be a true reflection of psychic reality. A striking example is of course the Oedipus complex. Freud believes in the actual truth of the Oedipus myth. The Oedipus myth articulates our unacknowledged desires. They are unacknowledged because any acknowledgment of their actuality would be an intolerable offence to humanity's quasi-divine self-image (surely as images of God we must not have any unconscious desire to be so depraved as to want to kill our father and to sleep with our mother).

Freud values art for "not daring to make any encroachments into the realm of reality."[30] As his reading of the Oedipus myth illustrates, Freud does, however, employ the self-professed illusion of art for a better understanding of psychic reality. As Beverley Clack has recently put it, "engagement with Freud's work is fruitful precisely because he takes seriously the power that phantasy has to shape one's experience of the world."[31] Freud's new science is far from being positivistic in so far as it attends to dreams and other forms of consciousness such as religious narratives or myths that are ostensibly illusory and cannot be proven in any quantitative way.

Freud's method, however, is empiricist: he observes the details of an illusory reality in a way similar to which a physicist or chemist depicts the progress of an experiment. The crucial point here is that Freud's new scientist dedicates such time and energy to the observation of false consciousness, because it forms such a substantial part of our psychic condition. In Spinozist terms false consciousness is a lamentable but necessary ingredient of humanity. Spinoza's rationalism consists in recognizing falsehood. Both Spinoza and Freud take issue with theology and philosophy, because these two disciplines tend to focus on the mind's perfection while paying scant attention to the where and when it makes mistakes. Psychoanalysis, instead, focuses on the mind's blind spots. It is, however, not judgmental but treats mental failures as inevitable or, in Spinoza's terms, necessary aspects of our humanity with which we have to reckon (rather to dismiss as unworthy of scientific discussion).

Against this background it is not surprising that next to the anthropomorphic conception of God as found in various religions, Freud discusses the

---

30 Freud, *Studienausgabe*, Vol. 1, p. 588.

31 Clack, "After Freud: Phantasy and Imagination in the Philosophy of Religion," *Philosophy Compass* 3 (January 2008), pp. 203–221 (p. 209).

discipline of philosophy as hostile to his "new science." Like religion, philosophy proclaims to be promulgating nothing less than the truth. One of its illusions, however, consists in its claim to "proffer an unbroken and consistent world view."[32] According to Freud philosophy's methodology is even more questionable, because it "overrates the cognitive value of our logical operation."[33] Philosophy shares with religion the illusion of an omniscient quasi-divine mind. Similar to the way in which Spinoza warns against electing either philosophy or theology as the key to a full understanding of biblical texts, Freud differentiates his "new science" from the lofty sphere of the pure mind as found in a secular form in philosophy and in a spiritual shape in religion. Rather than endowing our cognitive capacities with an infallible quasi-divine power, Freud asks us to be mindful of our mind.

Freud makes the mind mindful of its origination within the dark and unsavory sphere of the drives by attending to repressed memories. He sees a resistance to this work of remembrance not so much in the relatively small world of philosophy, but in the larger ambience of religion in general and Christianity in particular. "Philosophy, however," Freud writes, "does not have an immediate influence on a large amount of people; it only catches the interest of a small number and of that small number only a tiny elite of intellectuals; and philosophy is unfathomable for everyone else."[34] Religion, on the other hand, shapes the life of most people. Freud takes particular aim at Christian and Jewish salvation narratives in which he sees the nucleus of endowing morality with a quasi-divine force. As a post-traditional Jew, Freud sees in the foundation of Judaism an alternative to anthropomorphic conceptions of God. On this view Christianity relegates Spinoza's nature and Herder's historical past to the realm of the old Adam. According to Freud, Jewish culture, in contrast revolves around a "savage" (i.e. premodern) past. The recollection of this repressed memory of "savagery" enables a turning away from the ontogenetic and phylogenetic determinism of self-destructive drives. In this way the psychoanalytical cure assists self-preservation. Both Freud and Spinoza see an ethical force at work in heuristic endeavors.[35]

---

32 Freud, *Studienausgabe,* Vol. 1, p. 588.
33 Ibid.
34 Ibid.
35 As Hampshire has put: "The theory of knowledge is introduced as a necessary means of salvation, where salvation involves a state of complete and permanent well-being. The theory of knowledge is represented in this respect as parallel, and complementary, to medicine and to the theory of education of the young; all three are essential as providing practical methods of self-improvement." Hampshire, *Spinoza and Spinozism,* p. 89. This quote refers to Spinoza and not to Freud. Freud would bristle at the suggestion of salvation. However, the salvation in question here is a medical one. In this context it could also apply to Freud's psychoanalysis.

5. Psychoanalysis or Ethics Beyond the Salvation Principle

Freud's cultural critique is intricately bound up with his understanding of his "new science." Whereas the "old" science clings to a secularized Christian paradigm (Kant and Hegel), the "new" attempts to make this dogmatic account of humanity fluid, by advancing a "modern" or more precisely, post-traditional, version of Judaism's political and cultural heritage. Freud sees in the "old science" a modernized version of Christianity's narration about original sin. We are all born guilty and no one can liberate us from this determinism. John Milbank's analysis of scientific and political positivism as replacing religion only to "become itself religion" offers an explanation for Freud's critique of secularized Christianity.[36] Nothing can indemnify us, apart from death for a greater scientific or political good. The transcendent power of Christ's sacrifice disappears and what replaces it appears in the immanent and therefore "secularized" forms of nation and science. Significantly, Freud's new science sets out to serve particular individuals, rather than the other way round (particular individuals serving the non-particular good of science). Again there is a fascinating parallel between Spinoza and Freud's ethical program. As Hampshire has shown both thinkers focus on the individual: "For both Spinoza and Freud, the starting-point was the individual."[37] More importantly, Freud breaks with a theoretical framework that posits human life qua "natural" entity as intellectually and also spiritually meaningless. Psychoanalysis' newness initiates a turning away from philosophical, scientific and theological notions of a self-destructive determinism.

Freud reads this endorsement of a self-destructive determinism as the secularized Christian element within modernity. In his account, Christianity separates itself from Judaism by introducing a causal linkage between sin and grace: Christ's sacrificial death on the cross offers redemption from the state of original sin. As a result of this reinterpretation of religious history, innocence now comes to coincide not with human agency, but with belief in Christ. Sin and grace—the two main elements that constitute this belief system—share a disregard for human agency. In her fascinating interpretation of Christianity, Hannah Arendt speaks of "the Christian renunciation of any kind of action in this world."[38] Epistemology triumphs over ethics. The past determines present human actions. On account of original sin we cannot help but be guilty. On account of Christ's death, belief in Christ's sacrifice makes us partake of his redemption regardless of our everyday failings.

---

36 Milbank "Stories of Sacrifice: From Wellhausen to Girad," *Theory, Culture, Society* 12 (1995), pp. 15–46 (27).

37 Hampshire, *Spinoza and Spinozism*, p. 196.

38 Arendt, *Denktagebüch 1950–1973. Erster Band*, ed. by Ursula Ludz and Ingeborg Nordmann (Munich: Piper), 6.

Freud's new science on the other hand focuses on our everyday desires and actions. It does so in order to enable us to turn our actions and intentions away from encountering outer and, more importantly, inward (i.e. psychic) danger. Similar to the way Spinoza propounds in his *Ethics*, Freud's new science subjects the passions to scientific study. Here the mind performs its own mindfulness. Agency is here everything. This emphasis on agency is of course part and parcel of Spinoza's definition of the *conatus*, which is the "drive to self-maintenance, through degrees of complexity of interlocking parts, through balance of motion and rest in physical systems, through degrees of freedom and degrees of the power to act."[39] Acts of self-preservation in the human sphere give rise to acts of reflection.

Spinoza's conception of the mind as the idea of the body implies that the sphere of physical actions and thought upon them, are not separated realms of activity. Rather the physical and the cerebral are enfolded with each other. Similar to Freud afterwards, Spinoza sees in reflection a capacity that diminishes egotistic violence: "Reflection, the development of ideas of ideas, entails the suppression of egotism in our relations with the external world."[40] Freud focuses on the way the cerebral working through of violent acts may transform our lives. In *Moses and Monotheism* Freud compares deterministic tendencies within Christianity's theology of salvation with an emphasis on the transformative potential of deeds. This transformation, in turn, he argues, constitutes his new science.

In his discussion of psychoanalysis's distinctive relation to various anthropocentric and anthropomorphic conceptions of God, Freud focuses on modernity's conceptual triumph over a premodern past, as well as on the shift introduced by a different way of life. In the following section I will offer a new reading of Freud's work on the unconscious resistance to psychoanalytic treatment. In the course of this discussion it will become clear that Freud interprets the refusal to remember an unsavory experience as being culturally conditioned. By questioning this cultural resistance to an understanding of our psychic—and not merely physiological—nature, Freud introduces another shift into the naturalism of Spinozist thought.

6. Salvation Narratives or the Resistance to being Mindful of the Mind

Throughout most of his career Freud described the psychoanalytical cure as a process of conscious remembrance. As early as in his essay "Toward an Etiology of Hysteria" (1896), he focuses on memory. Here he voices his consternation that "hysterical symptoms can only come into existence with the assistance of memories."[41] This is all the more surprising "if one takes into

---

39 Hampshire, *Spinoza and Spinozism*, p. xxx.
40 Ibid., p. xxiii.
41 Freud, *Studienausgabe*, Vol. 6, 59.

account that, according to the patients, these memories did not come to consciousness at the moment at which the symptom first appeared."[42] In the course of "Toward an Etiology of Hysteria" Freud pursues the trajectory of this memory trace. An individual falls ill because she or he forgets a traumatic event.

Why then does memory cause illness? Here Freud distinguishes between unconscious and conscious remembrance. The patient attempts to disavow the existence of a traumatic past. His or her consciousness destroys evidence of its existence. However, this attempt to disavow unsavory aspects of one's past fails, as traces of the trauma remain, even though in distorted and displaced forms. The unconscious cannot help but shape those distortions and play with them within a displaced, seemingly unreal or surreal context. Freud's new science investigates how this surrealism of the unconscious sheds more accurate light on what really happened than the self-proclaimed rationality of consciousness might indicate. The distorted and displaced shapes produced by the unconsciousness lay open the spaces of disavowed memories.

Freud takes seriously what the rationalism of the "old science" belittles as trivia, superstition and non-sense. In the *Traumdeutung* (1899) he, in a non-apologetic mode, sides with the layman against the "scientist." Those who speak in the name of rationalism conflate dreams with the work of nature and thus denote them as the opposite of reason. According to scientific theories, "the dream is not at all a psychic act but a somatic process."[43] The layman, on the other hand, "cannot decide to deny the dream any form of meaning."[44] The *Traumdeutung* thus introduces the reader to Freud's new science, which examines the truth-content of dreams. Spinoza dedicates a substantial part of his *Ethics* to an analysis of the passion not with a view of dismissing them as unworthy of rational consideration but, on the contrary, in order to channel emotive energy into creative and nonviolent, or, in other words, rational directions. In a similar vein, Freud takes dreams seriously.

Dreams matter, because they are an enduring aspect of nature's immanent negativity: they instantiate a loss of reality that is common to all of us once we have fallen asleep. Dreams are the psyche's naturalistic heritage; no-one can liberate us from this heritage, not even the cognitive operations of either religion or philosophy. The old science clings to a Kantian division between the realms of freedom and nature. The rational here also denotes the moral. The very immorality of dreams proves their "natural" irrationality. In a witty move Freud argues that for the old scientist Kant's "categorical imperative extends into the realm of the dream." He undermines the rationalist mind-nature divide by referring to irony.[45] Freud says he hopes "their [i.e. the old scientists] own dreams, which are of such a debauched nature, do not make them disturbed

42 Ibid.
43 Freud, *Studienausgabe*, Vol. 2, 117.
44 Ibid.
45 For a discussion Freud's ironic response to Kantian moral philosophy, see Mack, *German Idealism and the Jew*.

[*irremachen*] about the otherwise confirmed appreciation of their own morality."[46] The self's self-image of moral rationality (*eigenen Sittlichkeit*) contrasts with the self's dream-life (*eigene Träume*). According to Kantian rational morality, this contrast only exemplifies the divide between reason and nature. Reason's autonomy enables the overcoming of the "natural." Freud's emphasis on the *eigen*, on the dream aspect of the self, unveils such categorical demand as an illusion.

Dreams thus proffer the material with which the new scientist debunks the concept of the "irrational." The supposed irrationality of dreams confirms the illusory claim advanced by the old scientists about reason's autonomous independence from nature's unsavory aspects. Freud's new science, in contrast, sees dreams as yielding memory traces of that which has been repressed by consciousness. Whereas the old science, operating along the lines of the categorical imperative, attempts to do without an analysis of dreams, Freud's new science examines their truth content. In this way, Freud's notion of the "old science" describes conscious attempts to resist a psychoanalytical re-presentation of a traumatic past. The work of dreams brings remote and unsavory realities to the surface in a surreal manner. Indeed, Freud treats dreams as memories of what consciousness does not want to remember. As he points out in his case study of the wolf-man (1914/1918), "to dream is nothing else but to remember, even though under the conditions of nightlife and dream-formation."[47] Someone falls ill due to loss of memory. The shock of past events shapes the patient's personality in an unconscious mode. The traumatic experience thus clings to the one who endured it, even though he or she is not aware of this. This absence of awareness describes the loss of conscious memory.

This loss is conditioned by certain cultural influences; influences that further repression. The repression in question here makes us forget that we actually lost touch with reality; that we are so determined by the past that we are unable to live in the present. This loss, however, intensifies the presence of a repressed past. Traumatic events inscribe their proximity onto the body of the patient in the form of symptoms. "*Hysterical symptoms*" are therefore "*descendants of memories that work unconsciously*."[48] In an apparently paradoxical way, illness chooses consciousness as its ally. Both resist any attempts at conscious remembrance and thus make the individual live out the after effects of trauma in the "inferior" sphere of his or her body. As a result, the cerebral part of oneself claims to be unaffected by any form of disturbance, while one's body turns into the site of illness.

Psychoanalysis addresses the seemingly mindless aspects of selfhood (dreams, slips of the tongue etc.) and seeks there the truth obfuscated by reason. More precisely, Freud argues for the translation of those "irrational", i.e. unconscious, manifestations into the sphere of consciousness. Once this transfer has been accomplished, the patient can embark on the road that leads to recovery.

---

46 Freud, *Studienausgabe*, Vol. 2, 90.
47 Freud, *Studienausgabe*, Vol. 8, 169.
48 Ibid., Vol. 6, 72.

The "practical goal of psychoanalytic treatment" consists in both "the revoca-
tion of symptoms and their replacement by thoughts."[49] On a theoretical level
Freud describes such practice when he argues for "the healing of the patient's
deficiency in memory (*Gedächtnisschäden*)."[50]

Why does our consciousness resist any attempt to remember events from a
traumatic past? Significantly, Freud seems to have characterized children to be
best prepared for psychoanalytical treatment. This might strike one as odd.
Does psychoanalytic practice not demand a high degree of intellectual engagement? The intellectual capacity of children can hardly be assessed as superior
to that of adults or so it seems, as Freud appears to have held a different view.
Why did he? This question can be best addressed through an examination of
his depiction of "little Hans" (1909).

If one of Freud's patients shows little signs of resistance to psychoanalysis
then it is "little Hans." Whenever his parents rebuke him for having voiced
"silly" ideas, he immediately refers to the usefulness of the irrational. After
all one could report such "silliness" to "the Professor [i.e. Freud]."[51] Freud in
turn praises children for their truthfulness, since, "on the whole, they have a
stronger inclination to the love of truth than those who have grown up."[52]
How can we explain the child's love of truthfulness? Freud locates the source
of this "childish" inclination in a not fully educated mind.

The child has not been fully exposed to the elevated conception of humanity as image of the Godhead. He/she does not indulge in what Spinoza has
criticized as anthropomorphic conceptions of God or nature. According to
Spinoza we tend to conflate our notion of rationality with that of God. This
conflation is dangerous, because it makes absolute the sometimes faulty work
done by our intellect. Anthropomorphic conceptions of God preclude being
mindful of the mind. Spinoza emphasizes the gulf between our limited understanding of reason and that of the universe at large: "For the intellect and
will which would constitute God's essence would have to differ entirely from
our intellect and will, and could not agree with them in anything except the
name."[53] The child cannot conflate one specific cultural view of intellect and
will with that of God or nature, because it has not fully been acculturated.

The child has not yet completely imbibed the moral and cultural norms of
his or her society. This implies that these standards further resistance to psychoanalysis. In his essay "Toward an Etiology of Hysteria," Freud underlines
this point when he refers to the absence of hysterical and neurotic symptoms
in members of the less educated classes. "We are now," he writes,

> no longer incapable of understanding the fact why hysteria occurs more rarely
> amongst lowly people (*beim niederen Volk*), than their specific etiology would

---

49   Ibid., Vol. 6, 97.
50   Ibid.
51   Cf.: Ibid., Vol. 8, 66.
52   Freud, *Studienausgabe*, Vol. 8, 90.
53   Spinoza, *Ethics*, p. 15.

allow for, because [we know] that the tendency of resistance depends on the whole moral and intellectual education of a person.[54]

Specific cultural formations of course precondition specific value systems. In what kind of cultural organization does Freud locate the values that prove resistant to psychoanalytic practice? Freud sees the location of resistance to psychoanalysis in the anthropomorphism of religion in general and of Christianity in particular.

This is not to say that Freud demonizes the Christian. Due to the free thinking environment of his father's home Freud was from early on exposed to Catholicism through his Czech nanny. So it is not surprising that in a letter of May 9, 1929 he writes to Pastor Oskar Pfister about his "special sympathy for St. Paul as a genuinely Jewish thinker."[55] In a similar way he seems to sympathize with Jesus and the early Christians. However, he takes issue with the Christian refusal to remember the "murderous deed"[56] [i.e. the primal scene where the sons kill their father] from which human history and society evolves. Therein consists the illusion of religion: to indulge in a feeling of innocence and quasi-divine perfection. This feeling of innocence and salvation is not peculiar to Christianity, it also pertains to various kinds of messianism (Jewish and Islamic) which propound different forms of soteriology (not having Jesus Christ but another soteriological figure that redeems humanity). This feeling of innocence and salvation is due to what Spinoza criticizes as anthropomorphic conception of God. In place of a conscious remembrance of a traumatic past, some Christians cling to "fantasy in form of a redemptive message (*Gospel*)."[57] This illusion of Christianity gives rise to resistance that makes a psychoanalytic confrontation with the sexual and aggressive dimension of the psyche more difficult than as it would "naturally" be.

Anthropomorphic conceptions of God shape a dogmatic approach, which psychoanalytic practice attempts to overcome. Where dogma offers certainty, Freud appreciates uncertainty. This is one of the reasons why he claims that the Jews killed Moses, arguably the founding figure of halachic Judaism: the cause of Jewish identity is murdered precisely by those whose identity he has founded. This account confounds causality. It is absurd and paradoxical. Freud's origin of Jewish identity is destabilizing. It is precisely this sense of uncertainty which is part and parcel of Spinoza's conception of God. As Žižek has put it, "Spinoza's own supreme example of 'God' is crucial here: conceived as a mighty person, God merely embodies our ignorance of causality."[58]

---

54 Freud, *Studienausgabe*, Vol. 6, 71.

55 *Psychoanalysis and Faith. The Letters of Sigmund Freud & Oskar Pfister*, ed. by Heinrich Meng and Ernst L. Freud, trans. by Eric Mosbacher (London: Hogarth Press, 1963), p. 76.

56 Freud, *Kulturtheoretische Schriften* (Frankfurt a. M.: Fischer, 1986) p. 534.

57 Ibid.

58 Žižek, *The Paralax View* (Cambridge, MA: The Massachusetts Institute of Technology Press, 2006), p. 39.

Various anthropomorphic conceptions of God, in contrast, depict those parts of humanity who share the same religion and identity as almost already redeemed and therefore morally unquestionable.

Any morally questionable aspects of human nature are projected onto those who are not part of one's community—a striking example are of course the Jews who, according to anti-Semitic stereotyping, are demonic rather than human. Freud sees the sources of anti-Semitism in the way modern European society raises its offspring. In the same case history, in which he describes children as less resistant to psychoanalysis, he elaborates on how the child's introduction to the symbolic sphere of culture goes hand in hand with entrance into the realm of prejudice and bigotry.

Morality demands of the child to become morally irreproachable. It does not allow for an open discussion of one's shortcomings but instead instructs the "educated" child to project these onto "the Jew" who represents the "other" of ones own culture. In this way, the child learns to perceive the Jews to be castrated as punishment for sexual and other "mundane" excesses. As Freud argues in the case history of "Little Hans," "the castration complex is the deepest unconscious root of anti-Semitism, because even during his upbringing a boy hears that something has been cut off from the Jew's penis."[59] The boy takes this to be "a part of the penis."[60] This castration complex "gives him the justification to despise Jews."[61] With reference to Otto Weininger's *Sex and Character* Freud compares anti-Semitism to misogyny. The accusation of having the penis cut off as punishment for "mundane" indulgences seems to justify both forms of hatred:

> The feeling of superiority over woman (*das Weib*) too does not have a stronger unconscious root [than in the anti-Semitic castration complex]. Weininger, this highly talented and sexually disturbed young philosopher, [. . .], has [. . .] treated Jews and woman (*das Weib*) with the same hostility and has hurled the same abuses against both.[62]

Freud detects such refusal to face up to the sexual aspect of one's own personality in the work of many Gentile writers (and self-hating Jewish ones like Weininger). Most famously, Jung's "retreat from inconvenient truths about the sexual drives inhabiting the human animal"[63] was the prime reason for his break with Freud.

The Jung affair in fact sheds light on the relation between resistance to psychoanalysis and modern European culture. Critics usually interpret Freud's insistent attempts to win over Jung and maintain his support as a strategic move. The commanding position of a Gentile served to prove that psychoanalysis

---

59 Freud, *Studienausgabe*, 7 (Frankfurt, 1969) 36, note 2.

60 Ibid., Vol. 7, 36, note 2.

61 Ibid.

62 Ibid.

63 Peter Gay, *Freud. A Life of Our Time* (New York: Norton, 1988), pp. 237–238.

was not a "Jewish science" and should therefore be taken as relevant for all sections of modern society.[64] Freud did his best to retain Jung's membership in the "new science." As Peter Gay put it, "when Jung was touchy, Freud was soothing."[65] Critics have, however, insufficiently discussed the reasons why Freud guarded against characterizing psychoanalysis as a "Jewish science."[66] Was it just because he attempted to be "universal" rather than be perceived as "particular?" His communications with Jung suggest that this was not the only reason. Here he depicts himself as "savage" and Jung as "civilized." This contrast has an important bearing on Freud's correlation between his new science and what he understands as Judaism's social and cultural relevance. We see in *Moses and Monotheism* that he employs this binary opposition in order to differentiate the Jews from the Egyptians.[67] In his communication with Jung he clearly refers to his position as a Jew within Western European society. Freud complements Jung and lays out before him the prospect of psychoanalytical conquests. All these achievements are due to Jung's membership in the "civilized world": "I leave you more to conquer than I could manage myself, all of psychiatry and the approval of the civilized world, which is accustomed to regard me as a savage!"[68] The German majority culture would dismiss Freud's psychoanalytical insights as alien, "other," in short, as Jewish and therefore "savage." Freud depicts this resistance to psychoanalysis with reference to his position as member of a minority.

In his communication with Jung, Freud emphasizes the public perception of himself as a "savage Jew." Writing to Karl Abraham, on the other hand, he elaborates on the truth-content within such perceived contrast between the Christian and the Jewish. Significantly, at this point the discussion focuses on resistance to psychoanalysis. In a letter of May 1908, he admonishes Abraham to "be tolerant"[69] in his dealings with Jung. Abraham as a Jew can easily accept psychoanalysis.[70] Jung, in contrast, has to find his way to Freud's new science "only against great inner resistance."[71] Freud attributes such resistance

---

64 For a discussion of Jung's "gentile façade" for Freud, see Gay's *Freud*, 231–240.

65 Ibid., p. 227.

66 Dennis B. Klein locate "Freud's desire to broaden the appeal of the science" in the years following 1908. Klein refers to Freud's fear about psychoanalysis "becoming a 'Jewish national affair.'" See Klein's *Jewish Origins of the Psychoanalytical Movement* (New York: Praeger, 1981), p. 94. Throughout his study Klein emphasizes that the "psychoanalytic movement stands out as an intellectual endeavor that invites misrepresentation and confusion, for it exhibited considerable particularistic tendencies" (*Jewish Origins of the Psychoanalytical Movement*, p. vii).

67 For a detailed discussion of this point see Mack, *German Idealism and the Jew*, pp. 136–155.

68 Quoted from Dennis B. Klein's *Jewish Origins of the Psychoanalytical Movement*, p. vii.

69 Quoted from Gay, *Freud*, p. 204.

70 See Ibid., p. 204.

71 Quoted from Gay's *Freud*, p. 204.

to precisely Jung's upbringing "as Christian and the son of a pastor."[72] Gay interprets Jung's break with psychoanalysis as an allegiance to Christian mysticism:

> To be happily free of the mystical element meant, in Freud's view, to be open to science, to have the only attitude suitable for an understanding of his ideas. Jung, the son of a pastor, harbored dangerous sympathies for mystics East and West, as so many Christians seemed to do.[73]

Nowhere does Freud mention mysticism in relation to Jung's break with psychoanalysis. Nor does he do so when he contrasts Judaism and Christianity. According to Freud, the real difference between the two cultural formations seems to lie in their respective capabilities of confronting sexuality and other unsavory aspects of human existence. Freud in fact affirms the anti-Semitic perception of the Jews as "savage." He does so, however, only to reverse the discriminatory charge advanced by anti-Semites. Psychoanalysis' savagery consists in conscious remembrance of humanity's irrationality. Only such facing up to the irrational enables a turn to the rational and thus non-violent in one's everyday actions. Anthropomorphic conceptions of God, by comparison, avoid a confrontation with specific human deeds and instead subscribe to a determinism that combines despair (original sin) with a concomitant joyful consciousness of innocence (salvation through belief in Christ's redeeming sacrifice).

As his exchange with his good friend Pastor Pfister makes clear, Freud, even though he distinguishes between the two entities, does not deny that there exist parallels between religious and psychoanalytical practice. "But you," he writes to Pfister in a letter of 2 September 1909, "are in the fortunate position of being able to lead them [i.e. your congregation] to God and bringing about what in this one respect was the happy state of earlier times when religious faith stifled the neuroses."[74] With a view to the present irreligious age he goes on to say, "for us this way of disposing of the matter does not exist."[75] Psychoanalysis does not include a relation to a deity into its sphere of operation. It thus operates on irreligious ground. Be it Jung, or be it Pfister, Freud takes issue with their inability to face up to the irrationality of sexuality. Those who (like Jung and Pfister) cling to an anthropomorphic conception of God, suffer from the "vice of virtue." As Freud puts it in his letter to Pfister of June 5, 1910:

> Well, then, I think your *Analysis* suffers from the hereditary vice of—virtue; it is the work of too decent a man, who feels himself bound to discretion. Now, these psychoanalytical matters are intelligible only if presented in pretty full and complete detail, just as an analysis really gets going only when the patient descends into minute details from the abstractions which are their surrogate.[76]

---

72 Ibid.
73 Ibid., p. 205.
74 *Psychoanalysis and Faith*, 16.
75 Ibid.
76 Ibid., 38.

Pastor Pfister's vice seems to have been passed on by his religious heritage ("hereditary"). He clings to abstractions of humanity's quasi-divine goodness that avoid direct confrontation with the minutiae of concrete actions.

From a Spinozist perspective, Pfister's anthropomorphic conception of God precludes a critique of the human passions. Those who conceive of intellect and will as pertaining to God transcribe human values and human cognition into the sphere of Divinity. This unduly aggrandizes the mind. The divinization of humanity's intellect prevents a critical engagement with the way the mind assists rather than checks the destructive and self-destructive life of the passions. Abstractions veil what is actually occurring at the interface that connects the cerebral with the emotive. These abstractions precisely constitute the resistance to psychoanalysis. The dismissal of Freud's new science is consubstantial with refusal to acknowledge humanity's sexual constitution. This "resistance to sexuality"[77] results from an anthropomorphic conception of God, which, in turn, eventuates in an inability to confront the unsavory and the irrational. Freud's psychoanalysis radicalizes Spinoza's demand to be mindful of the mind. The resistance to such mindfulness originates in a loss of reality, where the self has assumed the omniscience and omnipotence of God. This book has uncovered the so far hidden Enlightenment of diversity, by tracing the ways in which Spinoza has inspired a series of shifts in thought—shifts that focus on the thoughtlessness implicit in anthropomorphic attempts at enthroning the mind as redeemer of a secular and post-secular humanity.

---

77 Ibid., 63.

INDEX